UNDER THE FLAGS OF FREEDOM

PITT LATIN AMERICAN SERIES

George Reid Andrews, General Editor

Catherine M. Conaghan, Associate Editor

Peter Blanchard

UNDER THE FLAGS OF FREEDOM

SLAVE SOLDIERS AND THE WARS
OF INDEPENDENCE IN SPANISH
SOUTH AMERICA

University of Pittsburgh Press

Published by the University of Pittsburgh Press, Pittsburgh, PA 15260

Copyright © 2008, University of Pittsburgh Press

Manufactured in the United States of America

Printed on acid-free paper

10   9   8   7   6   5   4   3   2   1

LIBRARY OF CONGRESS CATALOGING-IN-PUBLICATION DATA

Blanchard, Peter, 1946–

 Under the flags of freedom : slave soldiers and the wars of independence
in Spanish South America / Peter Blanchard.

   p. cm. — (Pitt Latin American series)

   Includes bibliographical references and index.

   ISBN-13: 978-0-8229-4347-1 (cloth : alk. paper)

   ISBN-10: 0-8229-4347-6 (cloth : alk. paper)

   ISBN-13: 978-0-8229-5992-2 (pbk. : alk. paper)

   ISBN-10: 0-8229-5992-5 (pbk. : alk. paper)

  1. South America—History—Wars of Independence, 1806–1830.
2. Soldiers, Black—South America—History—19th century.   3. Slaves—
South America—History—19th century.   I. Title.   II. Series.

   F2235.B53 2008

   980′.02—dc22   2008003272

CONTENTS

ACKNOWLEDGMENTS

In the far too many years taken to complete this project, I have accumulated a long list of debts to institutions and people without whose assistance this work would have taken even longer and quite likely would never have seen the light of day. During the period of research and writing, I received almost universally positive responses to my overtures, inquiries, and requests. My experiences revealed the best of my profession, as people could not have been more generous in offering advice, encouragement, suggestions, and materials. I was sincerely touched by their generosity, and this book has benefited enormously from it; none of them is responsible for its shortcomings.

My first debt is to the staffs in the numerous archives and libraries whose materials I consulted. A not uncommon response to my queries about relevant information was, "We don't have anything on that subject." But, then, they almost invariably managed to locate something, to their own delight and satisfaction as well as my own. The information on slaves who fought varied enormously from archive to archive; it was particularly rich in the Archivo General de la Nación in Buenos Aires because of the nature of the local recruiting process. Other, untapped archives may be equally blessed so that in the future new information is likely to appear that may modify the points made in the following pages and add to what we know about the contributions of slaves to the independence struggles. The institutions whose materials I consulted include, in Argentina, the Archivo General de la Nación, the Biblioteca de la Academia de Historia, and the Biblioteca Nacional in Buenos Aires, the Archivo Histórico de la Provincia de Buenos Aires in La Plata, and the Biblioteca del Departamento de Filosofía y Letras of the Universidad Nacional de Cuyo in Mendoza; in Canada, the University of Toronto libraries in Toronto; in Chile, the Archivo Naciónal, the Biblioteca Nacional, and the Museo Histórico Nacional in Santiago; in Colombia, the Archivo General de la Nación and the Biblioteca Nacional in Bogotá; in Ecuador, the Archivo Nacional del Ecuador in Quito, and the Archivo Histórico del Guayas and the Archivo Histórico Municipal "Camilo Destruge" in Guayaquil; in England, the Public Record Office in London; in Peru, the Archivo Arzobispal, the Archivo General de la Nación, the Archivo Histórico Militar, and the Biblioteca Nacional in Lima; in Spain, the Archivo General de Indias and the Biblioteca de Estudios Hispano-Americanos in Seville; in Uruguay, the Casa Lavalleja in Montevideo; and in Venezuela, the Archivo de la Academia Nacional de Historia, the Archivo Arzobispal, the Archivo General de la Nación, and the Fundación John Boulton in Caracas.

A second debt is owed to the numerous individuals who went out of their way to assist me in a variety of ways, many of them unexpected. I wish to mention Reid Andrews, Maritza Arauz, Carmen Bernand, Rebecca Earle, Marta Goldberg, Maïté Klachko, Sylvia Mallo, Cristina Ana Mazzeo, Seth Meisel, Alberto Navas Sierra, Karen Racine, José Marcial Ramos Guédez, Pedro Sosa Llanos, and Camilla Townsend, who provided me with copies of notes and photocopies of materials, as well as books, articles, and theses that had a bearing on the project. Many of them, along with Ken Andrien, Ed and Ileana Early, Judy Ewell, the late Pedro Grases, Nils Jacobsen, John Lynch, Carlos Mayo, Tony McFarlane, Steinar Saether, Eduardo Saguier, Renée Soulodre-La France, Miguel Torrens, and Ann Twinam, helped me by recommending hotels in hitherto unknown cities, suggesting works to consult, and supplying the names of contacts to meet and archives and libraries to check. Carmen Torres de Martínez took me by the hand through the stacks of the Archivo de la Academia Nacional de Historia in Caracas, crawling on her knees at times to locate relevant documents, even though she was several months pregnant at the time. Benjamin Luján worked through some of the printed primary material on Peru in the University of Toronto library. Students in my courses over the years came across useful articles and questioned some of the conclusions that I presented in lectures and seminars. Conference commentators and participants also provided feedback on the few occasions that I turned some of my findings into papers. There are undoubtedly many others who helped and influenced me, and I hope they will forgive me for not remembering their names at this time.

The extensive research for this project was made possible by generous grants and fellowships from the Social Science and Humanities Research Council of Canada, the Connaught Research Fellowship in the Humanities at the University of Toronto, and Victoria College at the University of Toronto. A research grant from the Senate of Victoria University at the University of Toronto paid for the maps included with the text. They were composed by Mariange Beaudry of the Cartography Department of the University of Toronto.

Finally, I owe my biggest debts as always to my wife, Joanna, and our son, Adam, who put up with my several absences over the years and even longer hours in front of my computer screen trying to find the right word to explain what was happening in distant lands two hundred years ago. Joanna read through the manuscript with the eye of an outsider, finding discrepancies, raising questions about content, fact, and presentation, and correcting numerous errors in style and punctuation. She and Adam will be happy that yet another group of Latin Americans—fascinating though they may be—has finally found a home for themselves elsewhere.

UNDER THE FLAGS OF FREEDOM

CHAPTER 1

A HISTORICAL TRADITION

 WARFARE HAD BEEN RAGING throughout much of Spanish South America for three years when a slave by the name of Francisco Estrada appeared before a Buenos Aires court in 1813 to ask for his freedom. He based his claim on an offer made two years earlier by the commander of an army from revolutionary Buenos Aires that had invaded the neighboring Banda Oriental (modern Uruguay). The commander had declared that any slave belonging to a Spaniard and living in Montevideo (still held by royalist forces) would be freed upon joining his forces. At the time of the invasion, Francisco's owner had instructed him to leave his hometown of San José and head to Montevideo. Instead, Francisco, together with his wife and child, sought to join the invaders. He eloquently recalled, "We sought the opportune moment to place ourselves under the flags of freedom. . . . We chose the generous system of the *Patria* [homeland], we sang the hymns of freedom, and we linked our desires, our hearts, to the holy principles of the just system of Freedom. Together we renounced forever and with indignation that cruel, unhappy, and disorganized government that degrades men and refuses to permit those who are called slaves to reclaim, if they so wish, the rights of humanity."[1]

What Francisco meant by "flags" is not entirely clear. Was he referring to the colors of battalions and regiments that at that time played a central role in maneuvering troops in battle? Was he referring specifically to the flag of the Buenos Aires revolutionaries that prominently displayed a red Phrygian cap connoting liberty? Or was he making a more metaphorical allusion, with the flags representing both the cause of political freedom and the promise of personal emancipation, which by 1813 had become closely intertwined in the wake of the spreading insurrection? His meaning remains something of a mystery and, unfortunately for Francisco, his appeal for freedom remained in doubt, as his owner challenged the request and demanded his return. Nevertheless, his words expressed a common feeling among the Spanish American slave population at this time: they wanted to be free, and the wars had created unforeseen opportunities to achieve that goal.

Thousands of slaves, like Francisco, found themselves fighting in what was the most extensive mobilization of black slaves for military purposes during the colonial period. They took part in the independence struggles that chronologically spanned the years from 1808 to 1826 and, in the case of Spanish South America, stretched geographically the entire length of the continent from north to south, through the viceroyalties of New Granada, Peru, and Río de la Plata. In many areas the slaves' contributions proved vital to those struggles, yet they have attracted only limited attention from historians of the events. Reid Andrews, Núria Sales de Bohigas, and Peter Voelz are among the few who have placed these soldiers at the center of their works.[2] The neglect is surprising, since references to slave involvement appear in memoirs of the wars, and their involvement attracted both literary and artistic attention in the decades after independence was won. One of the best known is the story of "el negro Falucho," made famous by the Argentine president, soldier, and writer Bartolomé Mitre. It tells the tale of a heroic black soldier from Buenos Aires who, in 1824, while serving the patriot forces in the Peruvian port of Callao, refused first to join a military mutiny and then to honor the royalist flag that was being raised over the city's fortress. His resistance led to his execution, but as the muskets fired, he proclaimed with his last breath, "Viva Buenos Aires!" Today, the general view is that while a black soldier may have participated in resisting the mutiny, the noble death was a creation of Mitre's imagination.[3] Nevertheless, his choice of hero to represent the emerging Argentine nationalism is an interesting one.

An artistic rendering of a similar theme can be seen in the Museo Histórico Nacional in Santiago, where among the many exhibits illustrating Chile's colorful history is a rather striking painting entitled "Battle of Chacabuco," by José Tomás Vandorse. Completed in 1863, it presents a snapshot of the battle fought outside Santiago on February 12, 1817, which ended with victory for the invading patriot forces under the command of General José de San Martín. The blue and white flags flying above the columns of troops advancing from the left clearly indicate their Argentine origin. But what is most interesting about the picture is the race of the soldiers. While the mounted officers are white, virtually all the rank and file are black. It shows that forty-six years after the event, in one person's mind at least, patriot success had rested on the shoulders and the skills of black soldiers.

Black soldiers were not something new to Spanish America. They had been part of the military history of the region since the Spanish Conquest in the sixteenth century. But the scale of slave military service during the independence period was unprecedented. Previously, their participation in the colonies' military forces had been tightly circumscribed, largely because of concerns about arming enslaved men. However, as warfare spread and the need for soldiers grew, those concerns were conveniently ignored or minimized, and thousands of slaves in the three viceroyalties soon found themselves in the armed forces, fighting for both royalists and patriots. This is not to say that they were preferred over any other group; indeed, opposition to recruiting slaves was voiced almost everywhere. Nevertheless, slaves came to serve, and in numbers that far exceeded their percentage of the general population. For example, of the soldiers recruited in Ecuador, according to Sales de Bohigas, 30 percent were slaves.[4] They also joined armies that were relatively small by European standards. Whereas over a quarter million soldiers fought at the battle of Waterloo in 1815, at the 1819 Battle of Boyacá, which determined the fate of Colombia, the royalists fielded an army of 2,700 men against the patriots' 2,800; at Ayacucho, the concluding battle of the wars of independence, 6,000 men on the patriot side confronted 9,300 royalist soldiers.[5] As a result, in many instances slave recruits determined the difference between military success and failure. Without their involvement, the patriot cause in particular would have been greatly weakened, and the fight for independence would have taken even longer than it did, probably with a different trajectory, and consequently with different results.

The insatiable need for soldiers during the extended conflict was the obvious reason for slave recruitment, but other factors also came into play. At first glance, slaves seem to be far from the ideal soldiers. Commanders desired disciplined veteran troops who were accustomed to the rigors and demands of army life and required little training. The Liberator, Simón Bolívar, wistfully wrote of the Spanish enemy, "The worst is that all are divinely disciplined."[6] One of his solutions was to hire foreign mercenaries, veterans of the Napoleonic wars. However, European veterans were not available in adequate numbers, and those who came often lacked the desired experience and proved more trouble than they were worth. Even the Spanish crown was unable to provide sufficient Spanish veterans to meet its military needs in the colonies, in part because of the situation at home, and in part because of the logistics of moving large numbers of troops across the Atlantic. In eight years it sent only forty-one thousand soldiers to deal with the insurrections throughout all of Spanish America. As a result, it was forced to rely on locals.[7] Newly recruited slaves may have lacked the military skills of these veterans, but unlike other sectors of the population, they at least were accustomed to discipline. And they had other attractions: they were available, they were of the right age, and African-born slaves furthermore had a reputation for military experience gained in their homeland.[8] Moreover, slaves (again, unlike any other sector of the population) were considered property and could thus be purchased and compelled to serve for a certain length of time. Of equal importance was the fact that they could be sent to fight far from their home regions, a situation other sectors of the population frequently resisted.[9] In return, they received their personal freedom. The authorities hoped that this would not only secure the necessary recruits but also create feelings of loyalty toward their emancipators that would compel them to complete their assigned period of service and in the process develop the skills of the veteran soldier. They might even be convinced to reenlist. On the other hand, slaves' status as property created certain problems, since both the crown and the new creole, or American-born white rulers remained committed to protecting property rights. They frequently resorted to drafting slaves, but they still felt an obligation to compensate owners, and money was often in short supply. Fortunately for recruiters, many owners were prepared to sell for less than the slave's true value or with the promise of future compensation. Sometimes this was out of sense of loyalty, but it was also because in many parts of Spanish America slaves were not absolutely essential to local economic activities and, consequently, were available. In other instances, the interests of owners could be ignored, most notably if they supported the enemy side. Their property was considered forfeit, and their slaves could be expropriated and assigned to whatever task their new owners chose, including military service.

Also playing a role in the recruitment of slaves were the intellectual pressures of the time. Recruiting and freeing slaves satisfied the enlightened beliefs of some of the independence leaders. Their primary goal was political freedom, but a few came to the realization that true freedom could not be achieved as long as any sector of society remained in bondage. Freedom in return for military service thus satisfied various interests, and attacks upon the institution of slavery became a part of the independence struggles.

Indeed, the widespread participation of slaves unleashed an unanticipated and unwanted social movement in the midst of the political struggle.[10] While the majority of the slaves who served were drafted or donated by their owners, large numbers took advantage of the situation to act on their own: running away, claiming to be free, joining one of the armies, and even rebelling. Some may have been responding to feelings of loyalty to one side or another, but most were attracted by the offer of securing what until then had seemed an unattainable goal: personal freedom. Recruiters whetted their hopes with this offer, and news that runaways who signed up were being granted their freedom provided a further stimulus to follow suit. Slaves, to use Carlos Aguirre's phrase, became "agents of their own freedom."[11] In freeing thousands of slaves, recruiting slaves during the wars of independence had additional social repercussions. It reduced the numbers left in bondage and thereby helped to weaken a pillar of the system. At the same time, a flurry of antislavery legislation that was designed to win slave support for the cause further undermined the institution. The legislative attack, together with recruiting efforts and the growing commitment to the concept of freedom, aroused large sections of the slave population. In the words of John Lombardi, slaves "discovered a sense of power during these years as the contending armies wooed their support."[12] Recruits used their association with the increasingly influential military to try to achieve improvements for family members still in bondage, while those not in service, both men and women, used the changing circumstances to try to better their own lot. As the wars continued, slaves became increasingly aggressive and demanding, raising further questions about slavery's future. In one of the ironies of Latin American history, the evil of warfare helped undermine the evil of slavery.

Nevertheless, the institution survived. Except in the case of Chile, where abolition occurred in 1823, slavery remained too important and the slaveholders too powerful for the system to disappear at this time. Fearful of social unrest and racial warfare, the elites acted to ensure that their interests were protected. As John Lynch has written, "During the wars of independence popular revolt, while not successful, was menacing enough to compel the creoles to tighten their grip on the revolution."[13] Where slaves were concerned, recruiters had to figure out how to mobilize slaves without unleashing racial unrest and an abolitionist struggle that could lose slaveholder support. Their solution, in general, was to pursue a policy of gradualism, using legislation to wear away at slavery without destroying it. They were largely successful. In this they were assisted by the slaves themselves, who were prepared to risk their lives to secure their personal freedom but not to attack slavery as an institution. In large part this was because they, like other sectors of society, were found on both sides of the struggle. Many remained staunchly loyal to the crown, considering it more capable of defending their interests. Slaves, consequently, were making choices as the wars unfolded, but rather than being united by the common cause of the struggle against slavery, they confronted one another in the opposing armies. They fought one another, and they killed one another. Thus, while the actions of the slaves during the wars undoubtedly weakened slavery, another generation would pass before the institution was finally abolished in all of Spain's former mainland colonies.

The slaves who fought were descendants of the estimated one million who had been brought from Africa to Spanish America since the beginning of Spanish rule.[14] Imported largely as a replacement labor force for the declining Indian population, they may not have come to occupy the central economic role that they did in Brazil, the Caribbean islands, and the southern United States, yet they were of undoubted importance to Spanish America's economy, and vital in some areas. In common with the pattern of chattel slavery elsewhere in the Americas, tens of thousands of them were assigned to rural work on Peruvian sugar plantations and vineyards, Venezuelan cacao and sugar estates, Ecuadorian tobacco and cacao farms, livestock ranches in Argentina, Uruguay, and Venezuela, and Colombian gold mines. They were also prominent in the urban sector. As Frederick Bowser writes, in early colonial Peru "blacks were perhaps most conspicuous as retainers and household servants in the urban areas along the coast and in many parts of the highlands." In Argentina, according to Tulio Halperín-Donghi, they were a "predominantly urban group," while in Venezuela the largest concentration of slaves was located in and about Caracas.[15] In the urban centers they occupied a variety of skilled and unskilled jobs, in addition to domestic service. In Buenos Aires, for example, they worked in artisan shops as shoemakers, hatmakers, jewelers, bakers, barbers, and tailors. They were employed in tile factories, they worked as dentists, they cared for animals, and they were involved in all aspects of transport.[16]

In this vast and varied continent, the respective slavery systems differed according to region and economic activity, but, as in all American slaveholding societies, there were common features. Most notably, slaves had to cope with an institution that was inherently brutal and dehumanizing. Everywhere they were considered property and treated as such, so that whatever stability they may have established in their lives could easily be disrupted by sale or assignment elsewhere. Everywhere they were subject to harsh treatment and punishments. Rural slaves in late colonial Peru were reported to have particularly suffered, as owners sought to recoup their investment as quickly as possible.[17] In Quito the whipping, starving, and other mistreatment of young slaves prompted the comment in 1811 that in spite of the efforts of the crown to ease their servitude quietly, there were "still men who in an insult to religion and to humanity itself" treated the slaves "with all the rigor and cruelty of the ancient Romans. Considering them beasts or individuals of another species," such owners sacrificed their slaves "to the barbarous pleasure of seeing them die, devoured by the fiestas in the Circuses and Amphitheaters."[18] Even in Buenos Aires, where slavery in the late colonial period was described as "mild," slaves were assigned to "the least desirable, most degrading, unhealthiest, and worst-paying jobs," with little chance of improving themselves.[19] Not only that, but the conditions of slaves in some areas were actually deteriorating in the early nineteenth century as a result of local economic problems, higher slave prices, and other developments, including a sharp rise in the size of the slave population.

Changing slave demographics were a product of the expansion of the slave trade in the late colonial period, one aspect of a wide spectrum of administrative and economic reforms introduced by the crown beginning in the middle of the eighteenth century to attempt to reassert its control over its colonies and increase its financial returns. To meet the labor needs for the anticipated economic expansion, the slave trade was opened to all nations in 1789, which resulted in an influx of African slaves. Perhaps one-fifth of all colonial slave imports occurred after that year. In the south, an estimated 45,000 slaves were imported through Buenos Aires between 1750 and 1810 for sale both in the city and the interior.[20] Another 15,000 passed through Montevideo after 1770.[21] On the other side of the continent, 1,500 Africans were introduced into Peru annually between 1799 and 1810 from Buenos Aires and Chile.[22] In the north, in Venezuela over 26,000 slaves were imported legally and illegally after 1770.[23] Consequently, on the eve of the independence struggles, slaves numbered around 30,000 in the Viceroyalty of Río de la Plata, 78,000 in New Granada (modern Colombia), 87,800 in Venezuela, 5,000 in Quito (modern Ecuador), over 40,000 in Peru, and another 6,000 in Chile.[24] And while their percentage of the total colonial population remained small—nowhere in Spanish South America did they exceed more than 10 percent—their continuing concentration in certain regions and in urban centers added weight to their numbers. Thus, although the slave trade was halted early in the nineteenth century in response to crown directives and the disruptions of the Napoleonic wars, tens of thousands had recently arrived, and many of these remembered what it was like to be free.

Freedom, however, both for these new arrivals and for American-born slaves, was a scarce commodity. The opportunities were uncertain and in many areas virtually impossible to realize, even though no absolute barrier prevented slaves from securing their freedom, as the sizeable population of free blacks and free mulattoes—or *pardos,* as the latter were called in some regions—attested. In parts of Venezuela, opportunities for manumission actually grew in the late colonial period, as slaves who served as foremen on the expanding cacao estates were rewarded for several years of service with freedom, and many slaveholders freed slaves in their wills. But this seems to have been the exception. In Buenos Aires, with its "mild" system, for example, manumission was tolerated but not encouraged by either church or state. When it occurred, both here and elsewhere, more females than males benefited, and it more often involved slaves who bought or were granted conditional freedom in return for additional years of service than it did slaves who received their freedom outright.[25] Everywhere slaves had the legal right to self-purchase, but there were difficulties in accumulating the necessary funds. In Buenos Aires, women had greater access to cash than did men, but saving the sum of even 100 pesos was described as "an insurmountable obstacle," while the value of prime female slaves was several times this amount. The price of male slaves was similarly high: the average price for a young male in early nineteenth-century Buenos Aires and Lima was 300 pesos, and many sold for much more. Those prices rose even higher following disruptions to the slave trade in the final years of the colonial period, reaching as much as 650 pesos in some areas. Thus, even though new ways for buying one's freedom, such as gradual self-purchase over time, were introduced, and the earning capacity of slaves seems to have been growing in the declining years of colonial rule, the doors to freedom remained firmly closed to most. In Buenos Aires manumissions may have increased in the late colonial period, but by 1810 those freed still constituted only 1.3 percent of the population. In the province of Caracas the figure was higher but still less than 5 percent.[26]

With exploitation a fact of life and manumission rare, Spanish American slaves responded, as they did everywhere, by engaging in various forms of passive and active resistance.[27] In doing so they demonstrated an ability to overcome the numerous factors that divided them, such as place of birth, ethnic identity, work location, and occupation, as well as the actions of owners and local officials. Two things that united them were their unique legal status and their racial identity. So, too, did their wish to establish biological ties and families that linked the black and mulatto communities. Their place of work could foster ties as well, especially the "gang" nature of work on plantations and in mines. Such workplace ties of solidarity may have been less common in urban centers, but contacts could be made in streets, plazas, and marketplaces.[28] Equally important were the organizations and associations, some with African roots, that came to incorporate many members of the black community, both slave and free. Especially notable were the religious brotherhoods or *cofradías* that had appeared early in the colonial period under the auspices of the church for the purpose of caring for a particular church or religious image. These were originally established along African ethnic or racial lines but gradually broadened their membership to include slave and free, black and mulatto, African and American-born. They collected money that paid for members' funerals and in some cases to purchase the freedom of a member, although the beneficiaries were few in number.[29] In other words, slaves were not isolated from the rest of the community. They managed to meet, socialize, and exchange news, information, and rumors. They used the opportunity to establish their identity and to protect their interests, and these same activities created à milieu where they could consider and plan more active forms of resistance.

Slave agitation had been a part of colonial life from the time of the first arrivals and seemed to intensify in the waning years of the empire as a result of the disruptions of the era. The economic and administrative reforms that antagonized various sectors of the colonial population, the 1767 expulsion of the Jesuits (who were one of the major slaveholders in the region), and the influx of new slaves all served to provoke a response. Buenos Aires may have been spared serious slave unrest, but this was not the case elsewhere.[30] For example, slaves were drawn to the major rebellions that flared in the Andean region in the early 1780s. The number who actually participated in the Túpac Amaru and Túpac Katari rebellions in Peru and Upper Peru (modern Bolivia) was small, but the rebels' offer to free any who joined their cause and their issuance of abolition decrees did not go unnoticed.[31] The Comunero rebels in New Granada freed a small number of slaves and attracted many others. In both areas the rebellions failed, but in their aftermath slave unrest seemed to spread, with large numbers in New Granada reportedly fleeing their owners, establishing runaway communities (*palenques*), and engaging in conspiracies.[32] The crown recognized and attempted to address the source of the dissatisfaction, but its efforts may have only exacerbated the problem. In 1784 it approved but never promulgated a new slave code that offered some protections for the slave population. Five years later, when it finally issued a document that incorporated many of these reforms, opposition by colonial officials and slave owners prevented its implementation and led to its rapid withdrawal. This triggered a new round of protests and violence, as slaves believed that they had been denied an opportunity to improve their situation.[33]

Fear of slaves and slave agitation had always existed in the colonies and was a factor in limiting the number of imports over the years. Those fears intensified with the late colonial unrest, and then reached an entirely new plane with the outbreak of the slave rebellion in the French colony of Saint Domingue in 1791. Leading eventually to the destruction of both slavery and French rule on the Caribbean island and the establishment of the black republic of Haiti, the bloody events of the Haitian Revolution clearly indicated that slaves could be a revolutionary force—a terrifying thought for proponents of slave regimes throughout the Americas.[34] Although modern historians disagree over the impact of the Haitian example and its American and French revolutionary antecedents among slaves in Spanish America, local elites at the time seemed convinced that radical ideas were circulating and that slaves were responding to them. They almost invariably blamed the Haitian events for the subsequent slave uprisings and conspiracies.[35] Most threatening was the Chirino uprising of 1795 in Coro, Venezuela, which involved slaves and free blacks who cited the events in France and Saint Domingue in calling for emancipation. Two years later the northern coast of Venezuela was again the scene of agitation as the result of the conspiracy of Manuel Gual and José María España against Spanish rule. This movement, too, made reference to the rights of man and called for the abolition of slavery, attracting slaves and black militiamen whom the conspirators planned to arm and transform into a revolutionary militia. Further slave agitation occurred in parts of New Granada, as well as in Peru, where coastal estates were particularly affected.[36] Adding to the turmoil and providing a further indication of slave dissatisfaction was an explosion in the number of runaways, a product perhaps of the recent importation of large numbers of recently enslaved young African males. In Venezuela at the end of the colonial era, an astonishing thirty to forty thousand slaves were reported to have run away. Although the figure is probably exaggerated, it indicates a lack of control over the local slaves, as well as their desire to be free.[37] In the Banda Oriental, slaves were also running away and forming bands, and local officials accused black crewmen from French ships of spreading French revolutionary ideas.[38]

None of these developments equaled the magnitude of the Saint Domingue insurrection, but they did give further warning of the racial powder keg on which the Spanish colonies rested and ensured continuing attention to the slave population. They reinforced creole loyalty to the crown, in the belief that Spanish soldiers were the only protection against possible racial unrest. And they strengthened the conviction that the slave population had to be controlled. At different times throughout the colonial period, restrictive legislation had been introduced to achieve that end. Prominent among these laws were prohibitions on slaves carrying weapons or even tools, in the belief that these might be used to attack owners. The frequent reissuing of these laws indicates that they had little effect, but their reappearance is also a measure of the continuing fear—a barometer of racial apprehension.[39] In the aftermath of the Saint Domingue rebellion and various local uprisings, the authorities responded once again. In March 1803, free blacks and slaves in the Banda Oriental were prohibited from using all types of arms. In Venezuela, where in recent years creole owners had strongly opposed any concessions to the black and especially to the extensive free *pardo* population, slave imports from Africa were curtailed, and—in an attempt to isolate blacks from any sort of weaponry—creoles asked that *pardos* not be accepted into the local militia units.[40]

In the light of these fears and developments, one might be surprised by the fact that some colonial officials considered accepting slaves into the military. Peter Voelz's explanation for the change of attitude is that during the wars of independence the situation became "desperate."[41] This was certainly true, but it constitutes only part of the story. Paving the way for that desperate gamble was a history of ties between the black population and the military that can be traced back to the conquest. In the early sixteenth century, much of the region's defense had been provided by the conquistadors and their retainers, in a semifeudal pattern. As Spanish rule solidified, these forces were supplemented by a small number of Spanish regular soldiers stationed in a few vital locations, and by militia units drawn from various sectors of the growing local population. With the introduction of the militias, military training became part of the routine of colonial life, often occurring on Sundays in the central squares of the prominent towns. In keeping with a rather idealistic view of warfare, as well as the hierarchical and racist framework of the colony, the preference was to draw soldiers from those who were considered loyal and respectable. This restriction seemed to limit military service to men of European descent, and regulations were issued to try to maintain that selectivity.[42] However, the growing needs and the demographic realities of the colonies soon produced militia units that included increasing numbers of nonwhites. Prominent among them were units of free blacks and mulattoes. In Peru they operated throughout the colonial period, with free blacks actually dominating the coastal militias. Their slave roots led to questions about their loyalty in some areas, and in Venezuela the growing dislike and fear of *pardos* meant many opposed their recruitment. Nevertheless, a pattern was established, and their numbers expanded in the late colonial period, largely in response to Spain's military setbacks during the Seven Years' War (1756–1763) and, in particular, the loss of Havana to British forces in 1762. A flurry of military reforms was introduced that were designed to prevent future embarrassments. Fortifications were built and strengthened, the stationing of Spanish regular troops was formalized, military training was intensified, and new militia units that often incorporated free blacks and mulattoes were established to supplement the regulars.[43] In the viceroyalty of New Granada, for example, *pardos* came to be the preferred militiamen, with battalions formed in Cartagena, Panama, and elsewhere. In Venezuela, despite continuing reservations, the new militia groups included regiments of free blacks and mulattoes. In Peru, mulatto militia units from Lima played a role in crushing the Túpac Amaru rebellion. In Buenos Aires, free blacks comprised 10 percent of the city's 1,600 militiamen by 1801, serving in a battalion of *castas* (nonwhites) that included corps of Indians, *pardos*, and blacks. Elsewhere in the southern viceroyalty, Montevideo had companies of free *pardos* and free blacks in the artillery and the grenadiers, and Córdoba had two companies of *pardos*. To address the reiterated concerns about enlisting blacks, especially those questions about their loyalty that were raised frequently after the Haitian Revolution, controls were put in place. For example, commanders of the black regiments had to be white, a restriction in Venezuela that was extended to all ranks above captain. Nevertheless, free blacks and mulattoes volunteered, and they volunteered in greater numbers than whites, in part because other "respectable" professions were closed to them. They were also attracted by the privileges that came with military service, such as the military *fuero* that granted them their own courts, access to pensions, and other perquisites, as well as exemption from certain taxes, labor levies, and tribute payments. A further attraction was the possibility of social mobility that came with promotion through the ranks. Many blacks became noncommissioned officers, while some even reached officer rank. Indeed, there seemed to be no limitation on how high they could rise, except in Venezuela.[44] As a result, the military became a profession with a definite black link, so that in most parts of the colonies the sight of blacks in uniform, carrying arms, and even commanding units was not uncommon.

This recruitment of free blacks and *pardos* helped prepare the ground for the eventual consideration of slaves as soldiers. As Matt Childs has written, recruiting blacks and *pardos* into the militia "militated against the racial subordination a slave society demanded."[45] Other factors also made this possible, for despite the long-standing fears and prohibitions, slaves had not been completely cut off from the colonies' military history. In fact, they had been involved since the beginning of Spanish rule. During the conquest period they had been part of the conquistadors' armies and fought alongside them to establish Spanish rule.[46] They had then participated in securing Spanish dominion over the region and subsequently helped defend it against foreign incursions. They had also filled a number of quasi-military roles, such as serving on royal ships and as slave catchers.[47] In the eighteenth century they appear in the military records of different areas, although whether they performed a combat role is unclear. In the 1760s they were used as auxiliary support battalions for the Cuban forces, as well as in the ammunition and storage sections of the artillery. In late eighteenth-century Florida they served with the artillery, as well as in the navy as sailors and rowers transporting supplies. At the same time, Spaniards in Cuba "employed free and enslaved Africans in local self-defense, as plantation and town militias, as coastal sentinels, and even as sailors on locally organized patrol boats." This may, on occasion, have involved bearing arms.[48] The creation of black militia units also created opportunities for slaves. Some who served in these militias were slaves who were performing military service in place of their owners, others were runaways claiming to be free, and still others were slaves who had been donated to the crown. In Bogotá in 1805, Doña Petronila Cuenca asked for the return of her slave, Isidro, whom she had donated to a militia battalion.[49] Whether he was a soldier or a laborer is not stated.

Thus, despite the fears and the restrictions, slaves provided military service during the colonial era. And while the prohibition on slaves carrying weapons may have been raised once again following the events in Haiti, this proved to be anything but rigid. Events showed that exceptional circumstances could weaken even the most strongly held attitudes. Pragmatic realities could force officials and elites to make what were radical and—to many—unpopular decisions. Prominent among these were military threats, which on occasion led to the mobilization of virtually the entire local population, including slaves. For example, they were called upon to serve in the unsuccessful defense of Havana in 1762.[50] A more striking case occurred in 1806 and 1807, just before the outbreak of the independence struggles, when English forces invaded the viceroyalty of Río de la Plata. A footnote to the Napoleonic wars, these invasions involved the landing of several thousand English troops in the viceroyalty. In the face of the crisis, the authorities in Buenos Aires and Montevideo decided to arm slaves and accept them into the military, despite misgivings that they might join the enemy. In Buenos Aires, 688 volunteered to fight. They served alongside free blacks and *pardos* and played an important role in defeating the invaders. Carrying knives and lances, they displayed a "loyalty and courage which surprised those who had hesitated about arming them."[51] In accordance with accepted practices, all who distinguished themselves in the fighting were promised their freedom. However, following the victory two lotteries were held, and only seventy were granted the promised reward, with their owners receiving compensation. No one seems to have challenged the broken promise; some of the slaves who fought remained in the armed forces, perhaps in anticipation of future emancipation, and a number of those who had been freed also decided to continue their service.[52]

Yet, despite this precedent and firm evidence that slave recruiting would not lead to a Haitian-style bloodbath, there was no dramatic shift in attitude regarding the arming of slaves. Their use as soldiers in Río de la Plata did not alter fundamental realities. The failure to honor the promise to free the combatants certainly demonstrated that the views of slaves had not changed: they continued to be property, not citizens. They could be called on if needed and then returned to slavery. The desire not to alienate the slaveholders and thus undermine the slavery system remained constant, especially with the virtual termination of slave imports and accompanying rise in slave prices. Perhaps the only important lesson from the English invasions was that defense of the state was no longer perceived to be a "privilege and honor exclusive to the free man."[53] But at the same time, authorities and slave owners may have been right in wondering about the slaves' loyalties. Their defense of Río de la Plata had indicated some sense of patriotism, but was it loyalty to Spain, the king, or the local leaders? What could serve to arouse and mobilize them? Marixa Lasso posits that the Haitian example may have prompted Spanish American blacks to support the republican side during the wars of independence, in the hope of achieving similar changes.[54] This could be true, but it fails to account for the slaves' differing responses once the independence struggles began. At first glance, they seemed to have little reason to support the crown that had been behind their enslavement. But at the same time, they had little love for the creoles who were usually their masters. There was some appreciation of, and perhaps even commitment to, the *patria*, but probably not among those who had recently arrived from Africa. The one thing that could arouse and win them over was the offer of personal freedom, as the Buenos Aires example indicated. Haiti, republicanism, democracy, even independence—all were of little importance to the vast majority of slaves. What they wanted was the opportunity to become free. Until 1810 that seemed a faint hope, but in that year the situation changed, and it changed dramatically. Warfare erupted, and suddenly the most valuable colonial commodity became its soldiery.

Slaves were recruited into the opposing armies in various ways and participated in a variety of activities once in the ranks. In the case of the northern viceroyalty of New Granada, the cause of the king initially proved more attractive, while the growing conflict also provided an opportunity for those in Venezuela to rise in an antipatriot rebellion that remained a backdrop to the early struggles. In contrast, in the southern viceroyalty of Río de la Plata, the creole government in Buenos Aires was successful in drawing slaves into its military ranks through an effective recruiting program. The patriots' reliance on slaves was indicated by the prominent role of blacks in the army that José de San Martín began organizing in western Argentina, beginning in 1815, for the purpose of invading Chile. That same reliance also developed in Venezuela as the patriot cause under Simón Bolívar began to gain ground after 1816. His successes on the battlefield served to attract more and more slave volunteers, some who were former royalist soldiers, although far more continued to be secured through forced recruitment of one sort and another. Nevertheless, with their assistance Bolívar finally freed the northern region from Spanish rule. In like fashion, San Martín's largely black army defeated the royalist forces in Chile, but his efforts to recruit local slaves there for his pending invasion of Peru met with little success, as owners proved unwilling to accede to the Argentine general's requests. That same reticence was also evident once he arrived in Peru in 1820.

Nevertheless, as elsewhere, recruiting programs were introduced and slaves secured, ensuring that they continued to play a role as the independence wars came to a close. Thousands of slaves had been recruited, and their efforts to enlist were a sign of how strongly slaves sought the personal freedom that was being offered through military service. But the ex-slaves also wanted to enjoy that freedom, and many sought to limit their service once they discovered the hardships that military life involved. This response is an indicator of the slaves' aroused sensibilities and the ways in which the wars of independence had weakened slavery's traditional means of control. An increase in activism was evident among the female slave population as well. Their ties to black soldiers provided ways to improve their situation and further challenge the slavery system. But while the disruptions of the wars and the activities of the slaves did much to weaken slavery and initiate the processes leading to abolition, the postindependence period found the ex-slave soldiers unable to achieve that loftier goal. They were too divided, their owners too powerful, and slavery too important for it to disappear at this time. Slaves had helped to free their countries from Spanish rule, but they were not able to destroy the system that kept many of their families and friends in bondage.

CHAPTER 2

SERVING THE KING IN VENEZUELA
AND NEW GRANADA

 THE NAPOLEONIC INVASION OF SPAIN in 1808 set in motion the long and bloody process that shattered the centuries-old ties between the Iberian mother country and its American colonies. The forced abdications of Charles IV and Ferdinand VII from the Spanish throne, their replacement by Napoleon's brother Joseph, and the formation of Spanish juntas claiming to rule in Ferdinand's name produced uncertainties among the creole elites that radiated out to every sector of society. While most declared continuing loyalty to the crown, they had little confidence in the juntas and subsequent Regency Council that claimed to rule in Ferdinand's name. Divisions among those in positions of influence grew as they sought to protect their own interests, in some cases by assuming or demanding local control. Replacing Spanish administrators and challenging the leadership aspirations of fellow creoles became commonplace, but the political maneuvering led inexorably to violence that quickly infected more than the white elites.

Among the sectors affected were the colonies' slaves. In the uncertain early days after the French invasion of Spain, few colonial slaves had any reason to get involved in the political friction. If asked, they, like the majority of the nonslave population, probably would have expressed loyalty to the crown. Their ties were to the "father king," not to some imprecise concepts like self-government or independence or nation.[1] If they had an "imagined community," it included the king.[2] At the same time, their hopes were aroused by the frequently enunciated and apparently general commitment to the concept of "freedom." In Spain the word was used to describe the fight for liberation from French domination, while closer to home it was on the lips and in the writings of revolutionaries as they sought to justify separation from Spain. The latter's frequent reiteration of the concept must have attracted slaves' attention, but they quickly learned that the revolutionaries were wedded to political independence, not to the emancipation of those who were held in legal bondage. The patriot cause, consequently, seemed to offer them little, while serving the king promised some clear rewards.

This was particularly true in the northern viceroyalty of New Granada and its adjoining captaincy general of Venezuela. Here, declaring allegiance to the king provided a legal justification for slaves to strike back at their owners, many of whom were supporters of the revolutionary cause. Aroused by royalist agitators and promised their freedom in exchange for their loyalty, slaves rose against their rebel masters. Attempts were made to channel some of that animosity by incorporating slaves into the royalist forces, but the violence quickly exploded out of royalist control, producing very real fears of a Haitian-style social revolution. Similarly in need of soldiers, the patriots, too, began turning to slaves as possible recruits, although they did so grudgingly, fearful of losing the support of the slaveholding class. Their reticence proved a grave error, for time and again during these early years slaves fighting on their own or in the royalist ranks helped to ensure royalist military success. The patriots' failures on the battlefield reinforced the slaves' loyalty to the king, as he alone seemed capable of granting them the personal freedom that they desired. But it was not a comfortable alliance, and the arrival of the Spanish Expeditionary Army at the end of the Napoleonic wars brought a momentary pause to royalist slave recruiting in the area, despite the slaves' past contributions and their apparent willingness to continue to serve the king.

Developments in the viceroyalty of New Granada following the arrival of news of the crisis in Spain clearly revealed the creoles' desire for greater autonomy, as well as the firm determination of royalist officials not to grant any concessions. The city of Quito was the site of the first challenge to Spanish authority, as local creoles in August 1809 established a governing junta following the pattern in Spain. They claimed loyalty to the crown, yet despite this and their aristocratic background they soon found themselves confront-

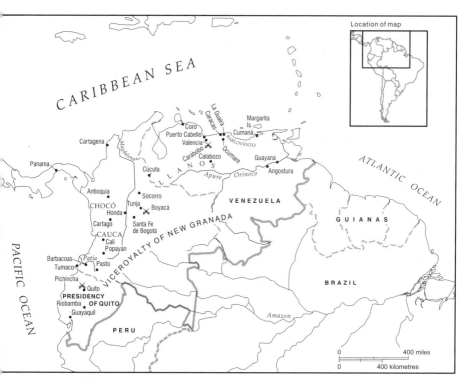

Northern South America

ing an army sent by the viceroy of Peru. The resignation of the junta failed to satisfy the authorities, who began arresting and executing the perceived ringleaders, indicating the depth of their fears and the extent of their willingness to resort to extreme measures to maintain order. Prominent in the repression was a *pardo* battalion from Lima, whose soldiers were reported to have behaved as conquerors, oppressing and threatening the population. They participated in a massacre of the movement's leaders and other citizens, and they plundered the city on August 2, 1810. As a result, they were withdrawn three days later, leaving other units composed of local black volunteers to maintain royalist control.[3] Their actions, however, failed to halt—and may even have stimulated—new uprisings and attempts at self-rule elsewhere in the viceroyalty. The most important of these took place in July 1810 in the capital, Santa Fe de Bogotá, where creoles deposed the viceroy, took over the government, and established a polity they called the republic of Cundinamarca. Other provinces and cities in the viceroyalty were equally keen to establish self-rule but were unwilling to accept Bogotá's leadership. Instead, they set about forming their own governments and in some cases declared independence, resulting in conflicts not only with the royalists but also among themselves.[4] One city that was determined to establish self-rule was the port of Cartagena, whose free blacks, *pardos,* and *zambos* (persons of mixed African and indigenous ancestry) played a prominent role in the local movement. Having suffered from recent rises in food prices, unemployment, and a decline in income, they joined with the local *pardo* militia and elements of the public in anti-Spanish uprisings in June 1810 and February 1811, and they backed the new regime's declaration of independence on November 11, 1811.[5]

The burgeoning crisis and spreading conflict created an obvious need for soldiers. Recruiters cast their eyes at different sectors of the population, but they were still hesitant where slaves were concerned. Haiti remained a powerful image, and its lessons were not far from peoples' minds, especially as the unrest spread. Maintaining social control was a paramount concern, so that in areas with large slave populations seemingly minor threats could provoke harsh responses. In 1809 a slave conspiracy was uncovered in the Chocó mining region of New Granada, a conspiracy that was nothing more than a discussion of freedom by five slaves, one of whom was described as a *"negrito"* (young black). Nevertheless, the prosecutor recommended that the leaders be sentenced to four years' imprisonment in Cartagena and prohibited from returning to Chocó, another participant to receive fifty lashes, and the remaining to be sold away from the region.[6] Yet not everyone saw slaves as a threat, and at least one official was prepared to use them to preserve royalist rule. The governor of Popayán, Miguel Tacón, in November 1810 began arming some slaves who worked in the area's mines for use against those demanding self-rule.[7] He may have been an exception, however, and even he may have wondered about the wisdom of his actions as he witnessed the neighboring captaincy of Venezuela begin to degenerate into what seemed to be racial warfare.

Creoles seized control of the Venezuelan capital of Caracas and established a self-governing junta in April 1810, similar to those that were being established elsewhere. Despite the fact that *pardo* troops played an important role in the political movement, the creoles' policies did nothing to promote racial harmony.[8] At first the junta may have been viewed favorably by nonwhites, for although it represented the more conservative elements of local society and, like juntas elsewhere, expressed its loyalty to the crown, it passed a number of liberal measures, including a law abolishing the African slave trade. However, the junta's more radical elements wanted nothing less than political separation. These radicals included men like the youthful aristocrat Simón Bolívar and the old revolutionary Francisco de Miranda who had recently returned from England. Together with other like-minded individuals they gradually gained control of the government and, on July 3, 1811, declared the First Republic.[9] The new leaders may have been progressive when it came to politics, but where race relations were concerned they were staunchly traditional. They were not willing to offer concessions that might have won over the black population, even though some, like those in Cartagena, supported the political shift. News of the brutal repression in Quito had resulted in *pardos* and blacks taking to the streets of Caracas on October 22, 1810, demanding that "lukewarm" Spaniards be exiled or imprisoned to avoid a similar confrontation. But the republicans refused to take advantage of their enthusiasm. Ten days after declaring independence, when the government called on all citizens to participate in its defense against the royalist forces that controlled other parts of the captaincy, it segregated the militia units according to color and retained the policy of placing white officers in command of black battalions. It also ordered slaves to remain with their masters. The republican constitution issued in December 1811 included a commitment to the concept of equality, but it effectively denied the vote to *pardos* by establishing high property requirements. Even black and *pardo* military officers were disenfranchised. With regard to slavery, the constitution abolished the African slave trade but continued to recognize the existence of the institution.[10] Many *pardos* consequently opposed the republic, and some expressed outright hatred toward its creole leaders. In July 1812, a handful participated in an unsuccessful attempt to overthrow the government. Similar hostility was evident among the black militias who pledged to fight against independence. They quickly followed up their words by joining the royalist forces in the captaincy.[11]

The radicals' alienation of the black population was particularly shortsighted in view of the fact that the acting rulers in Spain were doing very little to retain black support in the colonies. In the absence of the king, liberals came to dominate the Spanish governing apparatus, but where racial issues were concerned they proved to be almost as reactionary as Venezuela's creole radicals. Liberals were prominent on the Junta Central, a body set up by the regional juntas that appeared following the French invasion, and they came to dominate the Cortes, the parliament that was established in Cádiz by the Regency Council following the Junta Central's collapse in January 1810. Their liberalism was evident in various political and economic initiatives, as well as in their occasional attacks on slavery. For example, in November 1809 Antonio de Villavicencio, who was originally from Quito, called on the Junta Central to abolish slavery. This was not to occur immediately, as Villavicencio was a gradualist who anticipated an end to slavery around 1840; nevertheless, he believed that through reforms such as abolishing the African slave trade, introducing a free womb law that would grant freedom to all children born of slave mothers in Spanish territory, and setting a maximum price for slaves, violence along the road to emancipation would be avoided. These reforms, he argued, would also eliminate other horrors associated with slavery, such as infanticide and abortion, with the result that the birthrate would rise, providing more workers for national needs.

The issue was subsequently taken up in the Cortes, a body that included more representatives from the colonies. In May 1811, those from New Spain called for the immediate suppression of the African slave trade and the gradual abolition of slavery. However, the black population gained almost nothing. Confronted by spreading warfare in the colonies, members of the Cortes decided that political order required that slavery continue, at least for the time being. They also refused to recognize *pardos* as equals or to consider them part of the Spanish American population when determining the number of elected representatives to the Cortes. This had political, not ideological, roots, for it ensured Spanish domination of the body. Yet the American delegates supported the decision and in the process signaled their deep animosity toward this particular sector of the population. They described *pardos* as "worthless" and as "inebriates, incontinent, lax, lacking honor, gratitude, and fidelity, without a sense of religion or morality, without elegance, cleanliness, or decency."[12] Thus, the liberal constitution that the Cortes produced in 1812 may have ended royal absolutism by creating a constitutional monarchy, but it refused citizenship to individuals of African descent, except for those who had performed "meritorious services" to the nation and could prove that they were of good conduct, legitimate, and married, and exercised some useful profession.[13]

Nevertheless, despite the fact that the Cádiz resolutions did little for the black population in Spanish America, most blacks in Venezuela and elsewhere remained largely committed to the crown. Loyalty to the king was a powerful force in these uncertain times, and it had yet to be challenged by any viable or attractive alternative. Ferdinand's reputation remained largely unsullied, as the royalists could argue that he had been a French prisoner while the Cortes' decisions were being made and, therefore, he was not responsible for them. The captaincy's slaves reaffirmed their support for the king in various ways as political divisions in the area grew. At the same time, some, under the mantle of continuing loyalty, took advantage of the situation to act in their own interests. Offered nothing by the creoles and seeing that their owners were the ones making the decisions, they began to rise up. Priests and royalist agents, who were desperate to destroy the revolutionaries and prepared to risk social revolution in the process, spurred them on, contrasting Spanish rule with that of the creole slaveholders and hinting that personal freedom would follow the restoration of royalism. Racial confrontations consequently flared. In the Barlovento region east of the capital, slaves and free blacks in haciendas and in towns rose up against the creole government; the slaves expected to be freed for their actions. In the royalist stronghold of Valencia, free blacks and *pardos*, antagonized by the creoles' unwillingness to grant them equality, enthusiastically backed the royalist cause. To solidify their support, the royalists abolished slavery, proclaimed civil equality for all citizens, and, when attacked by republican troops under the command of Miranda, armed the *pardos* to defend the city. Their actions proved unsuccessful, and the city fell in August 1811, but Venezuela's free *pardos* now had a reputation of being faithful to the king.[14]

The same was true of the captaincy's slaves, who were discovering that the military conflict created new and unforeseen ways to secure personal freedom. Active participation in the royalist defense was an obvious route, but even verbal opposition to the revolutionaries could lead to the same goal. In October 1811, two slaves from the province of Nueva Barcelona fled following news of the declaration of what they called "fanatical independence," because, they said, "they did not like this system of government." Following the restoration of royalist rule in the area, they requested "royal protection of their freedom," a request that received serious attention, despite questions about the reasons behind their flight. Their owner demanded their return, pointing out that she had had nothing to do with the revolutionaries and alleging that the runaways had robbed her before escaping. The governor, however, seemed moved by the fact that the slaves had shown their opposition to independence. He considered freeing them, but lacked either the money to compensate the owner or the right to order their outright manumission. His compromise was to order their sale.[15]

Freedom may not have been granted in this case, but the loyalty of the slave population was generally accepted, and the idea of using them in other ways to bolster the royalist cause was gaining currency. Directing their apparent animosity to the creoles in a more structured way, such as military service, could pay other dividends. In addition to providing recruits, it would weaken their owners' economic strength and ability to resist by depriving them of their labor force. Thus, the royalist military commander Juan Domingo de Monteverde y Ribas, and some of his subordinates, began to recruit slaves.[16] Whether they considered the recruits as possible combatants is unclear, but military ties were being established. As for the slaves, joining the royalist forces offered the possibility of taking officially sanctioned revenge on their owners, an indication of the depth of their feelings. It also promised them their desired freedom.

Elsewhere in the north, the breakdown of civil order was also prompting slaves to participate more actively. Near Popayán, in southern New Granada, slaves from a local mine rebelled early in 1811; although the uprising was soon suppressed, it left fears of further unrest. That same year troops and members of the local elite were mobilized to suppress slave insubordination in different parts of the Cauca region. Around Chaparral, large numbers of slaves, claiming to be free, ran away and threatened to burn the parish and kill their masters. Slaves in different parts of Ecuador were also reported to be agitating.[17] Some of the unrest, like that in Venezuela, acquired a political complexion as slaves targeted the revolutionaries and began to be attached to royalist armies. In southern New Granada slaves expressed their loyalty throughout 1810 and then rose against the patriot regime in Bogotá in 1811. They invaded the valley of Patía, pillaging and robbing and killing stragglers from the patriot armies. Slaves from the provinces of Micay and Iscuandé assisted the royalist forces under Governor Tacón against the insurgents of Popayán. In 1812 Tacón planned to use some from local mines to capture the port of Buenaventura. One owner, José María de Mosquera y Figueroa, sent slaves from his mines for use by the royalist army in Quito, and in 1813 the viceroy was asked if slaves from northern Ecuador could be assigned to the military. To win their support, royalist officials offered freedom in exchange for participation, thereby formalizing the vital link between military service and personal liberty. Others were promised freedom if they betrayed owners who were known insurgents. Nevertheless, the authorities were not confident that they were in complete control. They knew of slaves who were brought into the royalist forces and exceeded the orders of their commanders. One charged that the slaves' "sole objective was robbery and murder, scarcely compatible with the defense of the Crown."[18] As the unrest spread, fears of a full-scale racial uprising increased.[19]

Meanwhile, despite the revolutionaries' apparent unwillingness to challenge the racial hierarchy, they had not entirely lost touch with the black community. This was true even in Venezuela, where some blacks were willing to assist in the fight for self-rule. José Antonio Andújar, a free black, enlisted in the republican forces in 1810, at the age of thirteen, and was still found serving them twelve years later. José de Jesús Suares was a runaway who had fled his owner because of mistreatment and then, claiming to be free, joined a patriot militia battalion that was en route to besiege royalist Valencia. When his owner demanded his return, he objected, describing himself as a "wretched man who has served the *patria* with love."[20] More often, slaves found themselves in the patriot forces without any say in the matter. Some were drafted and others were donated, while still others were forced to accompany their owners when the latter enlisted.[21] Fernando Suárez, on joining the army in 1810, offered three slaves and eighty-four animals, along with a house, to serve as a military hospital. Julián Carreño headed a company composed of the slaves from his haciendas, while General Juan Escalona brought along one of his slaves, also named Juan Escalona, who served from April 1810 as his "assistant." This description probably indicated a noncombat role, which seems to have been the pattern for much of this slave recruiting. The majority were used as laborers, servants, cooks, and the like, which meant they were neither armed nor risking their lives. But Juan may actually have fought, as he was wounded in the right arm at the first siege of Valencia.[22]

The Venezuelan republican leaders initially opposed more formal slave recruiting, but this stance finally gave way in May 1812 in response to military realities. Their political and battlefield failures—along with the catastrophic earthquake of March 1812 that destroyed wide areas of republican-held territory and was cited as proof that God was on the royalists' side—prompted large numbers of young men of all racial backgrounds to offer their services to the king. Confronted with royalist advances and an expanding slave revolt, as well as the increasing number of slaves joining the royalist forces, the patriot commander-in-chief, Francisco de Miranda, issued a proclamation on

May 14, 1812, that opened the way for enlisting slaves. He welcomed any who wished to fight against the Spaniards and offered freedom in return for ten years' service. It was hardly a radical gesture, but it flew in the face of slaveholder wishes, and they forced Miranda to modify his decree on June 19. The revised legislation limited the number of slave recruits to one thousand, reduced the term of service to four years, and promised compensation to the owners.[23] Nevertheless, even it aroused widespread hostility, being seen as an attack on property and the social order. The decree seriously undermined Miranda's support, as slaveholders showed that they were more concerned about maintaining slavery than achieving independence. Many of them hid their slaves to prevent their enlistment, while others went further and rose against the government. The decree also caused the archbishop of Caracas, Narciso Coll y Prat, secretly to instruct priests in areas of high slave density to encourage them to fight "for the king and religion." Their efforts convinced even more slaves and free blacks to join the unrest, and under their own commanders they began marching on Caracas to overthrow the rebel government. By late June they controlled much of the east coast, urged on by Spanish royalists who were promising slaves their freedom. The advance on Caracas seemed unstoppable, and on July 13 Miranda felt compelled to negotiate with the royalists. The First Republic fell twelve days later.[24]

The royalists were back in political control, but they had unleashed a racial maelstrom that showed no signs of abating. At heart they seemed as fearful as the republicans of slave unrest. They could have tried solidifying slave support by offering abolition or by recruiting more into the ranks of their armies, but instead they sought a scapegoat for the unrest. Ignoring his own complicity, Monteverde criticized the Caracas revolutionaries for offering freedom to any slave who took up arms. But he had little sympathy for the slaves. Referring to the continuing slave agitation, he warned that "almost certain ruin" would follow if the slaves were freed. He promised to pacify the areas in turmoil, return the slaves to their owners, and reestablish subordination.[25] The municipal government of Caracas also blamed the republicans for the unrest, charging that they had appealed to the slaves and planned to arm them, but "fortunately the greater part of the slaves of [the] province" had refused. At the same time, the city council recognized that the motivations of even apparently loyal slaves were mixed, commenting that while some may have risen against the insurgents, those in the east had taken up arms "not precisely to defend the just cause, but rather their personal interests."[26] Estate owners added their voices to the complaints but widened the target of responsibility. After a royalist officer enlisted local estate slaves into his forces, owners in the Barlovento area protested that the recruits' service had been of very little military value; indeed, they had sacked haciendas and attacked and mistreated owners. Owners reported that slaves were also fleeing estates, and while some may have joined the royalist forces, the general impression was that social control was slipping out of the hands of the slaveholders and the authorities.[27] Despite Monteverde's efforts and instructions to hacendados to reestablish authority over their slaves, slaves continued to act on their own, attacking masters, massacring whites, and destroying property, often regardless of the loyalties of the owner.[28] Priests—making offers supposedly on behalf of the king—managed to convince some to return to their plantations, but other runaways were hesitant, especially those who had killed their owners or other whites. They demanded their freedom, some pointing out that if they had joined Miranda, they would have received it. Many free blacks and *pardos* were also dissatisfied, adding to the atmosphere of uncertainty and fear. One royalist viewed what was happening in apocalyptic terms, describing it as a "revolution of the blacks," a term subsequently used by Simón Bolívar in his evaluation of this period.[29]

Thus, violence intensified in Venezuela as the patriots took advantage of the fragility of royalist control to stage a recovery in 1813. Bolívar's series of rapid military victories in the west, along with those of other patriot leaders in the east, permitted him to recapture Caracas in August and declare the Second Republic early in 1814. In an attempt to end the warfare between Venezuelans and transform the struggle into a nationalistic one, in June 1813 the charismatic and increasingly authoritarian Liberator issued his controversial declaration of "war to the death" against Spaniards and their supporters. His threat was also a response to the actions of royalists like Monteverde who considered the republicans rebels and therefore deserving of execution and who had mercilessly persecuted those perceived to be supporters of the patriot cause. But rather than polarizing the independence movement as a struggle between Americans and Spaniards and hastening its conclusion, Bolívar's pronouncement made the conflict even bloodier; the fighting intensified, with neither side giving quarter, and large numbers of innocent victims perishing at the hands of pitiless soldiers.[30]

One of Bolívar's failings was his blindness where the captaincy's slaves and free blacks were concerned. A slaveholder passionately committed to political freedom, he had developed a profound antipathy to the black population because they had opposed the cause of independence. In reference to their attacks during the First Republic, he described them as an "inhuman and atrocious people, feeding on the blood and property of the patriots, committing... the most horrible assassinations, robberies, violence, and destruction."[31] He recognized that they constituted a major opposition to his regime, but his solution was not a conciliatory one. Under pressure from landholders who called for the reinstitution of a national guard to track down runaways and to preserve plantations, he dispatched expeditions against the slaves, thereby ensuring their continuing enmity.[32]

Few slaves joined the republican forces fighting in the region. Of those who did, most were probably compelled to serve, accompanying their owners, as in the case of those enlisted by the patriot leader Santiago Mariño. In like fashion, when José Antonio Mújica, together with his brothers, joined the republican forces, he brought four slaves (who were granted their freedom).[33] Bolívar also failed to win over the free *pardo* militias, who remained loyal to the king and fought against the reinvigorated patriots. A factor in that loyalty may have been the 1812 Spanish constitution's offer of citizenship for those who provided distinguished service. In the months following its issuance, several free Venezuelan *pardos* asked for their citizenship. Among them was Agustín Amaya, a lieutenant in the *pardo* volunteers of Guayana who had joined the infantry in May 1809, fought in a number of battles, and had risen quickly through the ranks. In December 1812 he requested Spanish citizenship, and eventually received it after proving he was of legitimate birth.[34]

The continuing slave and free *pardo* animosity provided the royalists with a means to strike back at the Second Republic. Turning to slaves as recruits seemed an obvious choice for the royalists after their recent military setbacks, even though many remained skeptical about arming them. However, with the survival of the colony at stake, those concerns had to be ignored for the time being. Moreover, eliminating the republicans by using their former employees and slaves had a certain appeal to some. It certainly seemed to be the view of the most successful of the royalist military leaders who fought against the Second Republic, José Tomás Boves. Born in Asturias but a longtime resident of Venezuela's interior plains or llanos, Boves transformed the black and mixed-race residents of the region into an extraordinarily effective army. He appealed to the *llaneros'* racial and class feelings by promising to protect their style of life, offering them loot in the form of the plundered properties of patriots, and treating them as social equals.[35] He promoted mixed-race *llaneros* to officer rank, in some cases over lighter-skinned followers. He won over slaves by proclaiming their freedom as he attacked patriot plantations.[36] As elsewhere, some slaves accompanied their masters into Boves's army. The cavalry captain Juan Bautista Mendía brought more than thirty estate slaves with him when he joined Boves. However, his contribution was not entirely altruistic, for when two of them were killed in action, he asked for compensation.[37] Another slave owner, Juan de la Cruz Mena, had fled to Puerto Rico when Bolívar invaded; he later returned to join Boves, claiming that twenty-seven of his slaves had joined the royalist forces under Boves and Tomás Morales and that "some had died with weapons in their hands defending the legitimate authority."[38] Other slaves joined Boves on their own. José Silvestre, together with his wife and daughter, fled following an attack on his owner's property and subsequently enlisted in Boves's army. The estate slave Ramón Piñero and a fellow slave named Miguel chose to join the royalists in September 1813 after the "insurgents" arrested and jailed their owner. They served under Boves through a number of battles and entered Caracas with their leader in July 1814 as the Second Republic fell.[39] The irony of the slaves' actions was that while creoles claimed to be fighting for liberty, slaves chose to fight against them to achieve "the freedom that they were not finding in the republican ranks where their owners fought."[40]

Boves's military success was based largely on tactics that were notorious for their brutality, a brutality that was often linked to race. His forces were reported to go into battle shouting, "Death to the white exploiters of the *pardo* and the Indian!"[41] One of their bloodier massacres occurred at Ocumare early in 1814. Under the command of Boves's lieutenant Francisco Rosete, the royalist troops were reported to have raped the town's women, slaughtered more than three hundred inhabitants, and nailed the victims' severed noses, ears, sexual organs, and breasts to windows and doors.[42] Even the royalist authorities found Boves's willingness to put the elderly, children, and women "to the knife" unsettling. The political head of Cumaná, where the violence was extreme, commented, "Boves, by my count, has turned over twelve thousand beings into ashes, and the insurgents an equal number."[43] The municipal government in Caracas, after the royalist return to power, was also critical of Boves, charging that in attracting slaves, he had promoted insubordination among the entirety of the slave population. They were deserting their estates, engaging in theft and pillage, and paralyzing agriculture. Adding to the chaos was the response of the owners themselves, many of whom fled their properties, leaving their slaves unguarded.[44]

The concerns aroused by the actions of Boves and his forces help to explain the shift in royalist strategy that followed the arrival, early in 1815, of General Pablo Morillo and a Spanish Expeditionary Army of ten thousand soldiers. Confronted by an extraordinarily complex situation, Morillo was forced to make a number of contradictory decisions that secured immediate results but in time began to weaken royalist support among local blacks. His principal orders from the restored Ferdinand VII were to crush the separatist movements and destroy the rebels. But he was also under pressure to end the slave rebellion and bring the black population under control. He believed that despite their previous limited success, the "revolutionaries" were still capable of attracting slaves because of their adoption of what he referred to as "the detestable language of liberty and equality."[45] Some slaves, in fact, seemed to think that recent developments had ended slavery. Such, at least, was the claim of a Venezuelan estate slave named Juan Izaguirre, who told fellow slaves that they were as free as anyone else. These were words that both slaveholders and the authorities considered subversive, and Izaguirre was quickly arrested.[46]

Morillo's response to the racial conundrum was multifaceted. To reverse the decline in the size of the white population—a result of the high death toll during the insurgency and migration from the captaincy—and to reestablish a balance with the blacks, he recommended the importation of white families from Spain and the Canary Islands. At the same time, in order to maintain black support, he asked Madrid to reintroduce its earlier liberal gestures: abolish the slave trade, implement a policy of gradual manumission, and grant those free *pardos* and mestizos of legitimate birth the privileges enjoyed by whites.

The army of Boves was a particular cause of concern to both Spain and members of the Venezuelan elite. Morillo had been instructed to release those soldiers considered a threat to internal security, which meant disbanding the armies of Boves and his successor, Morales. Boves's death in battle at the time of the fall of the Second Republic eased Morillo's task somewhat, and with his large Spanish army and local white volunteers who enlisted following the royalist success, he had no need to recruit among the black population. In addition to disbanding Boves's forces, he disarmed and released many of the *pardo* rank and file, after an attempt to incorporate them into his army aroused criticism from those members of the elite who remained opposed to any sort of *pardo* equality. Free *pardos* who had commissions were reduced in rank, probably in the hope that this would convince them to resign. Where slaves were concerned, the shortage of funds caused by wartime destruction prevented the authorities from compensating owners; it provided justification for ending recruitment among this sector of the population. The only exception seemed to be those who had been serving in the rebel forces and wanted to change sides. In accordance with instructions, Morillo freed them, added them to his army, and compensated loyal owners. He also recognized the contribution of slaves who had served the king, declaring that those "who through faithfulness to his royal person" had "taken up arms in his cause" were now free.[47]

Thus, while formal recruiting may have ended, adherence to the royalist side had proven advantageous to the black population, which ensured their continuing support. Moreover, Morillo's recommendations to promote racial harmony were approved, as the constitutional offer of citizenship was reintroduced. A decree declared that every mulatto, black, and *zambo* who fought for the crown was to be offered Spanish citizenship, and those who were officers were to be decorated with a medal bearing the bust of Ferdinand. Three thousand letters requesting citizenship followed, along with orders for five hundred medals.[48] Slaves made their own appeals, responding to the promise "to free all the slaves who ha[d] fought in the armies in favor of the cause of His Majesty." Royal decrees in April and June 1815 freed those who could provide a certificate from their commander with proof and time of service, conduct, valor, merit, and other accomplishments.[49]

Since securing their personal freedom had been the principal reason for their willingness to risk their lives in military service, many slave soldiers now stepped forward to take advantage of the offer. Among them was the former estate slave and Boves soldier Ramón Piñero. After the capture of Caracas, his cohort Miguel went on to participate in a new campaign against Cartagena, but Ramón had decided to end his military career. More than forty years old and suffering from illnesses that were a result of his service and had required hospitalization, he asked for his freedom. "I have served with much love and faithfulness my King," he noted, "and I do not wish to lose the charity that his sovereign clemency has granted to those who like myself have defended his rights with weapons in hand." His request was granted, and his owner was compensated with 125 pesos.[50] Another supplicant was Juan Nepomuceno, a *moreno* (black) estate slave belonging to the *conde* de Tovar. He stated that he had served for nineteen months "with the greatest faithfulness and adhesion to the just cause of Spain." Presenting two witnesses who vouched for his service, Juan succeeded in his petition. Slaves who had served in other parts of the viceroyalty made similar requests. Mariano Antonio Rodalleja had been working in the Popayán mines when the area came under attack by the "insurgents." Donated along with other slaves to fight, he left his wife behind and marched off, urged by his owner "to die in the war." He served in the royalist army through numerous battles, sieges, and skirmishes, although probably not as a combatant, for when he asked for his "justly acquired" freedom in 1816, he claimed to be crippled and useless for any type of work as a result of carrying cannons on his shoulders.[51] The route to freedom of the Venezuelan slave Juan José Ledesma was somewhat different. Donated by his owner to the patriots for service, he had fled in October 1813 and joined the royalist army, which he served until 1815. José Gerónimo Ramires was another slave whose owner had donated him to the patriots and who, with other slaves, had fled "to show [his] loyalty to the King." He, like Juan, had continued to serve through defeats and victories and now wanted his freedom on the basis of the decrees.[52]

Even those who had provided the royalists with nonmilitary support in suppressing the insurgent movements were obtaining their freedom. When royalist troops landed at Cartagena in 1815, Ignacio de Maza offered to round up cattle from the hacienda where he was living and bring them to the royalist barracks. For this he was freed.[53] Some slaves pushed the parameters of the decrees by requesting their freedom on the grounds that their owners had joined the side of the insurgents while they had remained loyal to the king. A few even took their claims to Spain, although whether they were successful is unknown.[54] Nevertheless, the impression was that loyalty to the crown, however demonstrated, was a door to the freedom they craved.

Initiatives such as these did not go unchallenged. Complaints followed Morillo's actions, as the local commitment to slavery and to a racial hierarchy remained firm. In September 1815, the Caracas city council expressed concerns about the harm being done to agriculture because slaves were not being returned to their owners, and predicted that their release would have a detrimental effect on public order. It repeated its complaint the following year, this time to the king's advisory body on colonial affairs in Spain, the Council of the Indies. The council eventually responded in April 1818, dismissing the protest with the explanation that the granting of freedom was justified and the owners had been adequately compensated.[55] Slaveholders also tried to thwart Morillo by demanding the return of slaves who had served the king. Among the claimants was Mateo Montiel, whose slave Juan de la Paz had run away while working as a muleteer carrying fruit from the countryside to Caracas. Apprehended, he was taken to the city, where he claimed to be a free man and as such was assigned to the army. His owner, however, managed to track him down, and in March 1816 demanded his return.[56]

These complaints were but one aspect of the discontent that followed Morillo's arrival in the viceroyalty. His military campaigns may have been successful in quickly destroying most of the independent juntas and republican forces in Venezuela and elsewhere, but he had not eliminated their threat. In addition, his repressive measures targeting the patriots and their families left an atmosphere of fear, tension, and animosity. His efforts to end the racial unrest were also unsuccessful, as slaves continued to rebel. Moreover, despite his gestures in their direction, black loyalty was beginning to soften. Those who had been released from the royalist forces were particularly incensed and began turning against the crown. Some engaged in banditry, others found comfort among the rebelling slaves, while still others became a potentially bigger threat by joining the rebels.[57]

In switching sides, slaves tied their fortunes to patriot leaders, who, despite their frequent setbacks, had not been eliminated. But the patriots needed to be more successful on the battlefield, and some sought to recruit slaves to bolster to their depleted forces. In Ecuador, for example, rebel groups began granting slaves their freedom in return for their assistance.[58] In Venezuela, despite Miranda's lack of success in recruiting slaves, other patriot commanders sought their support as they fought to regain control of the captaincy. Santiago Mariño was only one of the patriot leaders in the east who had slaves under his command. Francisco Bermúdez and the *pardo* Manuel Piar were also recruiting nonwhites, and even Bolívar, despite his negative view of the black population, was beginning to accept them.[59]

However, not all were convinced, and some patriot leaders still had reservations about arming slaves. In contrast to Boves, republican recruiters seemed to view slaves primarily, if not exclusively, as noncombatant auxiliaries. For example, the Cundinamarca president, Antonio Nariño, turned to them for this purpose when he organized an expedition against royalist forces in southern Colombia in 1813. His requests for slaves from Antioquia,

Tunja, and Socorro were refused, but elsewhere he had some success. Twenty or twenty-one slaves were taken from the property of Domingo Caicedo in payment for a debt owed to the state, while others were obtained elsewhere. Nariño offered them their freedom if they served him "with honor" or, as one recruit recalled, "with valor." They were not armed; rather, they served as porters, carrying munitions and hauling cannons. Nevertheless, their presence proved invaluable, for when the patriot army suffered a crushing defeat in Pasto that resulted in the capture of their leader, the slaves stepped forward. They managed to haul away a number of muskets, a cask of powder, and over three thousand rounds of ammunition, which permitted the army to retreat in good order. A commentator noted, "Without this help we certainly would have had to surrender and would have perished." By their actions they had "saved the rest of the army."[60]

Unlike Nariño, more and more patriot leaders were beginning to recognize that they needed more substantial slave support if they were ever to achieve self-rule. The slaves' vehement anticreole agitation lay as a clear warning, while the passage of antislavery legislation elsewhere in the colonies, most notably a free womb law in Chile in 1811, indicated that at least some Spanish Americans had an appreciation of their demands and were developing ways to try to win them over. In Antioquia these concerns and pressures led to a serious debate of the issue by the local creole government in 1814. The conclusion was that the Chilean approach could not apply to New Granada because of the latter's greater number of slaves and their central role in agriculture and mining. But at the same time, there was a desire to avoid the disorder and discontent besetting Venezuela. One representative argued that slavery, being an institution created by the Spaniards, deserved to be challenged. He recommended the passage of a free womb law as well as other controls on slavery, such as preventing children from being separated from their parents, abolishing the slave trade into and out of the republic, establishing a manumission fund, and obliging owners in their wills to free 10 percent of their slaves. Convinced, the representatives urged the congress to adopt a policy of emancipation to prevent the royalists from winning slave support, and on July 15, 1814, they passed a manumission decree. The decree sparked renewed debate; one critic queried, "We are not yet free and already we wish to authorize freedom for our servants?" The law nonetheless remained in place, unique among the self-governing communities in New Granada, until the government eventually fell to royalist attack.[61]

In response to initiatives of this sort, some slaves chose to back the patriot cause. Perhaps, as Morillo believed, the revolutionaries' language of freedom was proving attractive. They remained supportive even after the fall of the Second Republic and Bolívar's flight, first to New Granada and eventually to Jamaica and Haiti. In his retreat from Caracas Bolívar recruited plantation slaves to assist him, including about fifteen of his own.[62] Others joined independently. Lino Rodríguez fled Caracas after it fell to Boves in July 1814 and made his way to the llanos of Barinas, where in August 1815 he joined one of the surviving patriot divisions. Still others, such as Bolívar's slaves, were accompanying their masters. When Félix Bastardo, a longtime officer, rejoined the insurgents on Margarita Island in November 1815, he brought along his son and two slaves to fight. They were part of the dispersed but still active units that would continue to fight—in Rodríguez's case—until the patriots' eventual victory.[63]

The numbers were limited, but commanders on both sides of the struggle were coming to the realization that military success in the area was going to depend on black troops. Even the royalists, despite the presence of Morillo and his Expeditionary Army, were moving to this way of thinking. Already, according to a rather exaggerated report written in July 1815 by the acting captain general of Venezuela, nonwhites made up almost the total force of both sides. With regard to "the armies that carry the Royal Standard," he wrote that they were "composed almost totally of *pardos* and those of the other castes." He believed that they should be rewarded for this in the same way as whites, including being put in command of whites. He noted that since the king had conceded "the inestimable benefit of freedom" to slave veterans, the free *pardos* should receive something equivalent.[64] The defeat of the Second Republic and the collapse of the other independent centers in New Granada in the months following the arrival of the Spanish army may have altered royalist views for a time, but Morillo soon saw that he was going to have to use locals. For one thing, they seemed best suited to the local environment. In discussing the state of the military force in Panama in 1814, a report to the royal authorities pointed out that this was an unhealthy area with high mortality rates from disease. There were insufficient whites to maintain the white companies in the royal army, but there were plenty of *pardos*, and they were "the most appropriate for the war in these countries." What was needed was a veteran battalion of light infantry composed of the "most abundant people here, *zambos*, mulattoes, and mestizos."[65] It was a recommendation that soon became the view of both sides, ensuring that the recruiting of slaves was going to continue and, indeed, intensify.

In these first years of the independence wars, the majority of slaves in Venezuela and New Granada had found the opportunities and rewards offered by the crown far more attractive than anything promised by the patriots. As a result, they had helped to defeat the two attempts at republican rule in Venezuela and to maintain royalist rule throughout the region. If the independence forces and their self-proclaimed leader, Simón Bolívar, were to change their fortunes, they were going to have to adopt a new strategy that would win slave loyalty. Bolívar was beginning to understand this as he headed off into exile in May 1815, arriving in Haiti in December. His stay in the world's first black republic confirmed the shift in his reasoning. Promising in February 1816 to free all the slaves in the lands that he liberated in exchange for the arms and supplies offered by President Alexandre Pétion, he linked his political objective with social transformation.[66] Political freedom was now inextricably tied to the personal freedom of the viceroyalty's slaves. He still had to show that he could defeat the royalists militarily, but a commitment to abolition provided at least an opening for greater slave support; with it came the prospect of more slave soldiers for his armies and less opposition to the cause of independence.

CHAPTER 3

FIGHTING FOR THE *PATRIA* IN
THE RÍO DE LA PLATA

 IN 1815 A SLAVE NAMED ANTONIO CASTRO presented himself before the authorities in Buenos Aires and asked to join the black Eighth Regiment. His desire was "to sacrifice himself for the just cause of his *patria*."[1] Antonio was one of over two thousand slaves who officially and unofficially joined the patriot armies in the Río de la Plata region after 1810. In contrast to slaves in Venezuela, the predominantly urban-based slaves of what is today Argentina displayed neither the antipathy toward the creole leaders nor the affection for the king that marked the northern struggle. For them, the *patria* (homeland), rather than the royalist cause, seemed to offer the more likely route to what one slave in Buenos Aires referred to as the "most sacred right of freedom."[2] Offered an opportunity to secure that freedom through service in the military, slaves like Antonio came forward and left an indelible mark on the independence struggles of the region.

The link between personal freedom and *patria* was reinforced by the Argentine revolutionaries. Very much aware of the racial conflict then occurring in Venezuela, they made a deliberate effort to win slave support, even though they had no intention of destroying slavery. Thus, their gestures to the slaves were balanced by a recognition of slaveholder rights, and granting freedom in return for military service developed gradually in response to military needs. The process began in the Banda Oriental in 1811, when patriot military leaders sought to fill gaps in their ranks and prevent the enemy from tapping this potential source of recruits by offering freedom to local slaves who joined their armies. They attracted far more volunteers than anticipated, as men, women, and children from throughout the region flocked to their forces, indicating the slaves' profound desire to be free and willingness to risk their lives to attain that goal. The success of the initiative opened the way for a formal recruiting program in Buenos Aires, where a series of laws was enacted that enlisted slaves from different parts of the country. Others were donated and forcibly drafted, while still others ran away to serve. They fought in many of the campaigns and battles of the region, establishing in the process a reputation as brave and effective soldiers that attracted the attention of commanders such as José de San Martín. As a result, in 1814, when he began organizing an army to invade royalist-held Chile and eventually to attack the center of royalist strength in Peru, he wanted slaves to be the nucleus of his forces.

The recruitment of slaves in the viceroyalty of Río de la Plata, as elsewhere, followed on the heels of the French invasion of Spain and the resulting creole demand for self-government. At first, news of the developments in Spain produced proclamations of loyalty to the crown, but disillusionment with the new rulers in Spain and local competition between European-born *peninsulares* and American-born creoles over political and commercial control fostered conspiracies in Buenos Aires, Montevideo, La Paz, and other viceregal centers. Royalists managed to maintain their authority in Montevideo, while in Upper Peru they achieved it through force of arms in 1809. In Buenos Aires, however, their attempt to take control of the government in January 1809 failed, largely because of the opposition of the creole militia. Concerns rose with news of French advances in Spain, the fall of the Central Junta, and its replacement by the Regency Council, leading to the creole-led "May Revolution" in Buenos Aires in 1810.[3] The new government's plans to establish its authority over the entire viceroyalty, however, were not welcomed in the neighboring provinces and regions. Royalists in Montevideo feared that despite the Buenos Aires revolutionaries' continued expressions of loyalty to the crown, their ultimate aim was independence. As the naval commander in Montevideo wrote in June 1810, "One can scarcely meet a creole, regardless of sex, age, or state, who does not desire the independence of these provinces, and some with a frenzy."[4] War was declared on the *porteños*, armies were mobilized, and fighting erupted everywhere.

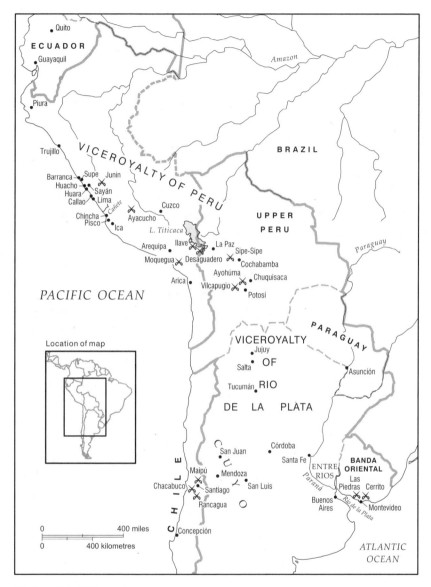

Quito

ECUADOR
Guayaquil

Piura

Amazon

Trujillo

VICEROYALTY OF PERU

BRAZIL

Barranca   Supe   Junín
Huacho
Huara   Sayán
Callao   Lima
                     Cuzco
Chincha   Ayacucho
Pisco   Ica
                     L. Titicaca

UPPER

PERU

Paraguay

Arequipa   Ilave   La Paz   Sipe-Sipe
Moquegua   Desaguadero   Cochabamba
                   Ayohúma   Chuquisaca
Arica   Vilcapugio
                   Potosí

PACIFIC OCEAN

PARAGUAY

VICEROYALTY

Jujuy

Salta   OF

Tucumán   RIO

DE   LA   PLATA

Asunción

Location of map

San Juan   Córdoba
                        Santa Fe
Maipú   BANDA
Mendoza   ORIENTAL
Chacabuco   ENTRE   Las
            Santiago   RIOS   Piedras   Cerrito
            Rancagua   Buenos
                                     Aires   Montevideo

CHILE

CUYO

San Luis

Paraná

Río de la Plata

0   400 miles

0   400 kilometres

Concepción

ATLANTIC
OCEAN

Río de la Plata, Chile, and Peru

39

With the focus on military needs, units of all sorts were organized, including those that incorporated free blacks and mulattoes. A battalion of free blacks under the command of José Superí was part of General Manuel Belgrano's army, while the Sixth Regiment of Pardos and Morenos, also known as the Regiment of Castes or the Regiment of Pardos and Morenos Patricios, included companies from Buenos Aires, Córdoba, and Salta.[5] Those regional differences may have been respected initially, but they soon broke down in the face of military realities. The creation of the all-black Sixth Regiment reflected the revolutionary junta's desire to maintain racial segregation within the forces, but like the regional exclusivity, this, too, soon disappeared. By 1811 several companies of free blacks were part of what had been the white Second Regiment. The junta recognized their importance by declaring that black officers and men were equal to whites and Indians and permitting them to use the honorific "Don" before their names, but it continued to insist that commanders be whites.[6]

In response to the increasingly threatening military situation, recruiting standards also shifted noticeably. The junta began drafting among "marginal sectors" of the population, including the poor, vagrants, the unemployed, and criminals. Expanding the boundaries to encompass the slave population seemed like the next logical step. Already a few slaves were serving, as owners donated their property after the May Revolution to demonstrate their patriotism and loyalty to the new regime. Among the first owners to do so was Father José Zambrana, whose donation in July 1810 of his slave Francisco Xavier attracted coverage in the local newspaper.[7] The donated slaves were freed and granted the privileges of the colonial military *fueros*. In addition, they were now part of an increasingly important institution, a fact recognized by the junta in September 1811, when it proclaimed that military virtues were to be "the path to distinctions, honors, and dignities" in the country, and added: "All citizens will be born as soldiers and will receive from their infancy an education appropriate to their destiny."[8]

The drift toward slave recruiting was gaining momentum, but it required the realities of a military campaign to formalize it. In 1811 the *porteño* authorities launched an invasion of the Banda Oriental after the viceroy, Francisco Xavier de Elío, declared war on Buenos Aires in February. The invading forces, commanded by General José Rondeau, established an alliance with a local, largely gaucho army under the Uruguayan nationalist José Gervasio Artigas; together with other commanders they began turning to local slaves largely for nonmilitary purposes, such as transportation, carpentry, and masonry. But they were not prevented from fighting. Rondeau reported in May, "Many of the slaves taken from the enemy are found in voluntary service, and others through their good disposition have been solicited by the commanders of the company who have used them to cover their respective losses." He inquired about paying them and was informed that slaves who joined voluntarily had to receive a full wage.[9] Far more joined him as he advanced on Montevideo and offered freedom to any slave belonging to Spaniards living in the city. It was this offer that prompted Francisco Estrada to place himself "under the flags of freedom," and many others to follow suit. Among them was Miguel García, whose Spanish owner had gone to Montevideo in 1810 in order to serve the royalists. The owner had left Miguel, his wife, and their two children in the town of Capilla de Mercedes with orders to stay put, but on the appearance of the invading troops, Miguel joined the Sixth Regiment of Pardos and Morenos, led by Colonel Miguel Estanislao Soler, and began a long service with the regiment.[10] Six other slaves, who claimed that they had fled Montevideo, arranged with Artigas and Rondeau to create a corps of lancers from the slaves belonging to "Europeans" (Spaniards). The wife of one of them later recalled that her husband had joined out of a sense of patriotism and his "decided love of his country." They collected over 350 for the corps, named themselves officers, and fought as guerrillas at the battle of Las Piedras in May 1811. They subsequently asked for, and in December were granted, freedom for both themselves and their wives, although the authorities were unwilling to recognize their self-assigned ranks and instructed that the captain not be promoted above more senior candidates.[11] Those assigned to the Sixth Regiment fought outside Montevideo at the battle of Cordón on June 4, 1811. Their "intrepidity and valor" drew the attention of their commander, who commented upon it in a report that subsequently appeared in the *Gaceta de Buenos Aires.*[12]

Lured by the patriots, slaves in the Banda Oriental found little reason to consider serving the king. In many ways, the situation was the reverse of that in Venezuela and New Granada, as the viceroy's authority was restricted largely to Montevideo and his military officers lacked the resources to alter the situation. In 1810 the royalist forces were described as short of veterans, unpaid, and with useless and bad officers. The local naval commander, José María Salazar, complained of the lack of volunteers and the quality of the creole troops. In August 1810 he asked for four thousand "good" European troops to pacify the provinces, or at least one thousand to defend Montevideo. But no reinforcements arrived, which undermined the morale of what troops he had. Desertion had already depleted his forces following rumors of a *porteño* invasion, and he lost even more once Rondeau's forces actually appeared. The royalist defeat at Las Piedras and the siege of Montevideo added to his problems. Royalist fortunes improved only after Doña Carlota, the sister of the imprisoned Ferdinand VII and wife of the regent of Portugal (who was then residing in the Brazilian capital of Rio de Janeiro), took upon herself the task of protecting her brother's patrimony. In response to a Spanish request, she ordered Portuguese troops south into the Banda Oriental. As a result, in September Salazar expressed greater confidence. In addition to the Portuguese, he now had a substantial navy, a corps of Catalans, *cazadores* from Seville (meaning hunters, the equivalent of French *chasseurs* or British rangers), and volunteers from Madrid, as well as militia units composed of royalist emigrants from Buenos Aires and elsewhere who were commanded by a worthy and loyal colonel. Volunteers also included some free blacks who served in the Regiment of Grenadiers of Ferdinand VII.[13]

The Portuguese intervention, together with Argentine military setbacks, set the stage in October 1811 for a formal truce between the Buenos Aires authorities and the royalist government in Montevideo. Its terms took into account the runaways who had joined the invading army and whose numbers had been substantial. "Over one thousand slaves have been removed," Salazar claimed, perhaps an exaggeration, as Lieutenant Colonel Nicolás Vedia of the Argentine forces gave a much smaller figure. He wrote that over three hundred of both sexes had "fled from the *Godos* [Goths, a pejorative term for Spaniards]."[14] Among the runaways were several from Brazil and others from Argentina. The truce declared that those who had fled Montevideo to the invading army would not be obliged to return to their owners unless they wished to do so, with lists to be drawn up of those affected. The rest, including the Brazilian runaways, were supposed to be returned to their owners once Portuguese troops evacuated Spanish territory.[15] Artigas, however, refused to recognize the agreement, and the Argentine commanders, too, were unwilling to comply. When Vedia embarked for Buenos Aires, two hundred slaves accompanied him. The royalists registered their displeasure. One of their generals, Gaspar Vigodet, complained, "Only twenty to twenty-five black slaves can be counted out of the eight hundred who fled from the dominion of their masters." He also claimed that the *porteños* were breaking the armistice by trying to assign a regiment of blacks to help "protect the rebel Artigas," who had no intention of withdrawing from the Banda Oriental along with the Buenos Aires forces. The Argentine junta responded that the runaways would be returned when the owners presented themselves and demanded their slaves.[16] At least one owner of an Argentine runaway made such a request. Her slave, named Pedro Miranda, was a blacksmith who had fled to the *porteño* army. However, she was willing to accept his wages in lieu of his return.[17]

The events of the first siege of Montevideo established a precedent for further slave recruiting when fighting quickly resumed in the region. Committed to securing his homeland's independence, Artigas was particularly welcoming. He turned to slaves to assist in his struggle against the Portuguese troops, expropriating them along with horses and muskets from the enemy and accepting runaways, including more from Brazil. He reported in February 1812 that they were "daily fleeing to our territories."[18] Slaves were also among the *porteño* forces when they invaded the Banda Oriental again when hostilities resumed late in 1812. They included veterans from the first siege, as well as recent donations, and were assigned largely to Soler's Sixth Regiment of Pardos and Morenos that was again part of the army.[19] Others were abducted by the invading army, usually for noncombat roles. A few were assigned to one unit's officers as servants. On hearing of this, the authorities ordered that they be released unless they voluntarily chose to apply for military service. The term was four years, indicating that they were viewed as long-term recruits and not just auxiliaries for the immediate campaign. Another abducted slave was José Antonio Moreno (or Pérez), who had been transporting vegetables into Montevideo when he was taken by a cavalry unit. Although he was declared free by the unit commander, Fernando Otorgués, he was ordered to work for the unit. After a time José returned to his owner, but then rejoined the besieging army as a soldier.[20] Argentine runaways were also part of the invading army. Mateo Vidal's slave Manuel enlisted with the Pardos y Morenos as they set out from Buenos Aires, but was apprehended in Córdoba. Petrona Fernández of Córdoba claimed that her slave Pedro Nolasco Rivas had joined the troops besieging Montevideo and then moved on to Artigas's army. She asked for his return on the grounds that he was not the property of those in Montevideo but rather of a patriot supporter. Another resident of Córdoba, Ambrosio Funes, claimed that his slave was also part of the siege of Montevideo, in the Second Regiment.[21]

As in the case of the previous invasion, the slaves most involved were those living in the Banda Oriental, although this time there was some competition for their services. The patriot army again proved particularly attractive, as Soler was given permission in September 1812 to free slaves of the enemy and enroll them in the Sixth Regiment. As before, large numbers flocked to his banners, including two from an estate near Montevideo owned by a supporter of the Buenos Aires cause. Because of this, the slaves should have been returned, but the owner desired "to contribute to the happy success" of the patriot armies and allowed them to remain. Nevertheless, his request that their wages for their time of service be donated to the *patria* indicated that he did not consider them to be free.[22] This was in sharp contrast to the understanding of the slaves who joined the invaders. They acted as they did precisely because freedom was being offered. An outbreak of disease and shortages of food and water in Montevideo provided further incentives for those living in that city to flee. In November Soler reported that so many were joining him that he lacked the weapons to arm them and asked the government to provide lances to equip companies of lancers. Rondeau decided to turn some of them into a separate company of sappers, and at the end of 1813 had a force of 115 ex-slaves being trained.[23]

In contrast to past practices, the royalists, too, began turning to the local slave population. At the time of the second invasion, their hopes had been momentarily aroused by the October 1813 arrival of a small contingent of troops from Spain, but repeated requests failed to produce further reinforcements. Desperate, the authorities formed a slave battalion, granting them their freedom in return for their service. But their initiative had little impact on the siege, as Montevideo fell in June 1814. Moreover, the promise of freedom proved to be largely a fiction, for the battalion was dissolved shortly before the surrender, and at least some of the slaves were returned to their owners. Weighing the options, more slaves decided that their future lay with the patriots. José Apolinario Sauco had been one of those selected to serve in the royalist battalion, but he chose instead to offer his services to the Argentine Tenth Battalion. Patriotism seemed to be a more important motivation than freedom in his case, as he explained, "It is more appealing to serve the *patria* than the masters who had given him freedom." Annoyance with his owner may also have been a factor, as his defection occurred after the latter failed to live up to a promise to buy José's wife.[24] Another Uruguayan slave who joined the invaders was Lucas Lezica. He participated in a battle against the royalists and managed to capture an enemy musket, which he personally presented to Rondeau. Then, "desirous of following a military career," he approached Soler, stating that he was "keen" (*gustoso*) to join the Sixth Regiment.[25]

As Lezica's case shows, many of the slave recruits were not simply auxiliaries supporting the troops but were actively involved in the action. At the battle of Cerrito on December 31, 1812, those serving in the Sixth Regiment, or Soler's "bizarre battalion," as it was called, came under heavy enemy attack. With their accompanying cavalry dispersed, they began to retreat, but behind Rondeau's leadership managed to recover their lost ground and then mounted a bayonet charge that broke the enemy's line. Victory was thus achieved through the "daring and bravery of the officers and soldiers of No. 6" and "the gallantry of those valiant soldiers." But the cost had been high. The regiment suffered the heaviest casualties of all the units in the battle, with thirty-six killed and seventy-two wounded. Seven more subsequently succumbed to their injuries. Among the casualties was Antonio Videla, a former slave who had served in the defense of Buenos Aires against the British and then in the Corps of Morenos. He was an officer—a captain—in the Sixth Regiment, as were some other black Argentines at this time. Earlier in the year, Soler had recommended that three of its members, all of whom had relatives still enslaved, be promoted: José Mariano San Martín to captain, Felipe Malaver to lieutenant, and Domingo Sosa to sublieutenant.[26] At Cerrito, Videla had commanded a company of *cazadores* that had maintained its position in the face of the enemy charge until all were killed. In recognition of his valor and sacrifice, the state ordered that his daughter be freed.[27]

The events in the Banda Oriental clearly revealed to the rulers in Buenos Aires the benefits of securing slave support. Ideological pressures were pushing them in the same direction. The May Revolutionaries espoused a liberal agenda that included weakening elements of colonial rule, including the institution of slavery. This did not mean abolition, for they were firmly committed to the preservation of property rights. To liberals like Manuel Belgrano, for example, liberalism meant "liberty, equality, security, and property." The challenge was to balance these contradictory elements in order to maintain the support of the slaveholders while controlling the masses and avoiding the social unrest that was threatening the cause of self-government in Venezuela.[28] The government's efforts to win over the black population, therefore, had to be limited yet significant, and its first gesture was to issue a decree on

April 9, 1812, ending the African slave trade. Couched in humanitarian and liberal terms, the decree was presented as a response to concerns about "the rights of afflicted humanity," and at the same time a reflection of "the common conduct of cultured nations, the claims of the respectable authorities of [the] capital, and . . . the liberal principles that the illustrious peoples of the United Provinces of Río de la Plata have proclaimed and [were] defending with valor and energy." The following month, as part of the celebrations of the May Revolution, the government provided 1,200 pesos to free two male and two female slaves. The action, a commentator wrote, would provide freedom to those who "could expect it only in the tomb," and "ultimately" slavery would disappear. However, this was not going to occur immediately, as property rights still had to be respected. It was not possible, the writer noted, "to extinguish slavery at a blow without attacking the sanctity of our properties and without exposing the homeland to grave dangers with the sudden emancipation of a race that, educated in servitude, would only use freedom to cause harm to itself."[29]

Slavery was thus being challenged, if rather hesitantly. At the same time the government was establishing further links between military service and the manumission of slaves. With great fanfare on July 22, 1812, it freed Ventura, a slave of Valentina Feijó, for denouncing a conspiracy that he had uncovered. He was presented with the uniform of the Second Regiment that bore a shield on the left sleeve with the inscription "For faithfulness to the Homeland." He was also to receive either fifty pesos and a sword or the wage of a soldier, while his owner was compensated with three hundred pesos.[30] The groundwork had been set, and eight days later the government unveiled plans to purchase slaves to create a new corps of *libertos*, or freedmen. The recruits were to receive a uniform and a wage of two reales (one-fourth of a peso) per day; in return they had to provide six years of "good service." But gradualism was still the order of the day, for eighteen months passed before thirty-nine slaves, ranging in price from 280 to 350 pesos, were acquired. The delay may have been caused by a lack of funds, or perhaps the authorities were unwilling to upset slave owners, as only thirty-four of them were eventually affected.[31] Nevertheless, the impression was emerging that slavery was under attack, a feeling that was reinforced by further gestures in the direction of the black population. The government publicly recognized them as good soldiers in September 1812 when it organized a militia regiment of *pardos* and free blacks to defend Buenos Aires. The enabling legislation noted the "desire for military honor and the fidelity" of the black community, who "in times past" had contributed to the city's defense and had "shown themselves energetically supportive of the holy cause of freedom from the day that these provinces proclaimed it and for whose achievement they continue to act with the greatest credit and bravery."[32] Of even more value to the slave population was a free womb law that the government issued early in 1813, which declared free all children born in the United Provinces of the Río de la Plata after January 31 of that year. In February a further law freed foreign slaves who set foot on the territory of the United Provinces, although it was later amended to exclude servants and runaways from Brazil. And in May, lotteries to award a chance at freedom were held in Buenos Aires and Mendoza to celebrate the May Revolution.[33]

These initiatives may have been expressed in humanitarian terms, but behind the rhetoric was the creole rulers' overriding worry about political survival. The future of the autonomous governments that they had established in the viceroyalty was becoming increasingly parlous in the face of military threats from neighboring areas and rumors of an imminent invasion of troops from Spain. The governments needed soldiers to confront these, as well as to establish control over the region, especially Upper Peru with its mineral wealth and its access to the royalist stronghold of Peru. One solution that was gaining support was to lay more of the military burden on the shoulders of slaves, who in the Banda Oriental had shown their willingness to serve and their mettle in battle. Consequently, on May 31, 1813, the constituent assembly of Buenos Aires, in response to the "dangers to the *patria*," requested that the executive issue a decree for the formation of a regiment of slaves between the ages of thirteen and sixty, whose owners would be compensated from public funds. The decree referred to the recruits as *"rescatados,"* or rescued ones, imbuing it with a moral tone. This was reinforced by the text of the legislation, which stated that it would free a portion of the men condemned to slavery by ancient laws. It would win their loyalty by raising them to the "dignity of free men" so that they would "defend with energy and enthusiasm a cause that secured their own freedom and that of their descendants." It thereby tied national liberation to personal freedom. The law recognized the "sacred right of property," but the drafters believed that the owners would not resent the "small" sacrifice being demanded of them. The law differentiated among slaves according to occupation: owners would lose one out of three male slaves in domestic service; one out of five slaves working in factories, warehouses, and bakeries; and one of eight slaves involved in agricultural labor. Owners were permitted to donate more. They were to be compensated in three years, although instead of taking the money they had the option of applying the value against various monthly contributions and taxes and thereby reduce them by one-quarter. And to ensure compliance, they were warned that any attempt to hide their slaves would result in losing them all. The recruits were to receive six pesos monthly in wages, just like other soldiers. They would serve for five years, although if owners reduced their selling price to the state, the period of service could be cut. And they were considered free from the time of inscription, but only if they served their five years, which left them in a somewhat nebulous legal situation.[34]

New military crises soon led to additional legislation. Belgrano's armies suffered serious defeats at the hands of royalist forces in Upper Peru in October and November 1813. At the battle of Vilcapugio his losses amounted to three thousand killed, wounded, and missing, including most of his militia and newly raised troops. A second defeat at the battle of Ayohúma cost him the lives of his commander and more soldiers, among them slave recruits. At the same time, the *porteño* forces besieging Montevideo were suffering. A British observer described them as "much weakened by disease and bad diet." In addition, they now faced the prospect of confronting Spanish veterans of the independence war against France, whose arrival was believed to be imminent and likely to have "a serious and decisive effect."[35] As a result, on December 24 the earlier recruiting law was extended to the entire province in order to complete the Regiment of Libertos. "The calamities that constantly accompany the war whose weight is still felt . . . demand heroic suffering. . . . A good peace is never made without having made a good war," it trumpeted. It divided owners into two groups. Those having more than one slave but who had not been affected by the earlier decree now had to contribute one slave regardless of his occupation. From each one hundred so named, a selection of fifteen would be taken. The second group comprised those who had previously contributed but still had slaves. They had to supply one slave, with thirty selected from each hundred identified. A third decree, on February 14, 1814, sought additional slaves to meet a critical shortage of troops of the line, producing three hundred soldiers for the regiment.[36]

The country was moving inexorably toward independence, and in its wake those targeted to supply the recruits came increasingly from a particular group of slaveholders. Casting Spain as the oppressive tyrant, on January 14, 1815, the government ordered the recruitment of all male slaves between the ages of sixteen and thirty belonging to Spaniards residing in the United Provinces without citizenship. It exempted only Buenos Aires bakeries, women slaveholders, and those described as "poor." In contrast to the earlier laws, the term of service was imprecise—continuing until one year after the end of the war, when the owners would be compensated.[37] The floating date may have been an indication of the present military uncertainties, or the government may have seen it as a means to compel the recruits to fight more bravely. In any event, troops were still needed, and on March 3 the government modified the earlier legislation to include bakery workers, as long as the bakery was not left with "an irreparable gap" in its workforce.[38] In May, it included slaves in a law that assigned "every African and free *pardo* in Buenos Aires and every individual American regardless of class, condition, or state" between the ages of fifteen and sixty for service in a new militia corps to prevent the reintroduction of "the barbarous colonial system."[39] In October the government hit Spanish owners again with the reintroduction of the January decree, following reports that Spain was about to launch its long-rumored expedition of ten thousand men.[40] With the declaration of independence in July 1816, there was even less need to curry favor among Spanish slaveholders, and on September 19 a decree called on Spanish bachelors to supply most of the slaves for a new battalion of *libertos*. They were to give up all their male slaves between the ages of twelve and forty. Meanwhile, the church, religious orders, priests, local and foreign bachelors, and Spanish married men had to supply one-third of their slaves, and local and foreign married men had to supply one-sixth. Again, the term of service was until one year after the end of the war, at which time owners would be paid.

The decree was suspended within three weeks on news that sufficient recruits were arriving from Córdoba and that there was no immediate threat to the city.[41] Yet, the government had not ended its recruitment of slaves. On December 3, 1816, it prohibited their removal from the United Provinces to ensure that they would be available should the need arise. Six days later it called on those Spaniards without citizenship living in the province of Buenos Aires to contribute four hundred more slaves for a battalion of *cazadores*, or alternatively provide 210 pesos each, with compensation two years after a peace treaty. The law stated that while Americans had carried the weight of the public cause, donating their wealth and their lives, Spaniards had benefited, "looking with pleasure on the conflicts."[42] A year later, on December 19, the government issued a new law that condemned Spain for continuing with the "abominable traffic of making men slaves" and for its brutality in Venezuela, destroying "with blood and fire the lives and homes of Americans" who had fought "to create a nation under the auspices of a rationally free, circumspect, and incorruptible government." The law called for the creation of a corps of slaves in the capital, commenting that this was "not to raise them to the rank of citizens, since in the price of their military actions they will have bought this precious gift." It applied to all slaves between the ages of fifteen and sixty in the precinct of Buenos Aires, regardless of the nationality of their owners, but they would see service only if the city came under attack. Freedom would follow three years of service.[43]

A Spanish invasion was by now highly unlikely, so that the offers of freedom and citizenship were almost meaningless and slave recruiting in the city began to lose its importance. The existing laws continued to be applied for the next three years, supplying some of the soldiers for the expeditionary army being organized in the western city of Mendoza for the invasion of Chile, but the size of the draw declined annually. In August 1819 a law designed to complete the corps described in the December 1816 law may have reduced the minimum age of recruits to ten; however, military needs were now less critical, and the number of available slaves was shrinking. Thus, when on November 3, 1821, the government officially ended the *rescate*, it merely recognized an existing reality.[44]

The series of recruiting laws was the principal mechanism for securing Argentine slaves for military service, but a handful of other official channels added to the numbers. Jails provided a few recruits. José Franciso Iturri, a convicted murderer, had been sentenced to ten years in prison and two hundred lashes, to be administered through the streets of the city, when officials decided that as a result of his good behavior he would be of more use to the *patria* in the army than in jail. Vagrants, who in some cases were migrants from the Banda Oriental with uncertain ownership, were also viewed as suitable for the army, with those believed to be the property of the enemy particularly susceptible. Other slaves were simply abducted. The commander of a raid on the island of Martín Garcia in 1814 asked that several local slaves who had been taken by his officers be placed in his battalion. His request was approved, provided that he supply their names, the names of their owners, and other details. Privateers, who in some cases had slaves among their crews, were licensed to capture slaves for military purposes. According to a decree of November 18, 1816, they were instructed to carry their captives back to Argentina, where the government would pay fifty pesos for every male between the ages of twelve and forty who was suited for military service. The slaves then had to serve for four years. However, only a small proportion may actually have served, for privateers seemed to prefer transporting their captives to Brazil, where they could obtain a much better price.[45]

Called upon to deliver their slaves for the good of the state, owners showed themselves to be generally supportive of the legislation, at least at first. Some chose not to accept compensation, out of either generosity or patriotism, transforming the selection into a donation. There were others who gave slaves independently of the recruiting laws, although their donations usually were included as part of the statistics, making differentiation impossible. Owners sometimes made their donation conditional on completing a period of service. José Francisco de Ugarteche freed his slave Joaquín on condition that he serve five years. The same period was demanded by Roque Pintos when he offered his slave Juan Bautista as "proof of his love of the cause." Juan was described as a man of twenty-two, healthy, without vices, and educated in the use of musket and cannon. Juan Antonio Costa asked for only two years when he donated his slave Joaquín, a man between twenty-two and twenty-five years of age, giving him his freedom along with two complete uniforms. Others specified no particular length of service. Domingo Mathew offered five out of the eight slaves who worked in his musket factory; Francisco Belgrano donated four slaves, worth a total of 1,170 pesos; and Antonio José Silveira donated a slave named Domingo worth 300 pesos. Juan Ortiz de Zarate offered Antonio, a slave between twenty-two and twenty-four years old, on account of his past good service and his owner's affection. However, that affection went only so far, for the donation stipulated that if Antonio failed to comply, the offer lapsed and he was to remain a slave until his owner's death.[46] Even those who did not own slaves became donors by providing money that could be used to purchase recruits. Among them was José Antonio Bustamante, a Spanish priest.[47]

The owners had some influence over the process, as they could select which of their slaves might be recruited, although the reasons for their choices are not always clear. Some claimed they chose on the basis of quality: in donating Joaquín, Juan Antonio Costa insisted he was "one of his best." Suitability for the military was also cited as a reason. Joaquín Belgrano selected Josef because of his "disposition and aptitude for the army," while Antonio Aremilla was described as "very brave." Other owners indicated that their slaves wanted to serve. Juan José Pérez claimed that Manuel, a twenty-year-old *pardo* valued at 290 pesos, was "healthy and without vices and with an inclination to military service." Lieutenant Colonel José Ortiz offered a slave who had "the most animated desire to follow a military career," while Antonio José Silveira claimed that four of his slaves were "determined on serving in the troops of the homeland," and he was not prepared to stand in their way. In similar fashion, Francisco de Eyzaga said his slave Antonio was "set on serving with the troops of the homeland" and he could not "deny him his wish." But why Gertrudis de Villegas chose to donate one of her slaves, Joaquín, after she had promised to free him on her death, remains a mystery. "It is indispensable that my name not be mentioned in public or secretly," she wrote, suggesting some pricking of her conscience as she sent him off to risk his life.[48]

Were these descriptions accurate? Might they have been designed to hide the flaws of the donated slaves? The recruitment laws provided an obvious opportunity for owners to unload slaves who were a problem or of limited value because of illness, infirmities, or old age, and officials were prepared to allow some leeway in this regard. Among the slaves accepted from the College of San Carlos was a runaway whose actions, it was reported, were a result of his "having no other motive than he did not wish to work as a slave." Apprehended after having survived in the city for some time by claiming to be a freeman and moving from work to work and barrio to barrio to avoid capture, he was described as "not only useless but prejudicial to the [College's] farm," hence his being made available to the military. Juan Parareda's donation was a slave named Cayetano, who was at the time in jail on account of what his owner called his "haughty disposition," a result of excessive drinking. Parareda seemed fearful of his slave, referring to him as his "capital enemy" and asking that he be kept in the barracks "to prevent him coming to insult [his owner's] face." But, in general, the authorities acted to prevent unsuitable donations. They insisted that every recruit had to be checked by a surgeon; only those deemed medically fit and apt were accepted, indicating that they wanted more than cannon fodder. Those found "useless" were returned, and the owner had to provide an alternative. The Convent of La Merced of Córdoba had to replace one slave who was discovered to be suffering from chest pains and was crippled. Juan Baptista Mújica supplied two of his six slaves, but one was rejected on account of his age, and his replacement was rejected because of chest problems. As a result, he had to present all of his slaves, out of whom Antonio, a blacksmith, was selected. Not wanting to lose this valuable artisan, Mújica offered to provide money instead, but was refused. He then offered to buy another slave as a substitute, an offer that was initially agreed to but then rejected, since Antonio had already been chosen.[49] But even "useless" slaves could be useful. When two of the four slaves Antonio Obligado provided from his estancias were rejected, they were nevertheless retained in the barracks, apparently to clean it. The other two proved less productive: one died and one fled.[50]

These cases indicate that the owners could not always get their way, and as time passed they became less supportive of the recruiting. Their initial enthusiasm was soon dampened by continuing demands and delays in paying compensation. But any opposition had to be muted. The laws and the various penalties prevented them from hiding slaves or removing them from the country. They may have been somewhat reassured by the authorities' reiteration that property rights would be respected, but the antislavery legislation and the expressions of liberalism produced fears that slavery might be abolished altogether, fears that were fed by rumors that on at least one occasion emanated from government circles.[51] The uncertainty was reflected in the slave market, which in July 1814 was described as having "many for sale but few buyers."[52] Some owners may have donated their slaves in an attempt to ensure the survival of a government that claimed to be committed to retaining slavery, but complaints and appeals soon began to be voiced. Exemptions were sought from the legislation, as in the case of one owner who described the slave as her husband's "right hand." Another, Luisa Estela, in June 1813 asked the state for a house whose rent would be covered by the money owed her. She referred to herself as "a poor woman charged with a family" whose large numbers could only be maintained with her slaves. She had "lost" two of her slaves—Benito, valued at 300 pesos, and Antonio, valued at 280—whom she claimed had provided her with an income. No house was immediately available, but she was assured that when one became available she would receive it. In a second letter in 1814 she added a third slave to her contributions and complained that after a year, she had still received not "the least amount," so that she was in "much misery," without bread to feed her children and money to maintain her house. She asked for 300 pesos to meet her "many needs." Similarly, Prudencio Zagari, writing for his brother who had provided two slaves, asked for at least some of the money owed. He noted that "love of the interests of the country was always worth more than his own convenience," and he would have remained indifferent to his reduced circumstances, but recent reverses in the Banda Oriental had ruined him, and he needed money in order to maintain his family of sixteen.[53] With compensation uncertain, many took advantage of the option to apply the value of their slaves to meet the various contributions and taxes that they owed, thereby securing at least some financial benefit.[54]

The only laws that owners challenged with some success were those that recruited slaves owned by Spaniards, usually on the grounds that the real owner was an American-born family member. Doña Carmen Sáenz made such a claim after Camilo Sáenz was assigned to the Eighth Regiment. She insisted that she, an American, was the owner of the slave, and not her Spanish husband. Manuela Tadea Pinazo asked for the return of her slave Anselmo, stating that she had inherited him from her parents and he was not the property of her Spanish husband. In a third case, the slave's owner claimed that she, and not her Spanish husband, had bought the slave some years earlier from a French slaver in Montevideo for three hundred pesos. She added that he was the only support for herself and her children, all of whom were minors.[55]

Ownership may have shifted suspiciously in response to the legislation, but the owners were not the only ones who were bending the truth and the law to protect their interests. Slaves had engaged in various forms of resistance since their introduction to America three hundred years earlier, and now with a new means to secure their freedom they were prepared to do whatever they could to facilitate their recruitment and remain in the military. Thus, some expressed a desire to serve in order to influence their owners, and one actually offered to pay for the privilege. Antonio Pavón of Buenos Aires made a contract with his owner to provide six pesos monthly from his wage as a soldier until his value was reached.[56] Still more slaves chose to run away to join, and then employed imaginative explanations to avoid being returned to their owners. The example of the runaways from the Banda Oriental who had been given their freedom in exchange for their military service served as motivation, and they found that Argentine recruiters, facing a growing demand for soldiers, were not too rigorous about demanding proof of status. Claiming to be a freeman was usually adequate, unless their owner made a complaint. The African-born shoemaker Juan Charras was twenty-two and single when he ran away to enlist. However, his owner managed to track him down and demanded his return. Some slaves recognized the growing nationalistic feelings in the area and tried to use ownership by a Spaniard as justification for their flight and request to enlist. Among them was Cipriano Suares, who in September 1813 appealed for permission to join the Seventh Regiment against the wishes of his Spanish owner. As for Francisco Agüero, he seemed to revise the nationality of his owner as the circumstances demanded. He had run away in April 1815, serving first in the Eighth Regiment and then in a regiment of dragoons. He claimed that when he had enlisted he told officials his owner was an American, but they had signed him up anyway. Later, as new legislation came into effect, he changed his story: his owner now was described as a European who had failed to deliver him according to the *rescate*, at which point he had fled and joined the Sixth Regiment.[57] His story was being checked by the authorities, but with freedom on the line, slaves seemed willing to provide any explanation as long as it kept their owners at bay.

The runaways, whose numbers are impossible to calculate, joined a cross-section of the area's male slaves who were recruited under the various laws. According to official statistics, 619 slaves were enlisted in 1813, another 364 the following year, and 567 more under the January 1815 decree. The *rescate* of 1816–1817 took over 400, with a further 37 produced by the March 1817 decree, totaling over 2,000 men. Most were in their twenties. Of those recruited under the 1816 and 1817 laws, the oldest was forty-five, while 13 were under the minimum age of fifteen and one was only eight years old. The latter were probably used as drummers and fifers, but as the August 1819 law indicated, slaves little more than children were considered possible soldiers. Their valuations reflected their differing ages, skills, and backgrounds. In the first round, the lowest price was 150 pesos and the highest 350, with most valued at either 280 or 300 pesos. The average price of those taken in 1815 was 260 pesos. The later recruiting that targeted the slaves of Spaniards set a single price of 210 pesos, although the amount paid was often much lower, thereby reducing the financial obligations of the state. Buenos Aires and its province were the source of most of the recruits, with the neighboring provinces adding others. Included in the first *rescate* were 81 slaves from Mendoza, 19 from San Juan, and others from Santa Fe and Córdoba. By September 1814, a further 31 slaves had been donated by twenty-six owners from Mendoza. Transported in the ubiquitous two-wheeled carts of the pampas, they made their way under military supervision to the capital for inscription and training. In October 1813, Sergeant Pedro Marcelio Rodrígues arrived in Buenos Aires in charge of carts carrying eight *libertos* and a quantity of *maté* (herbal tea). Many of the recruits were originally from Africa, listing themselves as natives of the Angola, Banguela, Congo, Costa de Mina, Hausa, Moro, Mozambique, and other nations. Some were described as being of the Portuguese nation, which could have referred to an African, European, or Brazilian background.[58] The large number of African-born slaves among the recruits might be taken to indicate that owners were trying to unload unmanageable foreign-born slaves, or it may point to the more personal connection between owners and those who had been born in their house. More likely, it simply reflected the extent of the late colonial influx of African slaves and the fact that a large percentage of them were of military age. None of the laws made reference to place of birth, and no commander expressed a preference for African- or American-born recruits.

Most of the slaves were recruited for the army, which included the attached artillery units, but the other branches of the military also had ex-slaves among their personnel. Some served in the cavalry, a few were assigned to the navy, and at least one served in more than one branch. Fernando Costa's slave Bonifacio was assigned to the brigantine *Nancy* as a cook, receiving a soldier's wage of six pesos per month. A condition of his service was that if the expedition lasted less than five years, he was to be enrolled in the Eighth Battalion. In fact, he was transferred almost immediately, as the expedition lasted less than a week.[59] The terms of Bonifacio's naval service indicated a noncombatant's role, which was true of other recruits as well. For example, the Regiment of Mounted Grenadiers bought three slaves who were blacksmiths, with the state paying their owners four hundred pesos each. They received clothing for fourteen months, plus wages of two reales daily. They were expected to provide six years of "good service" before being freed. The terms suggest that they were taken to shoe horses and not to serve as cavalrymen.[60]

Whether recruited, drafted, or abducted, these largely untrained troops were of doubtful quality, at least in the beginning. A British evaluation in September 1813 noted, "The troops collected for the defence of this place are very imperfectly disciplined, and the officers (speaking comparatively) are much worse than the men."[61] Government evaluations were equally critical. One written in the following month noted that in one barracks the effective force was only seventy-seven men: twenty-eight whites and forty-nine slaves. All were unarmed and lacking in discipline. Commenting on the blacks, the writer noted, "Their nature and quality demand that they be commanded by squadrons of whites, the only way that to my reckoning will make them useful."[62] These were men who might be armed and called upon to defend the city but could not really be considered soldiers. One black militia company that included slaves, the Company of Pardos of Punta Gorda, drew particular criticism. In November 1813 its commander, Eduardo Holmberg, reported that insubordination ran rife in the unit and only the most rigorous methods would restore discipline. On one occasion, a dispute between an ensign and five sergeants degenerated from insults, to blows, to a sword fight, to quarrelling in front of the troops. One soldier had struck his officer in the face, while many had deserted, taking their weapons with them. Holmberg, who was not opposed to black troops in general, asked that the soldiers be reassigned. "It would be a very great favor for me," he wrote, as well as a benefit to the state, because he feared "that these men, who I believe are capable of anything, will pass to the enemy in a battle and cause considerable disorder among others." Eventually the unit was integrated into the Tenth Battalion, but even more soldiers were lost to what Holmberg described as "scandalous desertions," so that what had been a company of fifty men was reduced to no more than ten.[63]

Circumstances such as these prompted some officers to express serious reservations about slave troops. The most notable was Manuel Belgrano, who commanded them in a number of his campaigns in the north. Writing to José de San Martín on December 25, 1815, he thanked him for some reinforcements, saying that they could serve as a model for others. But he added that he was not "happy with the troop of *libertos*." In a rather contradictory fashion, he complained, "The blacks and mulattoes are a canaille who are as cowardly as they are bloodthirsty, and in the five actions that I have had, they have been the first to break ranks and search for walls of bodies [to hide behind]." His solution to his army's problems was to have white officers.[64] His reservations may have had deep roots that preceded slave recruiting. In December 1811 he had had to contend with a mutiny in Buenos Aires that included black troops. According to a Spanish account, the troops objected when Belgrano was named their commander, demanded their pay before proceeding to Upper Peru, and then took over the barracks. Eventually the uprising had to be suppressed, through the use—ironically—of other black troops.[65] Belgrano may also have been searching for a scapegoat for his own series of military reversals. He quite likely shared the racist views that permeated Argentina's officer corps, for others also expressed doubts about black troops and their ability to lead. At the time of the first *rescate* law in June 1813, *pardo* officers, sergeants, and corporals were removed from the black units in Córdoba and replaced with whites, and a law was passed prohibiting ex-slaves from being promoted to noncommissioned officer rank.[66]

The reservations seemed unjustified, for black soldiers fought in numerous campaigns and battles in the area and, in general, acquitted themselves well, perhaps even displaying the bloodthirstiness that drew Belgrano's comment. The Sixth Regiment, for example, served throughout the region, in the northwest, Paraguay, Upper Peru, and the two sieges of Montevideo. It shared in the victories at Tucumán in September 1812 and Salta in February 1813 against invading royalist forces, as well as the defeats at Paraguarí, in Paraguay, in January 1811, Vilcapugio in October 1813, and Ayohúma the following month. In the aftermath of Ayohúma, San Martín, as commander of the Army of the North, incorporated all the remaining *pardos* and *morenos* into the Seventh Regiment. As a result, many were present at the shattering defeat at Sipe-Sipe, in Upper Peru, on November 29, 1815, when the Argentine army under General Rondeau was virtually destroyed, leading to the dissolution of regiments like the Seventh.[67] Individual accounts point to the valor of some of the black soldiers in these companies. Runaways in particular may have been determined to prove themselves in order to strengthen their request for freedom, should they be reclaimed by their owners. This may explain the conduct of Antonio Lima, a runaway from a hat factory who joined the Tenth Regiment of Libertos in December 1813 and then served for over two years in the Company of Pardos of Punta Gorda, where he established a reputation as a "good" soldier. He had served at the battle of Entre Ríos on February 22, 1814, and came to the rescue of his captain, José María de Ayuela, who had been shot in the knee. Ayuela subsequently reported, "This brave soldier came to where I was and without letting go of his musket, lifted me on his shoulders and carried me to our lines, returning immediately to occupy his post." He was subsequently captured but managed to escape and made his way to Santa Fe, where he resumed his duties. His sergeant referred to him as "one of the best soldiers in his corps."[68]

Actions such as these created supporters out of many commanders and countered the criticisms of people like Belgrano. Rondeau was favorably disposed, while José María Paz considered one black soldier to be worth at least three Europeans. In 1813, on the arrival of the Seventh Regiment in the northwest, he commented that they "served as a model to the rest of the infantry and cavalry."[69] Also impressed was José de San Martín. He had seen them in action in the north and, following his appointment in August 1814 as governor of the western region known as Cuyo and commander of the new Army of the Andes, he turned to blacks, and particularly slaves, to fill the ranks of the army that he was organizing to attack royalist Peru. His strategy was to avoid the sinkhole of Upper Peru that had produced so many defeats and cost the lives of so many Argentine soldiers, and to attack instead from the south through Chile. To do so he calculated that he needed an army of fourteen thousand men, with freed slaves to make up about ten thousand of the total. He preferred them because of what he described as "their uncontestable subordination and natural toughness in demanding tasks." In his view, "the infantry and even the artillery must be composed of slaves and *libertos*," for while Americans—that is, whites—were suited for the cavalry, "the best infantry soldier . . . is the black and the mulatto."[70] A slaveholder himself, San Martín had in his personal entourage at least one ex-slave: Andrés Ibáñez was the son of an African prince who had been brought to Buenos Aires when he was sixteen. A few years later he became a soldier and was among those who accompanied San Martín to the city of Mendoza, where the latter was establishing his base of operations.[71]

For San Martín, Mendoza seemed an ideal place to prepare his army. As well as being distant from the political machinations in Buenos Aires, it was the gateway to the Andean passes to Chile. The surrounding region of Cuyo, comprising the provinces of Mendoza, San Juan, and San Luis, had close commercial and personal ties with Chile that were reinforced following the defeat of the Chilean independence forces near Santiago in 1814 and the resulting influx of Chilean refugees.[72] The region had the resources to support his forces and boasted a slave population of 4,200 who worked on the region's fruit farms, vineyards, and livestock estates. San Martín wanted 1,190 of them as part of his 10,000 slave recruits, with Buenos Aires and its province providing another 5,000, 2,600 from Córdoba, and 1,000 from the rest of the country. Slaves from the area had already been recruited under earlier legislation, and following the Buenos Aires law that targeted the slaves of Spaniards, San Martín issued a similar law on January 26, 1815, that recruited slaves between the ages of sixteen and thirty belonging to Spaniards resident in Cuyo. The response was hardly what he expected, however, as only 23 slaves were collected from San Juan and sent by cart, along with other recruits, to Mendoza.[73]

The small number of recruits was one of several problems San Martín faced as he slowly put together his invasion force. In addition to filling the expeditionary army, he needed troops for local defense in case of a royalist invasion from Chile. But desertions depleted his forces almost as quickly as recruits were found. He was also short of weapons. In September 1815 he noted that the *pardo* companies that were part of the Mendoza militia had not a single musket among them and "would be useless in case of an attack." To meet this challenge, he set up local arms-making factories. At the same time he began transferring militia veterans into his army and replacing them with raw recruits. A January 1816 law assisted him by ordering the formation of two new militia companies of infantry, one of whites and the second of *pardos*. The latter would include urban and rural slaves between the ages of fourteen and forty-five. But this created a new problem: rural slaves were needed for the area's agricultural demands, especially during harvest. In response, in April 1816 San Martín agreed to a request from the *cabildo* of Mendoza that the military exercises of the slave corps be suspended for two months. Then, in a new effort to secure adequate numbers of recruits, he raised the maximum age to fifty-five and accepted free blacks and slaves from Chile into his forces. His hopes of securing ten thousand slaves by now had long faded, but San Martín continued to envision them as the centerpiece of his army, with those in Cuyo providing the core. Indeed, he was becoming increasingly reliant on them. On June 12 he wrote, "There is no recourse . . . , only the placing of every slave in arms can save us."[74]

San Martín's worries were expressed at a time of growing political and military chaos in the country. Provinces ruled independently of one another, while armies from Upper Peru and Brazil were threatening. In order to create a degree of unity and to challenge the atmosphere of pessimism, delegates from the various Argentine provinces met in Tucumán and, on July 9, 1816, declared independence, calling the new country the United Provinces of South America.[75] While failing to resolve internal differences over the nature of the new government or the continuing threats from forces in Upper Peru and the Banda Oriental, independence provided a degree of direction and momentary stability. But the survival of the new republic remained very much in doubt, putting even greater pressure on San Martín to succeed.

With the internal political situation somewhat resolved, San Martín could proceed with his efforts to acquire more slave recruits, although with now much-reduced expectations of four thousand men. His appeals to Cuyo politicians in August 1816 to pressure those who still had substantial numbers of slaves, particularly religious communities, at first met with firm refusals. He responded with a bit of deception. While negotiations with the local representatives were proceeding, he met with the new country's supreme director, Juan Martín de Pueyrredón, in Córdoba. He returned hinting that there were plans to abolish slavery in all of the United Provinces once one of the provinces took the lead. He urged the locals to show their generosity before the rumored law was introduced. This muted the opposition, and on September 2 he suggested the cession of two-thirds of the slaves of Cuyo, whose owners would receive a just price in compensation. Perhaps accepting the rumors as true and preferring some return on their property, the local deputies agreed unanimously.[76]

Having secured access to all slaves over the age of twenty, San Martín's army grew, but not without continuing problems. The Chilean independence leader Bernardo O'Higgins, who had fled from his homeland to Mendoza after the patriots' defeat two years earlier, wrote in September that there were six hundred men now serving who had been slaves, although he feared that they would not be ready in two months unless uniforms were delivered. Local slaveholders still had reservations. Those in San Luis reiterated concerns about the potential harmful effects on an economy that was already suffering and pointed out that since the enlisted included artisans as well as agricultural workers, various sectors were being affected. The head of the province tried to silence the complaints by pointing out that although people would suffer from the loss of their slaves, they would be "excessively remunerated" with the destruction of the "Tyrant of Chile" when they and "this virtuous pueblo received the sweet satisfaction of having participated in this work that will secure [their] future happiness." The *cabildo* agreed, and on October 8 all slaves between the ages of fourteen and fifty were called up. Forty-two eventually appeared, and twenty-eight were enlisted; the state paid 5,260 pesos in compensation.[77] Pueyrredón had thought that to secure the number of requested slaves would be impossible, but in response to the generosity of the western region, he suggested that five or six hundred more might be made available from the capital. He was unable to deliver, however, as his request for a donation of slaves from the country proportionate to what the *cuyanos* were offering resulted in "a hellish clamor by the patriots against the measure." He later elaborated, "As this pueblo has given so many already, a general discontent brewed that had to be suppressed, but in its place I am going to take another measure, that . . . will be borne by all the European Spaniards." The subsequent December decree was aimed at recruiting four hundred slaves for the army's needs, but it came too late to benefit the invasion force.[78]

As his army gradually grew to an effective size, San Martín also had to contend with the racist feelings that were evident in the army and had been reinforced by his heavy reliance on slave soldiers. He recognized that integrating the units would be impossible, noting early in 1816, "It is a chimera to believe that through an inconceivable revolution the master would present himself in the same line with his slave."[79] All the officers consequently were white, and there seemed to be no stigma attached to this, as individuals were applying for the positions.[80] But by law he was prevented from promoting ex-slaves to be even noncommissioned officers, and this seemed both iniquitous and unjustified. San Martín protested, writing, "There are many slaves who are educated, know how to write, and possess a nature capable of the best education." He urged that the authorities alter the law and open the way for their promotion, arguing that this measure would not hurt the nation, nor would it lead to what had occurred in Haiti. To try to resolve some of the concerns about the racial makeup of his forces, he also asked for five hundred reinforcements from Belgrano's army, who should be white, since it was "not suitable" to increase the number of those of the caste who composed the major part of the infantry. He failed to secure the white reinforcements, but on November 14 he wrote that he had in his hands a supreme resolution of October 30 declaring that slaves could be corporals and sergeants.[81]

Thus, by the end of the year the army was ready to break camp. Of the 4,000 soldiers and 1,000 auxiliaries, 1,554 were ex-slaves, constituting almost 40 percent of the total. In addition, freemen and runaways in militia battalions from Mendoza and San Juan were participating in the expedition, increasing the total number of blacks to over half the army. Cuyo had supplied half the slaves, with San Juan contributing 200, Mendoza, 248, and San Luis, 28. They included slaves who had been officially drafted or had been donated privately.[82] They were assigned to the Seventh and Eighth Regiments in about equal proportions, with others in the Eleventh Infantry.[83] San Martín later recognized Cuyo's contribution. Referring to it as the "immortal province," he commented on its contribution of war materiel, money, powder, and horses. Here was a province "of limited population without public treasury, commerce, or great capital, lacking wood and primary materials, [that] has been able to raise from its own breast an army of 3,000 men, depriving itself even of its slaves, its only agricultural workers," he wrote.[84] To arouse these soldiers he engaged in one further piece of deception. Prior to their departure he addressed them, waving papers that he claimed were letters from Chile stating that the Spanish leaders were so certain of victory that they already had plans for any captured black soldiers. They would then either be sent to work on local sugar plantations or sold for quantities of sugar.[85]

What the slaves thought as they prepared to invade Chile can only be surmised. Those who had been born in Africa probably were no longer surprised by anything. They had already experienced the physical and psychological turmoil of being brutally wrenched from their families and taken on a terrifying voyage across the Atlantic Ocean. Some had settled into the urban environment of Buenos Aires with the muddy Río de la Plata a ready signpost, unlike those who worked on the pampas with little to differentiate one region from the next. For both, that same featureless plain had stretched before them during the long weeks they had traveled to Mendoza. But now, off to the west, they could see a new natural feature that may have raised fears even among the most hardened of them. Before them lay the dark hills of the precordillera, and beyond the snow-capped mountains of the Andes. Their orders called for them to cross that barrier, and on January 9, 1817, they set out. A British report on the army was that it was "in a very good state of discipline, and extremely well equipped and appointed."[86] Whether they could successfully challenge the royalist forces in Chile was about to be tested.

CHAPTER 4

CHANGING LOYALTIES IN
THE NORTH

 IN 1816, AN EX-SLAVE by the name of Pedro Camejo joined the independence forces of Venezuelan *llanero* chief and future president José Antonio Páez. Camejo was no stranger to military service, having previously served under the royalist banners. He had done so, he later explained to Simón Bolívar, because it appeared that "everyone went to war without a shirt and without a peseta and returned afterwards dressed in a very fine uniform and with money in his pocket." His loyalties had shifted after the battle of Araure in December 1813, when an inferior patriot force under Bolívar defeated the royalist unit he served in. He deserted and eventually joined Páez, remaining a fiercely loyal companion until his death at the battle of Carabobo in 1821. His boldness and his race made him a widely recognized figure. The former earned him promotion to the rank of lieutenant; the two together produced his widely known sobriquet, "Negro Primero."[1]

Camejo's change of loyalty was the kind of response that Bolívar and other independence figures were keen to promote. For too long, the majority of slaves had either actively or passively supported the royalists, while large numbers had engaged in the racially motivated rebellion that had frequently exhibited a royalist hue. Few had joined the patriots. Following the arrival of Pablo Morillo and the Spanish Expeditionary Army, however, loyalty to the king lost some of its luster. The destruction of Venezuela's Second Republic and almost all the self-governing administrations in New Granada reduced the need for local recruiting, thereby closing what had been the primary route to personal freedom for male slaves. That setback did not alienate them completely from the royalist cause however, since the patriots were doing little to attract them. The struggle for independence continued, but it followed an uncertain path, often under the direction of regional leaders or caudillos whose political control was geographically restricted and whose careers in many cases seemed likely to be rather short. They were prepared to recruit slaves to meet their military needs, but they had access to limited numbers, and those few had little reason to join what in their eyes was a doomed cause.

Even the return from exile of the now widely recognized independence leader Simón Bolívar failed to ignite slave support for the independence effort. Bolívar's attitude to slaves appeared to be changing, in part because of his promise to the president of Haiti, and in part because he had begun to realize that to achieve his dream he had to make a more determined effort to win the support of the population of his homeland, including its slaves. His appreciation of them as soldiers was also growing, as was his recognition that slavery could not rationally or morally exist in a country that claimed to be free. However, his commitment to abolition was always secondary to his desire for independence, and his relationship with the slave population remained lukewarm at best. Although he preached abolition, he still owned slaves, and his offer of personal freedom was conditional upon fighting for his cause. Fortunately for Bolívar and the other independence leaders, the royalists allowed their earlier close relationship with the slave population to deteriorate, and they refused to introduce social policies equivalent to Bolívar's. At the same time, they alienated broad sections of the American population with the brutality of their reconquest and their failure to end the independence threat and the warfare.[2] Consequently, more and more slaves gravitated toward the patriots in the north, although without the enthusiasm seen in Argentina; loyalty to the king had not disappeared, and the program of the northern independence leaders were still viewed with some skepticism. Thus, while the latter managed to expand their appeal, most of their recruits still had to be compelled to serve. Bolívar sought to recruit thousands of them following his defeat of the royalists in New Granada in 1819, and as a result of his military successes growing numbers of them were attracted to his cause. That support helped him finally to secure the independence of his homeland and to establish the new nation that he called Gran Colombia.

In 1816 slaves remained a potent force in the north, but they lacked clear direction. Their agitation had not ended, despite the royalists' suppression of the creole governments in Venezuela and New Granada. In some areas the rebelling slaves, seeing that the royalists had failed to meet their demands, shifted their antagonism in the direction of the cause they had once supported. The years of brutal warfare and the attendant dislocations had left many slaves without a controlling hand. Owners had abandoned the area, especially after Bolívar's declaration of war to the death. While some returned when royalism was apparently restored, they found numerous obstacles to reclaiming their property. Records had been destroyed, and many slaves who had been left behind, along with those of recognized patriots, had been evaluated and sold at public action. Neither they, nor those ordered to work on lands that had been awarded to royalist supporters, had any reason to feel affection for their new masters. The same could be said of those who managed to avoid the assigned agricultural labor but found themselves without an alternative means of support. In 1816 Manuel de la Bastida, the slave of a captured republican, made his way to Bogotá to appeal for work or for assistance for himself and his family. The public prosecutor noted that although there were no precedents for his appeal, food should be found for him.[3] It was an ad hoc solution to what was probably a much wider problem. But the royalists seemed unwilling to address it, raising the possibility of further slave agitation.

Royalist inertia created an opportunity to shift slave opinion, and a rejuvenated Bolívar seemed aware of this when he returned to Venezuela in May 1816. As supreme chief of the republic and captain general of the armies of Venezuela and New Granada, he indicated his intention to keep his promise to the Haitian president. On May 23, on Margarita Island, he declared, "There will be no more slaves in Venezuela, except those who wish to be slaves. All those who prefer liberty to repose will take up arms to defend their sacred rights and will be citizens." A month later he announced to the inhabitants of Caracas, "Natural justice and political coherence demand the emancipation of the slaves. From now on, there will be only one class of men in Venezuela: citizens."[4] However, there was a price to be paid: the slaves had to fight. Decrees of June 2 and July 6, 1816, proclaimed the "absolute liberty of the slaves," but "all robust males from the age of fourteen until sixty years" had to serve. Adding teeth to the order was the threat that any slave who refused "to take up arms to comply with the sacred duty to defend his liberty" would remain in bondage, "not only he but also his children younger than fourteen years of age, his wife, and his elderly parents."[5]

The threat once again made clear that despite his stated sympathy, Bolívar had yet to accept slaves as equals. Indeed, he still viewed them largely in negative terms.[6] He commented on June 27 that while he had proclaimed the absolute emancipation of the slaves, "the tyranny of the Spaniards has reduced them to such a state of stupidity and instilled in their souls such a great sense of terror that they have lost even the desire to be free! Many of them have followed the Spaniards or have embarked on British vessels [whose owners] have sold them in the neighboring colonies. Scarcely a hundred of them have volunteered, whereas the number of free men who have voluntarily taken up arms is considerable."[7] Bolívar's antislavery proclamations had not affected their loyalties, which on the whole remained with the king. There was still little to convince them that his words and decrees would have any permanent effect, as his political control remained geographically limited. So, too, did his authority over his commanders, many of whom refused his orders to occupy areas outside their jurisdiction or to transfer their units to other commanders.[8] As a result, the military victories that might have widened his support were not forthcoming. On July 13, a serious defeat at the battle of Ocumare compelled him to flee Venezuela yet again. He returned later in the year to resume his offensive, but his fortunes remained uncertain, as defeat on the battlefield often followed apparent gains.

Nonetheless, Bolívar's situation was improving. His May invasion had split the royalist army, forcing Morillo to leave New Granada, along with much of his army. In the resulting vacuum, patriot guerrilla bands managed to regroup and resume operations, as the royalist offensive had not destroyed the desire for independence. In Venezuela, republican guerrillas and irregulars continued to operate in the east, while on the llanos, the inhabitants were gravitating toward a new leader who, like Boves, respected their traditional style of life and permitted them to loot the property of their enemies. But unlike Boves, José Antonio Páez was committed to independence.[9] Everywhere the royalist cause was losing favor because of the repressive acts of the Spanish army and its demands on the local population. One criticism was that local troops were being treated "with so much *hauteur* and contempt, that many of them seceded" and joined the patriot forces.[10] The royalists' failure to bring an end to the destructive warfare also undermined their support, as did their failure to recognize the black population's vital role in the defeat of the two Venezuelan republics. Blacks had also become the target of racist criticism that was probably linked to the excesses of Boves's army but which led to accusations that recalled the language of Bolívar. One royalist complained of their "sanguinary, arrogant, ferocious, perverse, and obstinate character," their uprisings, their disruption of communications and travel, and their demands for equality. Continuing slave unrest compelled Morillo to assign troops to contain it, and in September 1816 instructions were issued for the good order of the provinces. They insisted that slaves be quiet, peaceful, and subordinate, as well as obedient and respectful of their owners and foremen, but also that slaves must be well treated.[11] A related concern was that more and more slaves seemed to be joining the patriots. In Ocumare, Bolívar was reported to have attracted some two hundred, while one of his commanders, Antonio Briceño, had one hundred under his command, with similar numbers in the armies of the eastern independence leaders Santiago Mariño and Manuel Piar.[12]

Royalist reservations did not mean that black troops were being completely rejected. To replace losses from disease and the apparently unending Venezuelan campaign, Morillo was compelled to recruit locally, resulting in the gradual Americanization of his army. He had access to free black and *pardo* militia units that served as a conduit for soldiers to regiments of the line, and on occasion he specifically targeted them. In 1817, a shortage of sufficient Venezuelan whites for the artillery resulted in local men of color being recruited. The royalists continued to leave slaves and Indians more or less alone, in the case of the former because of the cost of compensating owners, demand for agricultural labor, local opposition, and an unwillingness to resort to forced recruiting, but even this restriction was breaking down. In some areas slaves and Indians constituted the entire population, as a failed attempt to raise four nonwhite companies in New Granada in March 1817 made abundantly clear.[13] As a result, slaves could still be found fighting for the king. Owners were donating them, and courts were prepared to assign an occasional slave who was in jail when mitigating factors could be introduced. A court sent Hermengildo Valencia of Quito to the army instead of to jail, believing that this would "correct his conduct," specifically a propensity for thievery, which, it recognized, was prompted by hunger.[14] Despite owner opposition, slaves were also abducted and forced to serve. After the Expeditionary Army passed through the region around Cartagena late in 1815, a number of landowners charged that it had taken all their slaves and animals, along with foodstuffs, jewelry, farm implements, and other belongings. They asked for the return of their possessions, a request that produced some mules and burros, a saddle, a canoe, and a single slave. One owner, who claimed that her slaves had been taken, asked that those not in the service of the king be returned, although she was prepared to give up the rest as a donation "for the service of the Expeditionary Army."[15]

As in the past, those obtained for royalist service were not necessarily used for fighting. Military requests for slaves in some cases specified a non-combat role. In response to one such request, José Antonio de Guendica, of Cartago, New Granada, donated a slave named Apolinario for work as a shoe-maker. Guendica had not given up ownership, so that on discovering that Apolinario was not being used, he asked that the slave be returned, along with his earnings. In the Cauca region, large numbers of slaves were taken for building and maintaining highways, although the repercussions were largely negative, as the recruiting disrupted the local economy and upset lo-cal slaveholders.[16] Apparently free blacks, who were actually runaways hiding their status, were also assigned to tasks that did not involve bearing arms. Ramón Sarmiento was a runaway who served in the artillery in Bogotá as a laborer for over a year until he was reclaimed by his owner in 1818. Ramón testified that he had fled five years earlier after receiving an excessive whip-ping of one hundred lashes. His owner stated that the reason for the pun-ishment, which he described as not excessive but "moderate," was for serving the independence leader Antonio Nariño. With regard to his military service, Ramón stated that it gave him "much satisfaction to serve our king," and he had no desire "to retire from the service of His Majesty." Instead, he asked that part of his wages be used to pay off his owner.[17]

Nonetheless, while many of the slaves in the royalist forces may have been serving as laborers, others were being armed and participated in the fighting. On occasion this occurred outside formal military service, as in the case of a patriot attack on the Colombian town of Honda in November 1816. A local official turned to the slaves of a former Jesuit estate to assist him in the counterattack. All "performed their duty," but four distinguished them-selves, and he asked that they be freed. The slaves then participated in the pursuit of the "rebels," capturing some of the leaders. Subsequently, they helped to maintain the "tranquility and subordination" of the area.[18] Own-ers' requests for compensation for slaves who had been recruited and were claiming their freedom also indicate that the latter were involved in fighting.

In 1817 Jacinta Álvarez of Venezuela asked for the value of her slave, Josef de Jesús, on the basis of what she called the "grace conceded by His Majesty to slaves who have fought for his just cause." A search of the archive of the captaincy failed to reveal such a concession, yet José de la Cruz Parra, the slave of Josefa Zabaleta, had the same impression, saying that he had been a slave but was no longer, "for reason of having fought in support of the cause of the King." The authorities, having heard the particulars of the case, decided not to return him to his owner.[19]

One group of slaves whom the royalists deliberately continued to target and who served as soldiers if recruited was the small but growing number fighting for the enemy. In July 1817, Morillo was given instructions to issue an amnesty that freed slaves who were armed if they became soldiers of the crown, using money set aside to compensate any owners who proved to be followers of the king.[20] They added to the number of slaves that Morillo had already ordered to be freed, described as those "who through faithfulness to his Royal person have taken up arms for his cause."[21]

By 1818 the hiatus in royalist slave recruiting had come to an end as a result of the now precipitous decline in the size of the Expeditionary Army and the improving fortunes of the independence forces. The seriousness of the situation was apparent in March 1818, when Morillo indicated his willingness to take all unmarried men, whether white, Indian, or *pardo*, between the ages of fifteen and forty-five. These recruits were destined primarily for the militia, but some were also needed for regiments of the line. Recruiters were so desperate that they drafted underage youths, leading to appeals from their mothers for their release.[22] Slaves had been excluded from this particular program, but they were not being ignored. In a step that reversed an earlier decision and further indicated the depth of the crisis, Morillo began drafting Boves's veterans and proposed creating a battalion of slaves in return for their freedom. His explanation was that he wanted to forestall the patriots, who were "recruiting largely among the slaves." He had also developed a positive view of slaves as soldiers, indicating that he had seen them in action in the field. Echoing the words of San Martín, he wrote that slaves were "subject to discipline, made excellent soldiers, and fought well in the climate." Extensive recruiting had begun, as "some two thousand were already serving in the royalist army," he wrote.[23] His efforts were confirmed by the patriots, whose resulting complaints hinted at continuing reservations about arming this sector of the population. The October 28, 1818, issue of the republican newspaper *Correo del Orinoco* charged that Morillo had instructions to collect every hacienda slave who might be militarily useful in order to prevent the enemy from taking them. The article went on to accuse the Spaniards of having freed slaves in the staunchly royalist region of Pasto in southern New Granada for the purpose of slaughtering republicans and to form royalist units to continue the fighting. It added that many of the royalist leaders had made proclamations freeing slaves. In December, Morillo was informed that in response to an earlier request, the king had authorized the formation of a battalion of one thousand slaves to serve in his army, despite the fact that the Caracas Audiencia saw such a step as "dangerous" and likely to harm the agricultural sector.[24] The source of these slaves was unclear, but donations continued to provide some. In 1819 José Antonio Suares, a man of advanced age and facing death, offered his twenty-five-year-old slave Joaquín. He painted a rather negative picture of Joaquín, stating that rather than taking advantage of his good breeding, he had become a vagrant, resulting in his having been enlisted in the militia with the hope that this would provide some order to his life. But militia service had proven far too lax, so now Suares was donating Joaquín to a veterans' corps in the hope that this would provide greater discipline and might even involve military action.[25]

As Morillo began turning more and more to slaves to replenish his depleted army and at the same time deny the enemy from using them, the patriots were adopting the same policy. They were driven to do so in large part because they faced the same problem as the royalists: a need for more troops. Battle losses, disease, and particularly desertion had created gaps in the ranks that had to be filled. After his defeat at Ocumare, Bolívar wrote that he had lost two hundred men as casualties, plus five hundred who deserted, "all the coastal inhabitants we had recruited." He subsequently described the rate of desertions as "frightful."[26] Marching to Calabozo in April and May 1818, the army, he reported to Páez, "almost disbanded."[27] He consequently introduced a recruiting decree in 1818 in republican-held territory that was similar to Morillo's, calling on every male between the ages of fourteen and sixty for military duty. But it was more draconian than the royalist decree, as Bolívar threatened to execute anyone who failed to appear or helped to conceal a potential recruit. Nevertheless, he was optimistic that military victories would serve as a lure. In August 1818, after a number of successes, he commented, "The enthusiasm with which the men come forward to enlist is indescribable."[28] His hopes also rested on foreign mercenaries, veterans of the Napoleonic Wars, whom he was aggressively recruiting. They began arriving early in 1818 and eventually totaled around four thousand men. Bolívar once said that his agent in London was the real liberator of South America, because of his role in securing these foreign soldiers. Yet they proved to be less than the perfect recruits that he had envisioned. For one thing, they had difficulty serving alongside the locals. Their numbers were also insufficient to fill the ever-present gaps in his ranks, forcing him to consider other groups, including slaves.[29]

More and more slaves were willing to consider the patriot cause. Bolívar's military advances made his offer of freedom in return for military service more than just a recruiting ploy. A few even began to volunteer. One was José Ambrosio Surarregui, who said that when he had heard that republican troops had taken Angostura in 1817, he immediately crossed by boat to join their forces on Margarita Island and subsequently served as a sailor along the coast and on the Orinoco River.[30] Paéz also had slaves among his *llanero* troops. The inhabitants of Apure, he recalled, "put their slaves at my disposal, whom I declared free when I liberated the territory."[31] By 1818 the growing extent of black support for the patriots compelled Morillo to order that hacendados withdraw their slaves to the safety of areas controlled by the royalist forces. However, Bolívar's invasion of the valleys of Aragua prevented this, "so that," Morillo reported, "all the slave groups remain at the disposition of the rebels who extract many men from them."[32]

Bolívar may have been enjoying greater success in recruiting slaves, yet his relationship with this group and with the black population in general remained cool. He was still suspicious of them, perhaps remembering their earlier opposition to republican rule, and he was determined to prevent any action that might divert attention from his primary goal of achieving independence. He also had to contend with challenges to his leadership from a number of caudillo generals who had maintained the independence struggle in his absence and were not convinced of either his military genius or his right to command. When confronted by what appeared to be a plot that combined both insubordination and a racial threat, his response was quick and brutal. In 1817, the mulatto general Manuel Piar refused to recognize Bolívar as supreme commander. According to a royalist commentator, Piar was one of their "most terrible enemies, adventurous, talented, and with great influence among the castes, to whom he belonged. He was thus one of the few Venezuelans who could inspire the greater part of the population."[33] He was now accused of heading a *pardo* conspiracy designed to transform the war into a racial one, or at least to lead an eastern separatist movement in Guayana with a racial focus. Evidence indicates that he had engaged in such discussions. According to intercepted letters from the Haitian president to Piar, a black conspiracy existed "to destroy the white ruling class throughout the Caribbean and create a series of Negro republics."[34] Determined to establish his authority and suppress any racial threat, Bolívar had Piar arrested. Tried for "insubordination" and found guilty, he was shot on October 16, 1817. The following day, Bolívar tried to defuse the issue by asking his soldiers, "Have not our arms broken the chains of the slaves? Has not the odious distinction between classes and colors been abolished for ever?"[35] His resolute action helped to establish some authority over the caudillos, but racial concerns were still very much alive.

Bolívar's uncertainties about the black population were apparent even as he launched what seemed to be a frontal attack on the whole institution of slavery. In 1819, from his headquarters at Angostura on the Orinoco River, he called a congress to organize his new republic and to plan the next step in the liberation of Venezuela. Among his proposals to the delegates who began meeting in mid-February was one for the complete abolition of "the dark mantle of barbarous and profane slavery."[36] The twenty-six delegates were largely members of the creole elite and were thus not prepared to take such a step. They supported ending the slave trade, but they rejected abolition, agreeing only to free those slaves who provided military service. Were they convinced that Bolívar was truly committed to abolition? He was still a slave owner, although his absence from his properties prevented him from correcting the anomaly. Yet, in justifying his proposal he sounded more opportunistic than humanitarian. In November he wrote to Francisco de Paula Santander, his commander in New Granada, "To gain some faithful partisans we need to free the slaves."[37] In other words, abolition seemed to be a means to an end, not an end in itself.

Independence and military demands, not the future of slavery, remained foremost in Bolívar's mind, and on the military front his situation was about to improve dramatically. In August 1819, to establish a base from which to liberate his homeland, he crossed the Andes into New Granada and advanced on the capital of Bogotá, in an extraordinarily risky and dangerous campaign that replicated San Martín's invasion of Chile. After a series of military successes, his army decisively defeated the royalists at the battle of Boyacá on August 7. The results were profound, as the victory essentially secured the independence of New Granada. The viceroy fled to the coast, the remaining royalist forces in the region were put on the defensive, and royalist control was soon limited to Cartagena in the north and Pasto in the south.[38] Bolívar now not only possessed a secure base to attack the royalist armies in Venezuela but also the support of large numbers of locals, as well as access to an extensive area from which to draw supplies and new troops. Slaves from the region became a particular target of his recruiting efforts. In October 1819 he explained to Santander, whom he had placed in charge of New Granada, that he wanted each freed province to supply one thousand slaves. He expected them particularly from Antioquia and Chocó, which had substantial slave populations, as well as Popayán, which was to supply two thousand. They were to be men "of the reserve and not troops of the line armed with lances."[39] The following February he reiterated his request, now asking for three thousand from Antioquia and Chocó and two thousand from Popayán, although he was prepared to accept more. All should be bachelors "if possible," indicating his desire not to break up families. Yet, he seemed to have doubts about their willingness to serve, as they were to receive their freedom only after they had left their home territories, and their absolute license would follow two years of service. A decree based upon "humanity, politics, and military interest for the salvation of the Republic" was to be issued subsequently confirming these instructions. A few weeks later he altered the terms slightly in orders to General Manuel Valdés. They now called for the recruitment of "all useful slaves," who would be freed after they completed three years of service.[40]

Why was Bolívar recruiting so many slaves from this particular region? One reason was his need to increase the size of his army. It had numbered less than three thousand at Boyacá, so that adding four to five thousand could be vital. Young men from other sectors of New Granada's population were available and were also subject to the patriots' imposed levees, but slaves were different.[41] Bolívar believed that he could win them over with the offer of personal freedom, which was not an option with any other group.[42] It proved a mistaken assumption, for most of his new slave recruits turned out to be conscripts, not volunteers, but he remained hopeful.[43] There were more concrete reasons for enlisting them as well: he had access to them, unlike the slaves of Venezuela, who were still largely under royalist control, and he shared Morillo's thinking that drawing the slaves into his army would prevent the enemy from using them. He may also have come to share the view of Morillo, San Martín, and others that slaves made well-disciplined soldiers. This was of increasing importance as he shifted from a cavalry-focused army to one based on infantry for his campaigns in Venezuela, Ecuador, and eventually Peru.[44] Another and perhaps more important factor was that slaves had a reputation for hardiness and seemed suited to the conditions in the areas that still had to be freed. Like Morillo, Bolívar was having to contend with the demands of campaigning in a harsh environment. Many of his losses were due to desertion, but disease and exhaustion accounted for countless others. What he needed, he wrote to Santander in April 1820, were "robust and vigorous men; men accustomed to harshness and fatigue; men who embrace the cause and the career with enthusiasm; men who identify their interest with the public interest and for whom the price of death is little different from that of life."[45] Slaves seemed to fit the description, but they had to be slaves who were suited to a particular climate. In July 1820 he urged Santander to obtain slaves from the south, as those from central New Granada were not ready to march, with 300 sick in bed and another 320 who had arrived "very feeble and worn out." He needed more to "sustain *independence and the war.*"[46] He believed that those from the south would be able to cope with campaigning first in Venezuela and then in Peru. He was geographically specific because, he noted, "men from the cold uplands will all die in Venezuela, as sadly we have learned. I am resolved not to lead a single one from this region."[47] Slaves were resilient, a view shared by Santander, who described those from Chocó as "the most patient and most resistant to privations."[48]

There was a further reason why Bolívar turned to slaves. His fears of the black population had not abated, and one of his goals was to reduce their numbers in the region. His writings in 1820 indicate a commitment to the abolition of slavery, with the consequent elimination of the class of slaves. The clearest evidence of this appears in his oft-repeated sentence in a letter of July 10 to Santander: "It seems to me madness that a revolution for freedom pretends to maintain slavery."[49] And in April, in a letter that stated his intention to "take" slaves who were "available for bearing arms," he cited Montesquieu and the link between political freedom and civil freedom, that all sectors of society must be free to achieve true freedom. However, he also seemed to think that killing off slaves would help to end the institution that he now frequently condemned. After citing Montesquieu in the April letter, he pointed out that free governments that maintained slavery were punished by slave rebellions that could lead to extermination, as in the case of Haiti. To prevent this, not only should slavery end, but also the number of slaves should be reduced. Recruiting and combat would achieve this. He asked, "What is a more fit and legitimate means to secure freedom than to fight for it? Is it just that only free men die to free the slaves? Will it not be useful that they acquire their rights on the field of battle and that their dangerous numbers be reduced by a necessary and legitimate method? In Venezuela we have seen the free population die and the captive remain." He did not want to see this repeated in Colombia.[50] He made no attempt to keep his views secret, which may help to explain why he still had difficulty attracting slave volunteers: they probably thought that they were going be used only for the most dangerous tasks or as cannon fodder.

Bolívar's plans did not go unchallenged. Slaves avoided recruiters by fleeing, and they deserted after being enlisted.[51] Owners, too, objected, as slaves filled an important economic niche in New Granada, and they found a sympathetic audience in Santander. To a great extent, political loyalties and existing slave employment determined what slaves were selected. Santander was prepared to free slaves in areas that the enemy still occupied, although not the southern Pacific coast of Colombia, fearing that this might provoke a slave rebellion that would be "dangerous."[52] But he had no qualms about taking slaves from a province like Cauca, where slave owners were largely followers of the king and the economy was not based on mining. In Chocó and Antioquia, however, the slaves belonged to wealthy miners who were independence supporters. In addition to alienating the owners, he was worried about the impact on the provincial budget. He explained that taking away three thousand mineworkers would reduce gold production, which would affect the treasury at a time when money was needed to meet an expanding army. Bolívar responded that Santander was confusing freeing slaves with securing slaves for military service, raising questions once again about his commitment to abolition. On April 18 he wrote that with regard to freeing slaves in the province of Cauca, the law should read that "all slaves useful for military service will be assigned to the army," reiterating the point that this was not a proclamation of emancipation but that freedom could be granted for "distinguished service." He assured his lieutenant that only those needed would be taken, and not an excessive number.[53] His demands continued, as he anticipated heavy losses in his Venezuelan campaign. He also required soldiers for Ecuador, where an expeditionary division that was sent against Quito in 1820 was almost destroyed and had to be replaced.[54]

The problem facing Santander was to provide slaves in numbers that did not exist. In effect, to satisfy the requests, he would have had to recruit over half the slave population in some areas. Local recruiters shared his views. Manuel Valdés, the commander of the Army of the South who was supposed to supply three thousand slaves for the Army of the North, reported that he might be able to provide half that number, as he needed some of the recruits for his own forces, and at the same time owners were not supplying the requested recruits. Some were hiding their slaves, while the slaves themselves were fleeing to the neighboring hills to avoid the recruiters. Moreover, of those supplied, the majority proved useless for military service and had to be returned to their owners. Even some of those enlisted proved to be less than ideal. In the case of one small town, the recruits began stealing when the corps failed to provide them with medicine and food, while others deserted.[55] Bolívar was prepared to accept anyone who showed up, even runaways, but Santander was more sensitive to owner concerns, returning those slaves who had been enlisted illegally if a request was made.[56]

Santander tried, but by September 1820 he was not prepared to recruit more. He complained that Colombians had contributed more than their fair share of slaves, in addition to food, money, and supplies. He noted the high cost of maintaining the troops, that one thousand blacks from Antioquia cost four thousand gold castellanos daily. This was money that had so far realized no return, and Antioquia was unwilling to provide any more slaves. "I do not know how battalions can be created unless women are recruited," he wrote. The withdrawal of one thousand slaves had resulted in a decline in gold production and produced complaints from the *antioquianos*. Santander also wondered about the resilience of the recruits, especially from Cauca or Chocó. The journey from these provinces to the Venezuela border, he noted, was "capable of damaging the machinery of a man of bronze."[57]

Despite the complaints and the opposition, the efforts in New Granada secured a significant number of soldiers for Bolívar's armies. In May 1820 one thousand arrived from Antioquia, recruited by the future historian of Colombia José Manuel Restrepo. They were "very robust and very content men," according to Santander.[58] Later in the year a report mentioned three hundred *liberto* recruits in Colombia.[59] Others were runaways from royalist territory. Early in 1820, slaves in the Barbacoas area, who might have been mobilized against the patriots, were reported by royalist officials to be "passing to the enemy," taking advantage of the lack of control to flee along the rivers flowing through the region to patriot-held areas. They attested to the changing loyalties in the slave community.[60] Slaves fighting as guerrillas in the Cali and Cauca regions gave further evidence of the growing popularity of the independence cause.[61]

As his army expanded, Bolívar was finally on the verge of ending Spanish rule in his homeland. He may have achieved it on his own, but a new crisis in Spain ensured his success. Opposition in Spain to the absolutist rule of Ferdinand VII and a mutiny by troops in Cádiz sparked a revolution in January 1820 that forced the king to reintroduce the 1812 liberal constitution and accept a renewed attempt at constitutional monarchy. The Spanish Cortes was effective once again, and it sought to negotiate a cessation to the overseas strife. A first step was the declaration of a unilateral ceasefire. The decision disrupted the flow of reinforcements and materiel to the royalist armies and prevented them from mounting new campaigns. In the north, the events undermined royalist morale, led to numerous desertions, and prompted Morillo to seek an armistice with Bolívar. Signed on November 26, 1820, it provided Morillo with justification to return to Spain, leaving the royalist command in much less capable hands. The armistice was supposed to last six months, but by January 1821 new republican uprisings were occurring, and Bolívar prepared to end the war in the north once and for all.[62]

The troops now facing Bolívar's men were no longer Morillo's Spanish veterans but rather recruits drawn increasingly from the viceroyalty. Denied reinforcements from Spain, the royalists had to rely more than ever on locals, including still-loyal black and *pardo* militias.[63] Trying to reconfirm their bond with the crown and at the same time arouse the morale of all American-born troops, Morillo had issued a decree in August 1820 that recognized their service. It granted the right of citizenship to all soldiers, including *pardo* and *moreno* officers, those of the rank and file who had at least three years' service, and those without the necessary years but who had been wounded or rendered useless in action. It was approved by the Spanish authorities at the end of November.[64] The existence of these militia units continued to provide slaves with a route to military service as in the past, and efforts to recruit them had not ended, despite their wavering support.[65] The royalist cause was still strong among slaves in some areas, although the majority, as in the case of those fighting for the patriots, were being compelled to serve. Donations from royalist adherents provided additional recruits, as did familiar sources such as jails. Among the ex-prisoners was Juan Eugenio, an American-born black from Valencia who had previously served under Boves and was described as "of very bad conduct and prejudicial in this jurisdiction." The authorities recommended that he be sent to work on the La Guaira road, indicating that the military was still a dumping ground for the incorrigible and that not all were going to serve as combatants.[66] Slaves arrested with deserters might also be assigned to the army, but this was no longer true of those owned by known rebels. Perhaps royalist officials were recognizing that Spanish rule was in its final days and property rights would have to be addressed once the fighting ended. Nevertheless, slaves continued to be taken to replace the royalist losses.[67]

With royalist fortunes floundering, more and more slaves embraced the patriot cause. A few who had served the patriots in the past now rejoined, men like José de Jesús Malpica, who had fought in Venezuela in 1814 and was back in the patriot ranks in 1821.[68] Expressions of loyalty to the *patria* began to be heard with greater frequency. After General Francisco Bermúdez captured Caracas in May 1821, with the assistance of slave soldiers whom he had recruited during his advance, he issued an invitation to all slaves to join him, offering them freedom and their owners compensation. Among those who responded to take up "arms in defense of the Republic" were two young men who said that they were motivated by "the sacred object to which they [were] called."[69]

The recruiting among the local population was producing armies with a significant black component. The captain general of Venezuela wrote with some exaggeration on January 1, 1821, that the insurgent forces "in their totality" were "composed of descendents from Africa, particularly in the provinces of Venezuela," while three-quarters of the royalist forces were similarly constituted. He viewed this with concern, fearing that it would lead to "the loss of the Provinces, the extermination of [the white] caste, and the domination of those [blacks]." White immigration was needed to prevent it. He warned that if the republicans won, the "African Provinces of Venezuela" would ally themselves with "those of the Island of Santo Domingo." To prevent this feared development, he argued that black loyalty needed to be solidified by granting more of them citizenship. He considered the existing constitutional article too "restricting" and urged that citizenship be granted to all those of this "caste" who had served for one year in the army, even dissidents, as long as they embraced the 1812 constitution.[70] A British commentator wrote at about the same time that the armies of the different patriot caudillos were composed "above all of blacks commanded by white officers. They are notably adapted to the climate and the country. They are not always clothed, but they do not need it."[71] In July 1821 the commissioners of the Spanish Pacification Junta, sent to negotiate with the patriots, noted a similar Americanization of the royalist army, although they gave a somewhat different racial composition. The army comprised 10,755 men, they wrote: 3,461 Europeans, 812 Venezuelan whites, and 6,481 Indians and castes. These last had been "taken by force and held by virtue of the most severe discipline and vigilance," as they were allegedly prone to stealing, returning to their homes, and escaping to the interior.[72]

A much-weakened royalist army confronted the increasingly confident Bolívar in 1821. Desertion was a particular problem for the royalists, as Morillo's successor, Miguel de la Torre, wrote to the government in January. He noted with a sense of frustration that even veteran units were afflicted by it and that the authorities were unable to do anything to prevent it. Any royalist offensive was unlikely without a significant injection of money and reinforcements, he added. A recruitment decree followed, enlisting all free bachelors between the ages of seventeen and thirty-six, and while it seemed to exclude slaves, recruits were permitted to provide a slave in their place or a sum of three hundred pesos. The decree failed to supply the necessary soldiers, however, and on the battlefield of Carabobo on June 24, Bolívar for the first time had the advantage of numerically superior forces: 6,500 versus the enemy's 5,000. The patriots secured a decisive victory, the royalist army was destroyed, and Venezuela's independence—after years of bloody warfare—was assured.[73]

Slave support had been vital to Bolívar's success, a debt that he recognized as he began organizing the new nation of Gran Colombia out of the ashes of the old viceroyalty and captaincy. The issue of slavery was on the agenda at the congress that began meeting at Cúcuta on July 21, 1821. The delegates had, as a template, the initiative taken by the earlier congress of Angostura, held in January 1820 after the battle of Boyacá. It had declared that no one could be the property of another, fixed a five-year schedule for total abolition in Venezuela, recognized the freedom of those who had already received it, offered it to those who volunteered to serve in the militia or provided some distinguished service, abolished the slave trade, and established a fund for indemnifying the owners.[74] Little had come from the earlier initiative, but now with independence guaranteed, the representatives were willing to apply the measures to the entirety of the new nation. Declaring that "a truly just and philanthropic republican government cannot exist without trying to lighten the load of all the classes of degraded and afflicted humanity," it issued a law of manumission. But this was not abolition. The object was gradualism, to achieve the extinction of slavery "without compromising public tranquility or violating the rights enjoyed by the owners." It declared free all children born in Gran Colombia, although those born of slaves had to serve their mother's owner until the age of eighteen. Bolívar noted that with regard to freeing the newborn, "in this manner property rights, political rights, and natural rights [would] be brought into harmony."[75] In addition, slaves could not be imported, nor could they be sold outside the country or their province, and children could not be separated from their parents until after puberty. Use of the lash was regulated, slaves were given the right to change owners, and owners were obliged to educate, feed, clothe, and house their slaves. Adults were to be freed through the creation of a manumission fund administered by local juntas and financed by a variety of taxes and duties.[76]

A common belief was that with the passage of this law, "there was no longer slavery in Colombia." However, the belief was unfounded, for the law contained a number of defects that worked against abolition, such as the requirement that children remain with their mothers' owners. Ultimately, the law proved of limited effectiveness, but at the time the gestures to the slave population managed to win their support. A British observer four years later noted that while previously "most of the slaves favoured the Spanish cause," following the free womb law and the creation of the manumission fund, "the Blacks immediately espoused with zeal the cause of the Colombians, and . . . rendered considerable service to the Republic."[77] Bolívar made his own personal commitment to the cause by authorizing the freedom of the last of his six slaves from his San Mateo hacienda.[78]

Slaves may have "rendered considerable service," but the route to freedom was not as smooth as many might have expected in this apparently more liberal environment. Military service was no longer the passport to freedom that it had been, for recruiting now required compensation, and the weak financial state of the new republic prevented it from paying for every slave. In mid-October, Santander amended the manumission law to read that they could be accepted for military service only if the government indemnified the owners, while those whose slaves had already been recruited would receive preference in the distribution of the manumission funds.[79] Bolívar approved. He wrote to Santander that he had ordered one thousand men to fill two battalions, and of these, three hundred would be slaves "who must be paid for with manumission funds."[80] With the state paying three hundred pesos for each recruit, the debt was extremely heavy.

Yet, despite the apparent obstacle to military service and, consequently, greater difficulty in obtaining one's freedom, slaves continued to make an effort to join. With warfare apparently on the wane, service may have appeared more attractive than before, as there was less likelihood of capture, injury, or something infinitely worse. A further incentive was an order of August 28, 1822, that permitted owners to recover slaves who were not in military service.[81] Many of those who had taken advantage of the long period of warfare to flee now had to consider their futures, and the military had certain attractions. Staying out of the hands of an old owner was the most obvious. In some cases, slaves' owners were not opposed to their serving and may even have encouraged them to enlist or to remain in the military because of the promise of compensation. Their actions suggest that, in the aftermath of wartime destruction, the money was worth more to them than the slaves' labor. Owners asking for compensation included Juan Bautista de Eraso, whose seven slaves had tried to enlist in the Orinoco Battalion; of these, only two, Miguel Melian, a married man of thirty-six, and Francisco Eraso, thirty-seven and also married, had been accepted. Another was the owner of Cirilo Pérez, who had been born on July 9, 1799, in La Guaira, baptized José Cirilo del Carmen, of unmarried parents. Cirilo had enlisted in December 1821 and fought in the battles of Santa Marta and La Guajira. A third was the owner of José Bonifacio, a slave described as being *sambo* in color and healthy in body, who had enlisted with the knowledge of his owner.[82] The owner of Martín Serrano, who was enrolled in the Orinoco Battalion, noted that by this "circumstance he ha[d] acquired his freedom, and the treasury must pay his value."[83] In September 1823, Narciso Ochoa asked for compensation for two of his slaves, setting their value at three hundred pesos each. Having previously received some gifts from the state, he was willing to accept four hundred pesos for the two, but he was not optimistic, as he considered the manumission funds insufficient to meet everyone's requests. In his view, the penury of the public coffers was "so notorious" that compensation was "not credible."[84]

In addition, and fortunately for the state of the treasury, slaves contin-ued to be drawn into the patriot forces through means that entailed no need for compensation. Bolívar managed to lure some from royalist-held territory with a law that freed slaves who had fled Spanish owners.[85] Many of them ended up in the Santander Battalion, a unit of black recruits created in 1821 and trained by British officers.[86] Some were deserters from the royalist forces. Páez recalled one, a slave named Julián, who in the siege of Puerto Cabello had been sent to spy on the patriots. However, they captured him and con-vinced him to serve them, at which point he revealed the weak points in the fortress.[87] And despite prohibitions, the patriot forces were still confiscating slaves to fill their ranks. In Colombia, Juana Josefa Aldana noted in her will that republican troops had taken thirty-four of her slaves, along with other possessions, from her estate near Cali. A Venezuelan owner claimed that her only two "useful" slaves had been removed from her hacienda for military service by the army besieging Puerto Cabello. Similarly, a group of owners protested that they had lost a total of fifty slaves, while the slaveholder Juan José Lander complained that despite government orders not to take slaves for military service except in the case of absolute necessity, his slave, Fran-cisco Antonio, had been called up by the local commander. He stated that he needed Francisco because other workers were not available for farming.[88]

With the patriot leaders securing more and more slaves for their armies, the royalists were now clearly aware that loyalty to the king was no longer the lure that it had been. They still needed soldiers, for their forces contin-ued to operate in the region despite the declaration of independence. In Ven-ezuela they were active on the northern coast, occupying Puerto Cabello and Coro. In southern Colombia, they enjoyed significant support around Pasto, where local forces managed to withstand Bolívar's advance for a time. How-ever, this was one of the few bright spots in an otherwise bleak picture, as elsewhere royalist efforts to mobilize the local population, including slaves, enjoyed little support. Everyone recognized that the tide had turned and the republicans were now dominant. Consequently, attempts to recruit slaves in previously loyal areas proved all but futile. In Riobamba, for example, officials reported that they had been unable to find even thirty slaves of the required quality. They focused on estate slaves who were bachelors, offering them their freedom, while compensating owners in order to maintain their loyalty. But the slaves resisted, fleeing to avoid the recruiting drive, so that in Barbacoas only fifty slaves and free coloreds were procured.[89]

As a result of the changing loyalties of the slaves, Bolívar enjoyed far more success than the royalists did in his efforts to obtain troops in southern Colombia and Ecuador for the next stage of the independence struggles.[90] In the port of Tumaco, Mauricio Quiñones provided six bachelor slaves, and he did so without complaint, as he was pleased "to increase the number of soldiers" for the benefit of the republican cause. One of the recruits, in the words of his wife, proved to be "a faithful soldier." In the parish of Palenque, a request in July 1821 for slave owners to provide information regarding the names, number, and sex of their slaves "for the urgent needs of the *patria*" drew a quick and positive response from patriotic owners.[91] Slaves were also conscripted; owners who possessed several slaves lost a percentage, while those who had only one had to give up their single slave. However, they received a generous three hundred pesos for each recruit.[92] The patriots secured sufficient recruits to form a separate battalion in John Illingsworth's division, the Vengadores de la Patria, which served in the Quito and Santo Domingo de los Colorados campaigns.[93] Other slaves volunteered, suggesting that they had confidence in a cause whose military might now seemed invincible. Fermín Padilla, a soldier in the First Company of Grenadiers of the Yaguachi Battalion and former slave of the *marqués* de Solanda y de Villarrocha explained, "Because of my devotion to and love of the homeland, I asked him to send me out of the city to free me from the claws of the Spaniards who despotically and forcibly had begun to recruit all the slaves to serve as soldiers." He eventually served under Bolívar's brilliant lieutenant Antonio José de Sucre, "fighting with valor and enthusiasm" at the crucial battle of Pichincha on May 24, 1822, that won Ecuador's independence.[94] Another slave, a runaway named Alejandro Campusano, was almost lyrical in recounting why he chose to join the independence cause. The property of a Spaniard, Alejandro came from the canton of Babaoyo in the department of Guayaquil. There, he explained, "the sweet voice of the *patria* came to my ears. And desiring to be one of its soldiers as much to shake off the yoke of general oppression as to free myself from the slavery in which I found myself, I swiftly ran to present myself to the liberating troops of Quito that passed through Babaoyo under the command of Señor General Sucre."[95] Love of king had given way to the appeal of the homeland and its more certain offer of freedom.

The battle of Pichincha opened the way for Bolívar to occupy Ecuador and prepare for his final destination, Peru. His advance south had rested heavily on the shoulders of slaves, and their contribution had not ended. Soldiers were now needed in Peru, where a powerful royalist army awaited. San Martín had challenged but not defeated it. At the famous meeting of the two men in Guayaquil on July 26 and 27, 1822, Bolívar offered to reinforce the Argentine with four thousand men.[96] Where they were to be obtained was not entirely clear. Ecuador seemed an unlikely source, as anyone suitable had been recruited already. A letter to the government in April 1822 claimed, "All the useful are enlisted, and only children, the old, and the useless remain."[97] In addition, laws had been passed prohibiting further slave recruitment except in extreme circumstances, and commanders sought to respect the wishes of landholders who were attempting to restore their agricultural activities and needed their workers. Recruits for the Peruvian campaign were going to have to be found elsewhere in the north, and once again slaves were to be part of the army. In Venezuela, General Carlos Soublette wrote to Páez in March 1823 of twenty-three former slaves who were employed in military service and did not want to return to their former status. To avoid this, they had agreed to serve either for eight years in the corps being organized for Peru or as guerrillas in Ocumare. They would be freed and their owners compensated from the manumission funds.[98] The same funds were being used to purchase slaves for the campaign. One was José Luciano López, a fifteen-year-old mulatto described as robust, young, of a good disposition, a shoemaker, and in good health. He had been sold in 1819 for 160 pesos, and now was bought for 300 pesos for military service.[99] He and others like him were now heading south as Bolívar prepared to confront the last royalist armies and bring the curtain down once and for all on the independence drama.

CHAPTER 5

CONTROLLING SLAVE RECRUITMENT IN CHILE AND PERU

 EARLY IN 1822, AN OBSERVER COMMENTING on José de San Martín's forces in Peru concluded that the "entire army" was composed of slaves.[1] He was either mistaken or exaggerating or trying to be provocative, for the army comprised a far more racially diverse group than he described. Nevertheless, his observation indicates that slaves were a strikingly visible part of the patriot armies fighting on the west coast of South America, just as they were elsewhere on the continent. A survey of the royalist armies at the time would have shown that they, too, had turned to the local slave population to meet some of their military needs, although with less success than the now increasingly dominant patriots. Yet, while slaves may have been serving as soldiers in Chile and Peru, the efforts to recruit them tended to be more controlled than elsewhere; this reflected the small number of slaves to be found in Chile, the availability of alternative recruits in Peru, and San Martín's policies in both areas. Military necessities and personal beliefs prompted him to issue antislavery legislation and to recruit slaves, but he was limited by slaveholder resistance and his desire not to alienate this specific group. The same concerns influenced Simón Bolívar to some extent when he took command in Peru in 1823, although a more important factor was his determination to rely on Colombian troops to defeat the remaining royalist armies. Thus, as the armies of the independence era marched toward their final climactic battles, slaves continued to participate. However, their importance as a military group had begun to wane. The post-war era was now in sight, and winning the support of the slave population was no longer a priority of the independence leaders.

In the southern captaincy of Chile, slaves, in spite of their small numbers, were drawn—like the rest of the population—into the political turmoil that followed news of the 1808 events in Spain. The initial Chilean response to Ferdinand's forced abdication was relatively peaceful, as members of elite families joined with reformist Spaniards in a national congress in 1810 that declared loyalty to the king. However, when the independence-minded José Miguel Carrera took control of the government the following year, royalist officials in Lima became alarmed, and early in 1813 the viceroy sent the first of a series of expeditionary forces to crush the perceived threat. The intervention led to splits within the patriot forces, resulting in Carrera's replacement by Bernardo O'Higgins, a man who was also committed to independence despite being the son of a former viceroy. But the patriots were divided among themselves and thus no match for the royalists, and they suffered a crushing defeat at the battle of Rancagua in October 1814. O'Higgins, Carrera, and two thousand others fled east to safety in Argentina, while those left behind suffered a long period of repression at the hands of the royalist authorities.[2]

During the brief period of Chilean self-government known as the *Patria Vieja*, the local creole leaders displayed a liberal bent that had significant repercussions where slaves were concerned. At the nascent state's first congress, delegates discussed and on October 15, 1811, approved proposals that included a free womb law, a law prohibiting the introduction of new slaves into Chile, and a law freeing recently arrived slaves after six months' residence. Abolition was out of the question, since prominent figures, including many in the government, were slave owners and all wished to avoid political dissension. The government also had little money for compensation, and delegates were not entirely certain what the slaves would do if they were freed. Their concerns seemed to have some basis in fact, for following the approval of the laws, three hundred slaves armed with knives marched through the streets of Santiago demanding that the government free them and offering to defend "the system of the *patria*." But the riot was out of character for local slaves, who on the whole were considered to be "contented," leading to questions about what lay behind it. Suspicions were voiced that the disturbance had been provoked by owners who wished to raise the specter of slave unrest and weaken support for abolition. Thus, while liberal sentiments influenced developments at the time and convinced some owners to free their slaves, others remained firmly committed to slavery and opposed efforts to implement the antislavery legislation.[3]

With owners determined to hold onto their human property, slaves seemed an unlikely group to play a role when fighting erupted in the region. But the situation created opportunities for them to become involved. As in other areas, Chilean blacks had a long history of military service, especially in militia units. Following the creole takeover in 1810, one Santiago unit that had been used for local police work in the past was renamed the Infantes de la Patria, and its two hundred free *pardos* were prepared for combat. The unit was not very effective, however, because of poor training, low morale, and frequent desertions, but it did serve as a magnet for runaways. Then, as fighting spread during the Carrera period, the government turned actively to slaves for military service. On August 29, 1814, it formed a regiment of slaves called the Ingenuos de la Patria. But like the militia unit, the new regiment was largely ineffective. Its formation also seemed to belie the picture of a contented slave population, for its soldiers were described as "miserable" slaves "who until now have borne the same yoke as animals." Men thirteen years old or older were permitted to join and were granted their freedom for their service, but they had to compensate their owners with half their wages, a unique measure designed to reduce the state's financial obligations. Anticipating opposition, the legislators threatened owners who prevented their slaves from enlisting with the loss of the value of their slave, half their goods, and two years' exile. Nonetheless, some owners did resist, leading to a rapid strengthening of the law—the penalty now increased to two times the value of the slave, who would be immediately freed. The law also laid out penalties for those slaves who preferred "to hide like cowards or to flee their homes to avoid enlisting in the legions of the motherland."[4] They would be punished with one hundred lashes, three years in jail, and perpetual slavery. The threat ensured that at least some slaves began to be enlisted, supplemented by others who had been donated, and by the omnipresent runaways who were covertly making their way into the ranks.[5]

The numbers were not large, but a few made their presence felt on the field of battle. Prominent among them was José Muñoz, a slave who served with such distinction that his superiors recommended that he be freed. They used his service as proof that the still widely accepted proslavery views of Aristotle and his sixteenth-century Spanish disciple, Juan Ginés de Sepúlveda, were completely unfounded.[6] A newspaper account in 1811 commented that in taking up his musket he had "made evident that souls do not have color, that no one excelled him in valor and patriotism. Assigned to defend a cannon, he was not willing to accept relief and only aspired to obtain in a glorious death all the honor that had been denied him in life."[7] Another local slave who left his mark was José Romero. Born in 1794 of a white father and slave mother, he joined the military before the war as a drummer and served with the Infantes from 1810, under Carrera in 1813–1814, and then in the Ingenuos de la Patria. He was assigned to recruit slaves for the latter regiment, although without much luck. He then returned to the Infantes and was at the battle of Rancagua, where he was captured. Through the intercession of some Spaniards he managed to secure his freedom and would fight again with the patriots. However, his earlier contributions, along with those of Muñoz and other slaves, were unable to stem the royalist advance. Creole rule collapsed, recruiting came to an end, and owners whose slaves had been enlisted requested their return.[8]

The hopes of Chilean slaves must have risen once again following San Martín's epic crossing of the Andes in January 1817 and his defeat of the royalists at the battle of Chacabuco, outside Santiago, on February 12, 1817. However, the restoration of creole rule failed to open many new routes to freedom. When slave recruiting resumed, slaveholders remained less than enthusiastic. They were willing to donate horses, wheat, straw, and money to the patriots, but they wanted compensation for their slaves, and money was in short supply. Only a few, motivated by patriotism, were prepared to be generous, receiving from San Martín his personal, written thanks in return. Among them were Francisco Xavier Gres, a militia captain, who donated five of his slaves for military service, and Antonio Urrutia y Mendiburu, who offered his two remaining slaves to the army in December 1817 to help free his country. One of them, named Luciano, already had some military experience, having accompanied his owner in the campaign of 1813, where he had displayed what was described as "a heroic bravery." His companion was also young and "of good disposition." Other slaves assigned to the army were the confiscated property of royalists. One, Faustino Ibarra, was also a petty thief who was in jail when the authorities decided that military service was preferable to keeping him locked up.[9]

Despite their small numbers, Chilean slaves fought in the pivotal battles of the Chilean campaign. Along with other black soldiers, they displayed a bravery that attracted the comments of observers and indicated a definite hostility to the old order. At Chacabuco, San Martín's previous warning of what might happen to ex-slaves if the expedition failed had not been forgotten by his Argentine recruits. One veteran of the battle, described as an "old African" when interviewed in Lima some decades later, "pulled from his pocket a paper in which he kept *the moustache of a Talavera* [Spanish soldier]." He explained that after upending him with his bayonet, he had shot him and "cut off his moustache with lip and everything," shouting, "'*No queré azuca, pues toma azuca.*'"[10] At Maipú, the second great battle of Chilean independence, fought outside Santiago on April 5, 1818, local slave recruits, primarily artisans and domestic servants, served in the recently reestablished Infantes de la Patria. According to one account, they displayed "audacity and discipline" in the battle. Equally noteworthy were African-born soldiers, who were reported to have fought "brilliantly."[11] Alongside them were other ex-slaves fighting under the Argentine colors, especially in the Eighth Regiment that composed much of the patriot left wing and suffered heavy casualties. The English observer Samuel Haigh recounted, "The carnage was very great, and I was told by some officers who had served in Europe that they never witnessed anything more bloody than occurred in this part of the field." Perhaps San Martín's warnings still rang in their ears, for according to Haigh, "Nothing could exceed the savage fury of the Black soldiers in the patriot army; they had borne the brunt of the action against the finest Spanish regiment and had lost the principal part of their forces; they were delighted with the idea of shooting their prisoners." He recalled, "I saw an old Negro actually crying with rage when he perceived the officers protected from his fury."[12]

The victory at Maipú guaranteed Chile's independence and permitted San Martín to begin preparing for his next challenge, the invasion of Peru, but this was to prove no easier than his earlier preparations for Chile. At first glance, his prospects seemed promising: he enjoyed a close relationship with his men, as the British admiral William Bowles remarked in February 1818. Bowles noted that the Argentine was "extremely beloved by all classes in his army, as although his discipline is rigorous, he knows how to conciliate their regard as well as to exact their obedience. The troops are well clothed and fed, regularly paid, and in point of order and instruction very superior to anything that has been hitherto seen in this country."[13] Yet, beneath that rapport was a nationalistic friction. Bowles referred to it later in the year when he informed the British Admiralty that "great animosities existed between the native troops and those of Buenos Ayres, and that during General San Martín's absence [in Mendoza] a total want of discipline prevailed in both armies."[14] Furthermore, his financial and material demands on the local population to meet the needs of the Peruvian invasion were provoking criticism, so that by early 1819 there was a "general hostility" toward the Argentine.[15]

Another of the problems San Martín faced was obtaining adequate numbers of soldiers. He needed them for his Peruvian expedition as well as local defense, as royalist forces remained active, particularly in the south. Reinforcements arrived from Argentina, but he still had to turn to local sources. He attracted some volunteers and reenlisted a number of patriot veterans who had been captured after the battles of Desaguadero, Vilcapugio, Ayohúma, and Sipe-Sipe and imprisoned in Chile. Found groaning "in the dungeons of *casas-matas*" (literally, killing houses but, in fact, fortifications), they were released to serve again.[16] His search for soldiers also prompted him to look to the local slave population, in keeping with his earlier efforts in Mendoza. With the reintroduction of the *Patria Vieja*'s recruiting law in October 1818, he had access to all Chilean slaves except domestics, a limitation that seriously reduced the number available. Some had served already, and at least one former soldier asked for his freedom on these grounds. The issue was deemed of sufficient importance that it was sent to the Chilean Senate; this body decided a law was necessary to resolve it, indicating that opposition to freeing slaves had not ended with the patriot success. The small numbers that were donated gave further evidence of the lack of local support. In some instances, the donations may have represented acts of self-preservation, as owners who had been drafted were permitted by law to assign a slave in their place. Other owners may have been unloading unwanted slaves, such as José María Pacheco, a slave of thirty-nine or forty described by his owner as "incorrigible." Pacheco, however, appeared to see some attraction in military service, for he asked to be enlisted. Another recruit was the runaway Ramón Niño, who had been arrested for stealing and was being held in jail awaiting assignment either to the Army of Peru or to public works in Mendoza.[17] San Martín's recruiting difficulties may be explained by the shortage of slaves, by the patriots' financial problems and the consequent low level of compensation, or by general Chilean hostility to a foreigner's request for their slaves. Whatever the reason, once the Argentine general departed north to Peru and the Chilean authorities offered a more generous 150 pesos to anyone who wished to redeem his or her slaves, donations multiplied.[18]

Despite the opposition, San Martín's expeditionary force grew. When their training and preparations finally came to an end in August 1820, between four and five thousand men were loaded onto eight men-of-war and thirteen transports, along with stores and supplies for two years.[19] According to Núria Sales de Bohigas, almost one-half, or around two thousand, of the soldiers, cavalrymen, artillerymen, and sailors under San Martín's command were manumitted slaves.[20] With the Santiago cabildo exhorting them to destroy "the tyrants who believed they could enslave with impunity the sons of liberty," on August 20 the ships set sail and headed north.[21] Some boarding the transports must have remembered their last experience with sea voyages. The recollections may have been painful, but this time they were part of a liberating expedition, whose added attraction was that victory would ensure their own personal freedom.

The ships sailed toward a country whose role in the independence wars lay in sharp contrast to that of Chile and most of the rest of Spanish South America. Throughout the years of conflict Peru had remained the bastion of royalist rule. Despite serious economic and financial problems that had afflicted the area in the late colonial period, Peru had managed to provide troops and resources to maintain the Spanish cause at home, eliminate threats in Ecuador and Chile, and prevent Argentine incursions through Upper Peru. Its army of Spanish regulars, backed by over forty thousand locals, had proven adequate to the task, and with the restoration of Ferdinand VII in 1814, more troops from Spain were promised.[22] As a result, the authorities had little need to consider slaves for military purposes. They probably were also sensitive to the racial concerns expressed by Peru's white minority. The latter's fears that had been aroused by the Túpac Amaru and Túpac Katari rebellions of the early 1780s resurfaced following a new Indian rebellion in 1814–1815, led by the previously loyal mestizo leader Mateo Pumacahua. The rebellion solidified creole support behind the royalist cause and aroused suspicions of even minor unrest involving any sector of the nonwhite population. Rumors of black conspiracies were, thus, widely believed. One in 1812 had the viceroy as its reported target, while another the same year claimed that slaves were planning to kill owners and destroy estates on the north coast. In 1817 there were new rumors that blacks in the southern Arica area, including an officer from a squadron of free *pardos* and blacks, were planning to seduce locals to the "cause of Buenos Aires." The stories had little foundation, but they produced accusations that some of the blacks in the area were *"revoltosos,"* once again strengthening royalist feelings. As a British observer noted in October 1818, "a slight attempt at an insurrection in Callao amongst the people of colour was quelled immediately," and he surmised it might "have the effect of inducing the white population to support the Viceroy."[23]

Despite the apparent black antipathy, the authorities showed little interest in appealing to the slaves and winning their support. For example, they introduced no antislavery legislation and did nothing to reduce slave prices, which remained high and even rose during this period, putting a serious roadblock in the way of slaves who wished to purchase their own freedom. In 1817, for example, a forty-nine-year-old male in Lima was valued at 500 pesos, while the price for a slave of sixty could range as high as 450 pesos. Females were equally expensive. Three of Pumacahua's slaves who were sold after his execution, a woman of over forty together with her two small children, were valued at 600 pesos.[24] The authorities' shortsightedness with regard to slaves provoked animosity that manifested itself in antisocial behavior. Court records of this period contain numerous cases of slaves who were tried for theft, murder, assault, and highway robbery. Marronage was common, and many runaways found a home among the highwaymen and bandits who infested the countryside, especially around Lima.[25] Resistance intensified in response to local challenges to Spanish rule, news that antislavery measures were being introduced elsewhere, and reports that San Martín was about to invade. The viceroy noted in 1818 that the black population was "openly decided for the rebels, from whose hands they expect liberty."[26] He could see the danger, but rather than addressing it, he directed his efforts at maintaining the loyalty of slave owners through imports of slaves from areas that remained under royalist control.[27]

The viceroy's reservations about the loyalty of the black population were largely misplaced, for despite their agitation most Peruvian blacks and mulattoes remained loyal to the king. They continued to serve in military units that had been established before the struggles began and staunchly defended Spanish rule both at home and in distant lands. A battalion of free *pardos* of Lima and a corps of free blacks played a prominent role in suppressing the Quito insurgent movements in 1810 and 1812 and were also active on the Upper Peru frontier against Argentine incursions.[28] Among those who served was a man by the name of Pedro Rosas, who may have been free when he enlisted in February 1811 but, according to his marriage certificate dated August 28, 1798, was of the Congo caste and had been a slave of María Antonia Rosas. He fought in Peru and Upper Peru on different campaigns and in numerous battles, including Desaguadero, Huaqui, Oruro, Vilcapugio, and Ayohúma, until his death at the battle of Ilave in 1814 against Buenos Aires troops.[29] As elsewhere, the existence of black units attracted runaways, lured perhaps by the pictures of military life described by members of the black militia and the other regiments with whom they mixed on a daily basis. One was Ramón Ovalle's slave, Rodulfo, who ran away and joined the Third Company of Grenadiers of the Royal Regiment of Lima, hiding his status by giving his name as José Jiménez.[30] Their participation indicates that despite the availability of Spanish veterans, blacks were fighting for the king; in fact, in some parts of the viceroyalty their involvement was vital, as the Spanish troops were insufficient to meet expanding military demands. Late in 1817 Admiral Bowles wrote that one Spanish regiment was "filled up a few days previous to their embarkation [for Chile] with prisoners, negroes, and recruits of the worst description." The following year the viceroy reported that five-sixths of the soldiers in the Lima garrison were blacks, mulattoes, and *zambos*.[31] He was now going to have to rely on them even more, as reinforcements from Spain could no longer be assured and the threat from the south was fast approaching.

What sort of military contribution San Martín expected from Peru's slaves is unclear. He could have easily justified expropriating and enlisting them, as most belonged to royalist sympathizers. Yet Bowles, for one, believed that he was averse to recruiting them. He reported that before setting sail from Chile, San Martín "expressed the greatest anxiety to prevent if possible any revolution in Lima which might occasion bloodshed and calamity." The British observer concluded, "I really believe that he has avoided all attempts to work upon the black population in that country from this very motive, and that he would now rather agree to a suspension of arms than undertake his expedition against that capital."[32] At the same time, the Argentine leader was being urged to recruit among the local slave population. An anonymous letter of July 22, 1818, suggested that on landing he should free seventy or eighty blacks from the coastal area south of Lima, if they agreed to provide information about their localities. To counter the recruiting plans of the viceroy, he should offer to arm slaves, who, he was assured, would desert to the patriots in exchange for their freedom. As a diversion, he should disembark one thousand men north of Lima and capture horses as well as two or three hundred slaves, giving them their freedom on joining the army. His correspondent claimed that the viceroy had already recruited hacienda slaves but described them as "totally undisciplined," unable to handle either a lance or stick, and likely to cause confusion in their own forces. Moreover, their true loyalty was to the patriots, from whom—he repeated—they expected their freedom. Patriotic hacendados, in addition, would donate their slaves to the army.[33] The information may be suspect, but it shows that long before his arrival, San Martín was aware of the issue. The letter also indicates that his reputation for freeing slaves in return for military service had preceded him and there was an expectation of the same in Peru. His own words may have played a role in arousing those beliefs. In his proclamation to the Peruvians before his invasion he declared, "The Spaniards want us not to be free but to be slaves; that is the only alternative that they have left us. I who know your sentiments have answered: *Free or dead, but never slaves.*"[34]

The actions of the patriots along the Peruvian coast before the arrival of the expeditionary force reinforced San Martín's antislavery reputation. Among the crew of the Chilean fleet under the command of Lord Thomas Cochrane, which from 1819 patrolled the Peruvian coast and attacked Spanish shipping, was a contingent of one hundred blacks from the Seventh Regiment. They were supplemented by slaves taken from coastal plantations. In May 1819, one raiding party of marines under William Miller took 150 slaves, along with sugar and a few oxen, from the estate of a royalist in the Supe area north of Lima. Eight or nine slaves from a nearby Augustinian estate joined them, while others from the region tried but were recaptured by royalist forces, who punished the runaways before returning them to their owners. According to a royalist source, not all the recruits were happy with their choice, as two (one from Guayaquil and the other from Lima) shortly afterwards deserted Cochrane's squadron and were returned to their owners. Their decision prompted the comment, "The chains of slavery among us are amiable and gentle when compared with the terrible freedom that the insurgents offer."[35] Nevertheless, many remained and provided the patriots with invaluable assistance. On their return with the invasion force, they were permitted to visit their relatives and friends, and, according to Miller, their reports "induced many slaves to enlist."[36]

San Martín may have arrived in Peru hesitant about recruiting slaves, but military realities and the small size of his army soon forced him to revise his thinking. In addition, the region that he invaded and controlled was home to most of the country's slaves, whose owners had long supported the king. He disembarked in the Pisco area south of Lima in September 1820, and while his initial attempts to attract slaves from the surrounding estates may have failed simply because most had been moved away, within weeks he was enjoying remarkable success. A correspondent of Bernardo O'Higgins reported that by October over six hundred blacks had been taken from the area. From nearby Ica, Francisco Mateo Cabezudo wrote to his brother in late December that the invading force had "expanded in a grand manner with rural slaves who were willingly attracted with the offer of freedom that was given in the name of their government." Miller claimed that upon San Martín's landing near the former Jesuit estate of Caucato, in the Chincha Valley, many of the estate's nine hundred slaves fled to join the patriots. The following March another thirty, "the most able-bodied," joined. North of Lima, in the Chancay Valley, the newly appointed political governor and military commander ordered all the slaves of the Quispico estate to appear, offering them freedom in return for military service. Ten of eleven slaves expressed their wish to serve and were taken to the barracks in the town of Sayán for training. On the nearby Andahuasi estate, the governor found that all the slaves had fled except for one who wished to serve, but he managed to obtain thirty-five more in the town.[37] Royalist commentators confirmed the recruiting, and one noted that as San Martín's troops marched to Ica, "he supplemented his army with some blacks from that locale, from the valley's sugarcane haciendas and vineyards after destroying the larger part of them." In addition, he took supplies, horses, and mules.[38] Royalists in New Granada also observed that San Martín was attracting Peruvian blacks, although the reported source of the recruits seems unlikely. Captain Francisco Mercadillo wrote in May 1821 that blacks had "come from the sierra" to occupy the northern coast of Peru and that San Martín had sent 120 blacks to Piura in the north to challenge a royalist movement from Quito.[39]

Local slaves could provide obvious benefits to the invaders. In addition to filling the ranks, they could cope with the coastal climate that proved deadly to those from more temperate zones.[40] They could also be used as guides and spies. One employed in this manner was a man named Ildefonso, who had been born a slave at Chincha and later became Miller's servant, dying in 1821 while on a mission to acquire information behind enemy lines. Another was Antonio Salazar, who was recruited in 1820 as a spy, as well as to carry correspondence, guide troops along on the coast, and help recruit others. He also fought, serving with the Guides Regiment at the battle of Pampa Grande in 1821, where he was wounded in the chest by a musket ball and then further injured when an unspecified animal fell on him. Hilario Pío was a third. Recruited by the Division of Arenales, which needed a guide when it landed at Pisco, he, like Ildefonso, served as a spy under Miller. He was captured and confined in stocks but was eventually released by the patriots and, after being granted his freedom, continued to serve on the coast as a guide and letter carrier in royalist-controlled territory.[41]

Peruvian slaves also assisted the patriots through their involvement in the bands of proindependence guerrillas or *montoneros* that operated on the coast and in the interior, occasionally under black leadership. Many of the slaves were runaways, while others of their cohorts had previously been bandits and highwaymen. They now assumed a political mantle, but they had not entirely abandoned their old ways, as looting seemed to remain the primary objective of many, and victims of their depredations must have questioned their supposed commitment to the cause of independence. Nevertheless, they helped observe and harass the enemy, they cut royalist communications and supply lines, and they provided information and supplies for the patriot forces.[42]

Confronted by San Martín's expanding invasion force, the royalists' military needs became critical. On the eve of the patriot landings in August 1820, they issued a call-up that initially excluded slaves but soon had to be expanded, as San Martín advanced along the coast and news of the liberal revolution in Spain raised doubts about further reinforcements from overseas.[43] The royalists also had to replace losses from disease and desertion. Late in the year the entire Numancia Battalion, comprising 650 Colombian and Venezuelan soldiers, deserted, and others followed. When the patriots captured Callao in September 1821, 1,400 South Americans were reported to have changed sides.[44] Desperate, the royalists finally turned to slaves to try to fill the gaps. They had a small base on which to build from past donations, which continued to provide a trickle of new recruits. In March 1820 José Ramón Rodil, the commander of the Arequipa Battalion, paid José Gabriel Hidalgo three hundred pesos to free his slave Salvador, "with the precise conditions that he [Salvador] serve His Majesty for ten years from today."[45]

But more were needed, and late in January 1821 the royalists made a deliberate move in this direction. The new viceroy, José de La Serna, who had recently taken over the position through a coup d'état, turned to slaves to defend Lima. He issued an order on January 31 whose aim was ultimately to arm 1,500 of them. He recognized the economic cost of this measure, calling it "a ruinous method," but he believed that it was necessary in his situation. His target was rural slaves between the ages of fifteen and sixty, living in the valleys south of Lima that were still under viceregal control. They were to be "agile, robust, and of the given age." They had to serve six years, although they would be freed at the time of their incorporation after being valued and their owners paid. "The blacks by this act . . . remain free, this freedom will not be taken away except for the crime of desertion, and on the war's conclusion they will receive their licenses [of freedom]." Three hundred were supposed to be recruited immediately, but within three weeks owners from Ica, Pisco, and Chincha reported that they had lost so many of their slaves because of the enemy occupation that it was impossible to provide the requested numbers. La Serna switched his focus to the nearby valleys of Cañete and Mala and their 2,460 slaves of both sexes and all ages, of whom he proposed to take 10 percent.[46] However, 250 raw slave recruits could not save the viceroyalty or even protect Lima, and early in July he evacuated the capital.

The precariousness of the royalist position was a factor in San Martín's decision to hold back and instead allow the Peruvians to declare their own independence and negotiate with the Spaniards to avoid bloodshed. While his strategy did not forestall troop movements and occasional confrontations, it prevented the decisive battle that might have ended the war. It also alienated many of his officers, but it won over prominent Peruvians and secured control of parts of the country where men and supplies could be obtained.[47] One of San Martín's desires was to maintain much of the existing social order and thereby prevent the racial unrest that had rent Venezuela. On entering Peru, he seemed to have developed some of the same racial fears that Bolívar expressed, and he certainly was aware of local slave animosity. Following his occupation of Lima in July he was told "that the slave population of the city meant to take advantage of the absence of the troops, to rise in a body and massacre the whites."[48] Their target was unlikely to have been the entire white population but, rather, local royalists who were probably slaveholders and the object of frequent patriot criticism. A British observer reported in September that when about 1,300 Spaniards were confined in the convent of La Merced to protect them and prevent them operating against the patriots at a time when a royalist attack appeared imminent, "the black population and lower orders assembled in the Plaza and demanded the lives of the Spaniards confined in the Convent." The authorities managed to avoid a massacre, but only just.[49]

In order to curb this animosity, appease the slaveholders, and at the same time maintain slave support, the conciliatory San Martín tried balancing the opposing forces without provoking outright opposition. He prepared a series of laws whose importance was evident from the fact that he drafted them at the same time that he was composing his declaration of Peruvian independence. On July 23, 1821, five days before that historic pronouncement, he issued an edict that was designed to compel runaways to return to their owners. It noted that many of them had assumed that the freedom granted those who had enlisted applied to them, and, as a result, they had "not simply left their houses and slave quarters but abandoned themselves to committing the greatest excesses." The edict gave slaves who had not been incorporated into the army before July 5 fifteen days to return to their owners. Those who complied would not be punished. A subsequent decree on July 31 also aimed at controlling slaves, specifically those whose owners had left the country or fled to the royalist-held fortresses in Callao, by ordering owners to present themselves to the authorities or be fined the value of their slaves and face expulsion from the country. At the same time, it prepared the ground for recruiting slaves. According to the decree, slaves who presented themselves and were deemed to belong to the enemy or to émigrés would be accepted into the army and freed. More important to slaves was his free womb law issued on August 12, which declared free all children born in Peru after independence day, July 28, 1821. Its preamble indicated that like Bolívar, San Martín had become committed to humanitarian goals:

When humanity has been greatly abused and their rights violated for a long time, a singular act of justice is, if not to compensate them entirely, at least to take the first steps in complying with the holiest of all obligations. A substantial portion of our species has until today been looked on as a permutable asset, and subject to the calculations of a criminal traffic: men have bought men and have not been ashamed of debasing the family to which they belong, selling one to others. . . . I shall not try to attack this ancient abuse with a single blow: it is necessary that time itself which has sanctioned it will destroy it, but I would not be responsible to my public conscience and to my private feelings were I not to prepare for the future with this merciful reform, reconciling for the present the interests of the proprietors with the vote of reason and of nature.

On November 24 he struck at the institution again by ending the African slave trade. The law declared free all slaves who arrived in Peru, "in keeping with the philanthropic principles that all the governments of the civilized world have now adopted."[50]

Over the same period San Martín issued several laws and decrees that were designed to bring slaves into his forces, with freedom being offered to attract them. The legislation indicated that he had confidence in their loyalty to the patriot cause and in their military capabilities, but again also hinted at his desire to avoid racial unrest. On September 2, in a general call-up, San Martín declared that every slave who fought against the enemy and distinguished himself by his bravery would be freed. Later that month, with the royalists advancing on Lima, he ordered that the slaves of the city be armed. When the threat passed, he recognized their contribution by decreeing that twenty-five of those who had shown their loyalty and then returned to their masters would be rewarded with their freedom, and that a like number "of the slaves who shone so generously in the defense of the capital and exterminated the oppressor" would be freed on September 7 in succeeding years. A selection would be made from those who had served, and the owners compensated.[51] On hearing that owners were preventing their slaves from enlisting, he decreed on October 25 that any owner who caused to desert, hid in his house, or apprehended an enlisted individual would lose his possessions on the first occasion and be exiled in perpetuity in the second. The law sought to involve the public in preventing this "abuse" by offering a reward of one-quarter of the guilty party's possessions to the person who denounced the crime, and freedom for any slave who did the same.[52] On November 17, declaring that "one of the duties of the government is to promote the freedom of those who have inhumanely suffered until today the usurpation of that inadmissible right," San Martín freed all the slaves belonging to Spaniards and enemy Americans. Those who were between the ages of fifteen and fifty were to present themselves for military service, while women and males who could not bear arms would receive their freedom papers from the departmental authorities.[53] On November 23, concerned about the large number of slaves around Lima who were deserters from the royalist army, he ordered the owners of those who had returned home to deliver them to the departmental authorities or lose all their property. The deserters who did not return to their owners were ordered to report to the authorities or face six months' imprisonment.[54] Owners attempted to lure back deserting slave recruits and runaways, leading to a further decree of January 8, 1822, that gave hacendados fifteen days to provide a list of their slaves who had fled since the army had entered Lima. These would be compared with military lists, and any slaves who joined the army after that date were to be restored to their owners, but those who had enlisted previously were to remain. As with its predecessor, the law declared anyone found hiding a slave would lose his or her possessions.[55]

Further legislation along the same lines was introduced after San Martín assigned local political authority to the Peruvian aristocrat, the *marqués* de Torre Tagle, in January 1822.[56] On January 31, after all Spanish bachelors had been ordered to leave the country, Torre Tagle decreed that their slaves had to present themselves to the military authorities. Those found useful for service would be incorporated into the army for three years, at the conclusion of which they would be freed, while the rest would be assigned to public works projects. On March 8, in response to "the obstinacy of the agents of the Spanish government that still conserve the hope of subjecting the country to the most abominable slavery," he directed all of Lima's slaves to enroll in the urban artillery, a militia unit. At the same time, a list of the rural slaves between the ages of fifteen and fifty living within three leagues of Lima was to be drawn up. Any slave whose owner tried to hide him would receive his freedom on condition that he served in the urban militia, while a slave who connived with his owner would be assigned to a line regiment. On April 11 the government instructed urban and rural owners to supply the names of their slaves for possible military service that could last six years, but the order was revoked two weeks later in response to owner protests and concerns about the likely impact on agriculture. A decree of May 13 enlisted all of Lima's slaves in the urban militia and instructed those whose owners ignored the law to present themselves to the authorities for assignment to the army. They would receive their freedom after two years' service.[57]

To oversee the recruiting aspects of the various laws the authorities turned to an institution whose name would have been familiar to those conversant with Argentine military developments. Early in 1822 a commission of *rescate* was established. As in Buenos Aires, it collected the slaves, determined their suitability, and returned those deemed useless or else assigned them to more appropriate duties. The commission also dealt with owners who requested the return of their slaves or demanded exemptions from the legislation.[58] The commission's appearance seemed to stimulate owners' generosity and desire to demonstrate support for the patriot cause, for the numbers of recruits multiplied, especially between March and May 1822. The head of the commission reported that in April alone sixty-three slaves had been taken from the valleys near Lima. The slaves surrendered were not only males: Pedro Mariano Goyeneche's donation was fourteen slaves of both sexes. The males were assigned to the army, while the fate of the women is unknown.[59]

The new recruits added to what was already a significantly black army. In January 1822, even before the commission started operating, the commentator quoted at the beginning of this chapter made his observation that "the entire army of 4,800 men was composed of slaves."[60] It was wildly inaccurate, for local slave recruits comprised about one-seventh of the army, and only a portion of the soldiers brought from Argentina and Chile had been slaves. Yet, the numbers, who included conscripts, donations, captured runaways, and deserters from both their own forces and the Spanish army, were substantial, even if no one seems to have made an actual count.[61] They were assigned to various units, including the black regiments from the Río de la Plata and Chile, the Army of Peru, the artillery, the cavalry, and even the navy, as donors sometimes specified the unit. Most were destined for the militia, and to this end a new regiment, the Unión Peruana, was established in Lima in April 1822 to accommodate those recruited from the city. Comprising 657 men, exclusive of officers, and divided into two battalions, it was under the command of Lieutenant Colonel Juan Pardo de Zela. His officers were drawn from existing battalions that were also supposed to provide the regiment's sergeants and corporals, although he was permitted to promote some of the slave recruits if the former proved insufficient. Other black militia units, such as the Battalion of Cívicos Patricios and the Battalion of Morenos, were also operating in Lima and probably incorporating slaves. Their principal duty seemed to be to patrol the city; in addition, they were expected to defend it in the case of royalist attack.[62] However, they were basically part-time soldiers, remaining with their owners while they were trained on weekends, if training actually occurred. In September 1822, the Minister of War and Navy reported that the training of 1,916 slaves enrolled as sappers had not been realized because of the difficulty in assembling them and because of their importance as workers in the countryside.[63]

Comments such as these suggest that many of the recruits existed only on paper, which may explain another contemporary writer's observation that San Martín was disappointed by the local slaves' lack of enthusiasm for service.[64] Perhaps he had expected a more positive response from those belonging to departing Spaniards, whom he had specifically tried to recruit. He also had to cope with the continuing opposition of those owners who prevented their slaves from serving, as the frequent and repeated introduction of legal sanctions to punish this clearly indicates.

The owners' reaction is understandable, for until recently they had been spared most of the disruptions of war. Now they had to cope with both military demands and challenges that were undermining their style of life. At a petty level, for example, urban dwellers found themselves the victims of thefts and home invasions by armed slaves.[65] More seriously affected were rural slaveholders. Following San Martín's invasion, they had suffered substantial and continuing losses. A British account after the war reported that of the 1,200 slaves on one estate, recruiting and flight had reduced the number to 300, primarily the elderly and children. Other hacienda owners reported more modest but nevertheless significant losses as San Martín's forces passed through their areas. In one case 40 slaves were taken, in another 60 were donated, and guerrillas made off with still others.[66] Owners objected to their loss of property, the resulting financial setbacks, and the challenges to their authority. They complained to San Martín that the removal of "the most useful slaves for soldiers" had resulted in the "ruin" of sown fields and led to slave unrest. In the Ica Valley, according to one observer, slaves, demonstrating a "desire to be free, were refusing absolutely to comply with their obligations," resulting in a loss of the harvest. The same was true of estates in the Lima area, where owners claimed that "slaves, abusing the political freedom, were applying it to the individual" and refusing to recognize any dominion. They expressed fears that slaves would go further and "make attempts against [owners'] lives."[67]

Slaveholders in the Cañete Valley were equally upset, complaining that agriculture was suffering because slaves were being taken for service in Lima. Domingo Orué, a slaveholding plantation owner who initially supported the royalists but after independence became a congressional deputy, recalled the disruption and damage caused by slave recruiting. He claimed that in response to San Martín's requests for mules, horses, cattle, and then slaves and money, he had provided more than fifty slaves for military service, with the promise that no more would be demanded. But then he was asked for half of any slaves remaining who were useful for military service, and was compensated only one hundred pesos for each. The viceroy's order to arm blacks had

had a further negative impact, as San Martín retaliated with a law freeing any of these who passed to his ranks. This was then followed with further legislation compelling all blacks to enlist.[68]

Slaveholder animosity added to the mounting chorus of opposition to the beleaguered San Martín. His inability or unwillingness to destroy the remaining royalist armies left him particularly vulnerable, causing him to look north to Simón Bolívar in the hope of some sort of assistance. But the famous meeting of the two great liberators in Guayaquil in July 1822 proved profoundly discouraging for the Argentine. His proposals were rejected, and his only accomplishment was an offer of reinforcements. He returned to Lima, where he found that his influence had declined even more, convincing him that others would have to resolve Peru's independence issues. He resigned his authority in favor of the Peruvian congress and set sail for home on September 21, marking a rather undistinguished end to his long, selfless, and quite extraordinary contributions to the independence struggles and to the liberation of Spanish America's slaves.[69]

With the patriot government now in the hands of local creoles, Peru's slaveholders faced a more favorable situation. They must have been pleased when late in 1822, with the military situation around Lima apparently under control, the government disbanded the *rescate* commission and dissolved the Unión Peruana. Their slaves continued to offer their services in the hope of eventual freedom, and some were still being drafted to fill gaps in the ranks. Nevertheless, when a commander of a unit of sappers became particularly active in this regard, owners tried to rein him in by making their concerns known about the possible impact on agriculture.[70] In another instance, when slaves on an estate south of Lima, who were "devoted to" the cause, were permitted to be recruited for a company of the Guides Regiment, the authorities conciliated the owners by ordering that every slave missing from the hacienda, whether male or female, should be apprehended and those not working should be punished.[71] On the whole, recruiting slaves was no longer a priority; by the end of January 1823 they were no longer being enlisted in the militia, and those still enrolled were being made available for public works.[72]

The hiatus, however, proved to be brief, for the military situation had not been resolved and the royalists still boasted a formidable army. In August 1822 they had 5,000 troops operating in the environs of Lima, while another 15,000 were available in the interior.[73] The independence forces, in contrast, numbered only 5,000, and reinforcements were not at all certain.

The 2,500 dispatched by Bolívar late in the year returned to Guayaquil almost immediately, following disagreements with the Peruvian government.[74] The royalists, consequently, could move more or less at will and scored notable military successes, including a crushing defeat of the patriots at the battle of Moquegua in January 1823, where the remaining Argentine and Chilean troops were almost destroyed. They also recaptured Lima for a brief period in June 1823.[75] In these circumstances, military concerns resumed their importance. Soldiers were needed, and the Peruvian governing junta focused its attention on slaves once again. On February 11, 1823, it reintroduced the decree compelling urban and rural owners to supply a list of their slaves, with the addendum that one-third of the urban slaves and one-fifth of the rural slaves were to be chosen by lottery for evaluation and enlistment. The decree also declared that any slave who was concealed but then denounced his owner would receive fifty pesos, plus his freedom, after two years' military service.[76] To oversee the recruiting, the government reactivated the *rescate* commission, which enthusiastically carried out its mandate over a period of six weeks, until it suspended its activities in response to concerns about ruining proprietors and hurting poor families. But during that brief period it considered every slave, including those of deputies, and selected 122. They ranged in value from 150 to 450 pesos, totaling 23,680 pesos, and all but 11 of them were enlisted. At the same time individuals continued to donate slaves, although not necessarily with military service in mind. Ysidora de las Barcera, lacking money or things of value, offered her eleven-year-old slave Miguel, noting, "The State needs our help in securing its ultimate goal, just freedom." The government planned to sell him, but as there were no buyers, he was assigned to the army.[77]

As well as reactivating the *rescate* commission, the government obtained slave recruits through mechanisms it introduced to try to resolve its horrendous financial situation. For example, it gave taxpayers the option of supplying corn, livestock, or slaves to meet their taxes and other financial burdens. Seven bakeries, in response, donated seventeen slaves worth 4,450 pesos, as did a number of hacendados and a chocolate maker. In like manner, a group of Spanish merchants—who together were levied a forced loan of 60,000 pesos—were permitted to provide slaves as an alternative. One who took advantage of the option was Manuel Ibáñez Pacheco, who was unable to pay his portion of 200 pesos because of his "deplorable situation." Instead, he offered a slave named Domingo to achieve "the total pacification of Peru."[78]

Other owners managed to meet their obligations and thereby retained control of their property. The need for soldiers also prompted military officers to draft hacienda slaves, until the government stepped in and ordered them returned. Nonetheless, the various methods put at least two hundred more slaves into the ranks. They were supposed to be assigned to the Patricios Battalion, but some ended up in other units, including the remnants of the Río de la Plata regiment and the revitalized Unión Peruana, which was reestablished under the command of Pardo de Zela on April 1, 1823, in response to a new threat to Lima. At that time, all those who had previously served in the unit were also recalled to duty.[79]

The end of the threat by mid-May brought an end to the organized recruiting of slaves in Peru, even though they continued to be called up as new crises arose. A decree ordering that slaves be returned to their owners permitted those who wished to remain in service to do so if they were purchased by the state.[80] In July, after Lima was recaptured from the royalists, a new decree ordered runaways to return to their owners; those whose ownership was unclear would be assigned to the army. In early August, slaves who had served in the artillery attached to the militia were called up again, only to be returned to their owners in December after the Chilean expeditionary army offered to leave its artillery, presumably with its artillerymen, in the service of Peru.[81] By that point, alternative soldiers were becoming available, and slave owners were again voicing complaints that recruiting was causing them economic distress. Among them was the mint, which had provided five slaves for the military and now claimed that foundry output was suffering because of the loss of their skills.[82] It asked for the return of its property, as did other owners. Most claimed that their slaves were not actually in military service, but on occasion provided other reasons. One owner wrote that her slave who was in the artillery should be returned because he was sick and she would cure him, while another, in asking for the return of two slaves in the army, mentioned a recent donation of firewood to the military hospital.[83]

The formal recruiting of slaves was thus a thing of the past as Bolívar made his plans to enter the Peruvian fray, and he was not going to turn back the clock. He had indicated long before his arrival that he intended to rely on Colombian troops for the final stages of the war. He had confidence in them, and he also believed that using Colombians gave him greater control over the entire army. In his view, locally recruited troops were too tied to their locales, which made them less easy to command. He preferred those that he could move at will and who had few local connections.[84] But he also wanted troops who could cope with the local environment. In writing to Santander in April 1823 that he was planning to send six thousand troops from Colombia to Lima, he asked his vice president to provide "recruits from a warmer climate, as those from these parts [of highland Ecuador] all die off to the last man." He added, "Unless men are sent from Venezuela and the Magdalena, we cannot form an army here. I might be able to send the entire available population to Lima, but I could not raise a single corps capable of defending the South, for, as you very well know, recruits are of no use in their own country." Commenting on men being recruited from Tumaco, he noted, "As these men are from a warm country, they are especially useful, that is, far from home, the only place where they are fit for anything."[85]

Bolívar's reliance on Colombians also rested on doubts that he had about the quality of the existing troops in Peru and the unlikelihood of reinforcements arriving from elsewhere. The political situation there had deteriorated into factionalism that made mounting a successful attack on the Spanish forces using Peruvian resources virtually impossible. San Martín's Army of the Andes had almost ceased to exist. As a British report in May 1823 noted, "the remnant of the original invading force" amounted to only about 1,500 Argentines and Chileans, of whom many had been redistributed among other regiments to try to raise them to full strength.[86] And their homelands had no intention of replacing them. On July 19, 1823, Bolívar wrote, "The government of Chile like that of Buenos Aires declines to participate further in the war of Peru. That of Buenos Aires not only refuses its cooperation but also assures me that it does not know how many troops it has here that bear the blue and white colors." He also had doubts about their political loyalty.[87] Therefore, he mobilized Colombians for his Peruvian campaign and sent his able lieutenant Antonio José de Sucre ahead with four thousand men.[88]

Bolívar's view of the situation remained unchanged following his own arrival in Peru in September. Reports about his allies were discouraging. In December he was informed that the Argentines and Chileans would "depart and the governments on which they rely [would] limit themselves to defending and preserving their own territories." The Chilean congress was asking for the return of its soldiers, including the slaves in the Chilean division, while the Peruvians seemed prepared to fall back under Spanish rule, so that "the Colombians [would] remain alone."[89] As a result, Bolívar became even more reliant on his own troops, establishing a flow of reinforcements from the north by sea via Panama and Guayaquil. He hoped to obtain up to five thousand, ordering each of the cantons of Gran Colombia to supply a specified proportion according to their population. Local officials may have resented the demands and failed to provide all that he requested, but they nevertheless drafted as many as they could, since they preferred that the fighting take place in Peru and not at home. They also wanted to see the end of the Spanish threat, fearing that a patriot defeat could lead to a new Spanish invasion of Colombia.[90] The reinforcements consequently continued to arrive, with slaves among their number. A British observer reporting on Colombia late in 1824 noted, "Of the 2000 soldiers whom I saw in Carthagena going to Peru [earlier in the year], at least one half were more or less of the African tinge."[91]

Bolívar's reservations about the non-Colombian troops in his multinational army proved remarkably prescient, for in February 1824 the garrison defending Callao mutinied and defected to the enemy. According to initial reports, a group of disaffected soldiers from the Río de la Plata Regiment took advantage of the small number of troops in the port to hand control of both Lima and the fortresses of Callao over to the Spanish forces. British reports blamed men of the Buenos Aires Seventh and Eighth Regiments, "the greater part emancipated slaves," men "who had distinguished themselves under General San Martin." The reports traced the soldiers' discontent to the fact that they had not been paid for over eleven months because of government neglect and officers stealing their wages. The British minister in Buenos Aires wrote that the garrison in Callao, "disgusted with the ill usage of their officers and having in vain demanded their long standing arrears of pay, released some Spanish prisoners" and placed themselves under their command. Subsequent information fleshed out the early reports, without entirely clarifying what occurred. It indicated that troops who had recently been assigned to Callao mutinied and took over the fortresses on February 5. Other troops joined them, so that between 1,200 and 1,400 from two Argentine and one Chilean regiment were involved, under the command of a mulatto sergeant. They demanded one hundred thousand pesos from the government and nine vessels to carry them to Buenos Aires; their requests were refused, and subsequent attempts at negotiations also failed. At this point the mutineers declared in favor of Spain. They released thirty Spanish prisoners being held in the fortresses, who quickly assumed command, and the Spanish flag was raised on February 11. The ex-prisoners then contacted the royalist army under General José Rodil, operating nearby in Ica. He marched on Lima and Callao with two thousand men and occupied the cities on February 27. In the meantime, the mutineers had been plundering houses in Callao, Lima, and the environs and fired on ships in the harbor. Bolívar tried to end the crisis by sending an envoy to Lima with money to pay the mutineers, and he managed to convince two hundred to rejoin their units. He also offered one hundred pesos and emancipation to any black soldier who returned to duty and extended the offer to all of the soldier's relations. However, he failed to win over the majority, who remained entrenched in Callao.[92]

A later Argentine account of the mutiny agreed on many of the salient points but laid much of the blame on the Peruvian government. It pointed out that the animosity had been building for some time because of a lack of local provisioning. As a result, soldiers were so short of food and clothing that they had taken to stealing simply in order to survive. Their situation had improved with the arrival of Bolívar, but his departure to deal with strife elsewhere led to a resurgence of discontent. Numerous desertions had occurred as early as November 1823, and by the end of the month shortages and the poor quality of the rations had reached such a point that the increasingly demoralized soldiers began to engage in even further excesses, little worried by the possible consequences. An attempted mutiny by soldiers in the black regiment of Río de la Plata in January was a warning of the state of affairs. The lack of wages, compounded by a failure to implement an offer to pay them a fraction of what they were owed, seemed to be the last straw. Three sergeants of the Río de la Plata grenadiers, headed by Sergeant Dámaso Moyano, led the mutiny, along with officers and noncommissioned officers of the Regiment of Río de la Plata and the Eleventh Battalion. They managed to seduce about one hundred others with the hope of being paid, men that included Chileans, Colombians, and Peruvians. Initially they had no intention of joining the enemy, but Spaniards took advantage "of the opportunity to seduce the stupidity of the mutinous troops" and took over. The report concluded that if the soldiers had been paid, the mutiny would never have occurred. It also pointed out that the mutineers numbered one thousand, and hardly one hundred were troops of the Army of the Andes; the rest, it stated, were blacks recruited from Peruvian haciendas.[93]

The mutineers remained discontented, despite royalist control, but they now had to deal with a much less conciliatory commander. On June 12 they engaged in a new outburst, and the conclusion was far more sanguinary.

Rodil made no attempt to negotiate with them, and many of the mutineers were shot, either during the uprising or shortly thereafter. The British minister wrote that fifty to sixty men were executed, of whom thirty-five were shot immediately and their bodies burned outside the fort. They seemed to be "chiefly" blacks "and probably of the party who surrendered these forts to the Spanish party." A local newspaper report claimed that the new plot involved the Arequipa and Río de la Plata battalions, the former a royalist unit and the latter a patriot.[94]

In the context of the campaign, the mutiny had very little impact. Bolívar made no attempt to recapture Lima and Callao, realizing that success depended on destroying the main royalist forces and not on occupying Lima and its port, which could easily be bypassed. Rodil remained in command of the fortresses but was unable to influence the outcome of the struggles. The only significant results were the dissolution of the Division of the Andes and Bolívar's even stronger dependence on his Colombians, although realities forced him to turn to locals as well. North of Lima, near Trujillo, he organized an army of about seven thousand Colombian troops and five thousand Peruvians, including many *montoneros*. He was named dictator by the Peruvian congress in February 1824 but still had to contend with numerous problems as he prepared his forces. One was the simmering nationalist hostility between sectors of his army, which had been a factor in the Callao mutiny. In March, a confrontation between Colombian and Peruvian troops resulted in a number of casualties. The royalists tried to foment divisions by claiming that the Colombians intended to remain in Peru, prompting Sucre to issue a rebuttal. Fortunately for Bolívar, the royalist forces were even more divided. The restoration of absolutism in Spain in October 1823 split the commanders between constitutionalists and absolutists and prevented a united attack on the patriot army as it readied for the final battles.[95]

During this period, Bolívar made few direct appeals to the black population of Peru. Extensive antislavery legislation had been passed already so that his opportunities were limited. His initiatives were confined to recognizing the existence of local slaves among his soldiers and occasionally intervening on their behalf. For example, he rebuked Torre Tagle in January 1824 for a decree passed by the Peruvian congress that made possible the reenslavement of soldiers. He commented, "Congress has issued a decree that justice, liberty, and good policy will forever disapprove. Is it not outrageous that free soldiers, in reward for their faithfulness to my banners, would again be consigned to chains? Is it possible or politic that, at a time when every ally is making great sacrifices for Peru, she should order the freedmen to be withdrawn from service?"[96] But he made no effort to increase the numbers in his service. A supreme resolution of March 24, 1824, gave slaves the right to change owners but had no impact on recruiting.[97] Geopolitical and environmental factors were of greater concern to him. Since his Peruvian resource base was confined largely to the province of Trujillo, he had to recruit from the immediate area, unlike irregular groups that could recruit slaves wherever they operated. But how many slaves were available to him, both in Trujillo and elsewhere? The British minister noted in June 1824 that "the bulk" of the black and mulatto population in Lima had "been greatly taken away for military service."[98] There were still slaves working on the sugar plantations of the Trujillo area, but Bolívar may have been loath to alienate their owners. Plus, these were coastal inhabitants, and his campaign called for a movement into the highlands where the royalist armies were operating. Local slave involvement was thus minor and seemed primarily to involve the collection of information. In one case, slaves on an estate in the Sayán area provided details about the size of the enemy force that served as the basis for a successful attack.[99]

Thus, slaves continued to provide military service, but they were not the dominant sector that they had been both elsewhere and earlier during the Peruvian struggle. Some of the recruits from Argentina, Chile, and Peru could still be found in the patriot army, supplemented now by those from Gran Colombia who had accompanied and followed Bolívar, but the comments about black participation that had marked the campaigns in Argentina, Venezuela, Chile, and even Peru during the period of San Martín's leadership were no longer heard. Similarly, separate black units were not a prominent part of the army, as the recruits seem to have been dispersed among the various regiments. Yet they were certainly present, as they were in the royalist army. In the latter case, the numbers were very small, eliciting the briefest of comments. In July 1824, as he prepared for what proved to be the final battles, the royalist commander in chief, José de Canterac, described his army as composed of "creoles and Indians, with some negroes."[100]

As a result, the armies that met at Junín on August 6 and at Ayacucho on December 8 to decide the fate of Peru and of Spanish rule in South America were not notable for their slave contingents. The slave recruits had disappeared into the largely American-born, multiethnic armies of both sides.[101] The reports of the battles describe the contributions of the national contingents and not the racial groupings. Even the term "slavery" at this late date was as likely to be heard in reference to Spanish rule in America as to describe the status of a particular sector of Spanish American society. Just before the battle of Junín, Bolívar exhorted his troops in typically grandiloquent style, "You are going to complete the greatest task that heaven has been able to entrust to man, that of saving the entire world from slavery."[102] He was not referring to the black population of Spanish America, and his choice of words relegated to a secondary role the long-standing social struggle that had been occurring alongside the independence wars. In a way, it was a warning of what was to come, for with the final battles fought and won the ex-slaves were about to learn that while they had helped to secure the freedom of their homelands, they had not destroyed slavery. The institution continued to exist, and large numbers of their family members remained in bondage. Even more disturbing for many of the ex-slave veterans was the fact that with slavery's survival, their own status as freemen was about to be challenged—despite their years of military service, hardship, and sacrifice. They had helped to secure the independence of their countries, but their personal struggle for freedom and equality had not ended.

RECRUITMENT AND RESISTANCE

 WILLIAM MILLER, THE ENGLISHMAN who fought for the independence forces in different parts of South America, has left an instructive, although somewhat misleading, picture of the slaves who served under him. Of those recruited in Buenos Aires, he wrote, most had been domestic slaves before the revolution. Yet, he observed, "they were distinguished throughout the war for their valour, constancy, and patriotism. They were docile, easy to instruct and devotedly attached to their officers. Many were remarkable for their intelligence, cleanliness, and good conduct. They went through their evolutions exceedingly well, and it was generally allowed that they marched better than the corps formed of whites. Many of them rose to be good non-commissioned officers; some had taught themselves to read and write, while others had been instructed by a kind owner, or by some part of his family."[1]

Miller's intent was probably to leave a positive impression, and his obvious paternalism can be seen as a product of his era and his profession. However, to describe the recruits as *docile* seems out of place, since the story of slave soldiers was often the antithesis of the word, from their efforts to enlist, to their service in the field, to their actions in defense of their personal freedom. The outbreak of warfare and subsequent recruiting fundamentally altered the lives of countless slaves and in the process provided them with opportunities to challenge openly both their owners and the slavery system in general. Slave agitation was hardly a new phenomenon in Spanish America, but the crisis that fractured the links with the mother country and widened divisions between Spaniards and creoles created an exceptional environment in which slaves could test the chains that bound them. They enthusiastically responded by running away to enlist, hiding their identities to avoid being reclaimed, and using their military connections to protect the freedom that they coveted. For those recruited, the restrictions of the military proved to be no particular obstacle to their growing activism. Indeed, the realities of military service stimulated slaves to flex their muscles in new directions, producing, by the end of the war, a group who seemed anything but obedient, and a slavery system that had been greatly weakened. In the midst of the political revolution, a social transformation was taking place, and slaves were often in the forefront of that process.

Even before recruiting began, slaves saw in the unfolding political crisis a chance to act and to strike back at their owners. In 1810 one slave in Buenos Aires played on the fears of imminent warfare by accusing his master of concealing a stash of more than three hundred muskets. His falsehood was soon revealed, and for his temerity he was sentenced to be whipped one hundred times through the streets of the city.[2] However, punishments such as these failed to deter others, for more accusations of this sort surfaced with the spread of warfare and the growth of anti-Spanish sentiments, especially in those areas under creole control. In 1813 another Buenos Aires slave, Domingo Apirón, accused his owner, Antonio Apirón, a Spaniard, of having treated him with great cruelty since the May Revolution and of having spoken intolerantly of the "sons of the nation." Apirón was arrested but soon released, as witnesses appearing on his behalf refuted the accusations of disloyalty. The reason for Domingo's charges seemed to be a recent punishment that he considered unjustified and destroyed a twenty-three-year relationship. Apirón's wife decided that she wanted nothing more to do with the slave and put him up for sale. The army seems to have attracted her attention as an option, for Domingo's name appears on a list of slaves made available for military service.[3]

In areas under royalist control slaves were similarly prepared to accuse owners—in this case patriots—of disloyalty. After the royalist restoration in Chile in 1814, José Antonio Ovalle asked for his freedom on the grounds that his master of ten years, Francisco Ovalle, had supported the insurgents. He claimed that during the period of the *Patria Vieja*, Ovalle had brought him to

Santiago to serve as "a soldier of the *patria*." However, even though the insurgents were offering slaves freedom for service, he chose "to suffer the punishment handed out to deserters" and after one day returned home. His owner was hardly welcoming, treating him like an animal, hitting and kicking him and rejecting him for his "ingratitude and perfidy." José Antonio cited his desertion as proof of his lack of interest in the military and, by implication, his continuing loyalty to the crown, and he claimed that he had little desire for freedom, as indicated by his return to his owner's house. Ovalle provided quite a different account. He denied being disloyal and claimed that he had always treated José Antonio as a son, making few demands on him and punishing him only twice, notably on one occasion when he had slapped José Antonio for embarrassing him. He noted that the insurgents had turned to slaves to bolster their forces, offering them freedom and compelling owners to deliver them under the threat of serious penalties. When officials in his village had demanded that José Antonio be delivered, he had complied, but hid another slave. José Antonio had tried to take advantage of this in order to obtain his freedom by reporting on the hidden slave. Witnesses testified that there was no evidence of the owner making donations to the insurgents, although some of these were *inquilinos,* or tenant workers, of Ovalle, who might have been hesitant to criticize their employer.[4]

Who was telling the truth in this case remains uncertain, and despite his protestations to the contrary, there seems little doubt that José Antonio's ultimate aim was to achieve what the vast majority of slaves wanted: personal freedom.[5] In the words of a bricklayer from Buenos Aires, it was "the most sacred right," a right that assumed increasing relevance as it became the byword of the independence era.[6] Dangled before them as recruiting began, the offer must have been almost irresistible, as the reaction of slaves in the Banda Oriental indicated. They may have couched their wish to serve in terms of love of king, or commitment to the *patria,* or loyalty to an owner, but behind the rhetoric was the wish to be free. As a result, even though most slaves had little control over whether they were recruited or not, they did what they could to serve in the military, since this seemed the surest way to alter their legal status.

Yet, while freedom was the principal reason why slaves considered joining the military, other aspects of military service contributed to their interest in enlisting and probably helped to offset some of the negative reports that must have been circulating about life in the ranks. The military life may have appeared no worse than the work that some were doing already, and military discipline may have sounded no more restrictive than living under a dominating master. In fact, getting recruited could serve as a means to defy an owner. Antonio Castro, a Buenos Aires slave, stated that his reason for offering himself to the patriot army was his "desire" to "sacrifice himself for the just cause of his *patria*." It also provided an opportunity to get even with his owner, who had recently sought to sell him after he had indicated a wish to marry.[7] Military service also put weapons in slaves' hands, which they could now use against masters who were fighting for the enemy. That slaves would risk their lives for the side that gave them an opportunity and a legal justification to kill their exploiters was a factor in winning white support for slave recruiting, albeit reluctantly, and in some areas it worked, as in the case of Venezuela.

How long this served as a lure is not clear, for the recruits must have soon realized that the soldiers facing them were not white slave owners but mestizos, Indians, and blacks and mulattoes like themselves. Nonetheless, they continued to serve with distinction, as their record and the testimonials of their commanders attest. Moreover, bearing arms challenged the long-standing prohibition that had set them apart from others and reinforced their claim to both humanity and equality.[8]

Yet, while some slaves may have seen in military service an opportunity to kill members of the class of masters, or whites in general, or to achieve some sort of "glorious death" in battle, or, as some said, to sacrifice themselves for king or country, the vast majority probably had different ideas. Their goal was personal freedom, but they also wanted an opportunity to enjoy that freedom, which meant avoiding getting killed on a near or distant battlefield. Fortunately for many of them, military service did not necessarily mean fighting, as they were recruited or donated for one of the various noncombat roles and became part of the extensive group of auxiliaries who were an essential part of any army and who determined to a great extent the success—or failure—of the campaign. They were the artisans, such as carpenters, caulkers, blacksmiths, cooks, and armorers. They were the common laborers who were needed to build roads and to collect and transport food, coal, firewood, and other necessities, including artillery and munitions. They were the wranglers who handled the herds of horses, mules, cattle, and other livestock that accompanied armies.[9]

One particular noncombat role for slaves arose from their reputation as skilled musicians. An essential part of armies of the era was the corps of drummers and fifers who, along with buglers and flag bearers, played a central role in the intricate choreography of early nineteenth-century warfare. They assisted in the positioning of units on the battlefield, they set the pace of marching, and they sounded the beat to charge into battle.[10] That they were not expected to fight was indicated by the fact that, as in Europe, the drummers and fifers were often children. Andrés Salas was only eight when he began serving in the Buenos Aires Eighth Regiment as a drummer, and Manuel González at fifteen had only just left childhood. Slaves were also employed in these duties, although not all of them were children. Juan Joaquín del Valle, the son of unknown slave parents from Guinea, was twenty-one when he was arrested as a vagrant in 1817 and assigned to serve the Argentine forces as a drummer.[11] In addition, a handful of Argentine slaves with advanced musical training supplied more formal musical duties. The most famous were the sixteen slaves of Rafael Vargas of Mendoza, who were sent to Buenos Aires to learn to play and to become teachers. After three or four years they returned, comprising a complete band that performed for their owner, as well as in church and on public occasions, when they played martial marches, *pasos dobles*, and waltzes. In April 1816 Vargas donated them to the Eleventh Battalion, complete with uniforms, instruments, and music. They may have been part of San Martín's expedition to Chile, for his army in Santiago in 1817 had at least two bands. One belonging to the Eighth Regiment was composed totally of blacks from Buenos Aires who were uniformed as Turks. They played when O'Higgins was acclaimed Supreme Director of Chile in 1818; according to his accounts, when the people heard the music, "they thought they were in heaven." General Miller recalled that the band was composed of twenty-seven musicians, all except three who played by ear. His evaluation was that they played "exceedingly well."[12]

The prospect of performing in a band or in some other musical capacity may have appealed to some slaves. Far more were drawn by an element that "Negro Primero" mentioned when he explained the success of royalist recruiting in Venezuela: the offer of a uniform. Uniforms provided slaves with a sense of pride and, like bearing arms, indicated that they had moved from property to royal or citizen soldier.[13] Armies usually allotted recruits a clothing ration that could be quite generous. Troops in Buenos Aires in January 1813 were supposed to receive a wool military coat and jacket, one pair of canvas trousers and another of wool, one wool and one linen vest, two ties, two shirts, one wool barracks cap, two pairs of shoes, four pairs of socks, and a braided cap bearing the corps' badge. Cavalry recruits received the same, along with a canvas knapsack or case, a pair of strong boots, and a wooden wardrobe.[14] In most regular units an attempt was made to create an identifiable uniform, although the common elements may have been quite minimal. The uniform of the Buenos Aires army in May 1811 was described as a poncho, jacket, wool pants, and shirt.[15] It seems little different from what irregulars and guerrillas were wearing, although they, too, might have some elements in common. At the extreme end in this regard were Boves's soldiers, who were described as wearing short breeches, sandals if they had anything at all on their feet, a *llanero* sombrero hanging over their shoulders, and a human ear as a rosette.[16] Some commanders were keen that their troops make a more distinctive fashion statement and not only designed the uniform but also may have supplied it. Eduardo Holmberg, when head of the Company of Pardos of Punta Gorda, proposed that the uniform of the Tenth Battalion be a tan cap with a white badge listing the number of the corps, a tan bow tie, a blue jacket with green facings and collar and red piping, a white cape, blue woolen trousers, and black and white boots.[17] The Buenos Aires decree of December 1816 creating a corps of slaves in the capital described their uniform as a blue jacket with a scarlet collar, green piping, and gold braid.[18] Miller wrote that in the Peruvian army there was a deliberate effort, through the uniform, to convey the impression that blacks were a distinctive and honored sector of the army. Black companies of the Río de La Plata Regiment that had fought in Chile and served in Peru under Andrés de Santa Cruz, the future president of Bolivia and Peru, were dressed in scarlet caps and ponchos, from which they acquired the nickname "the *infernales*" (the damned ones). Páez's soldiers were reported to have been so enamored of their uniforms that they changed out of them before going into battle.[19]

In addition to the uniform, the promise of wages and regular meals made the military an attractive possibility for potential recruits. Monthly wages for soldiers were fairly standard throughout Spanish America. As a rule, the common soldier received six pesos, though at times it was less. The wages for the company of *pardos* of Salta in October 1813 were listed as six pesos per month for sergeants, four pesos and four reales for corporals, and three pesos and four reales for the soldiers, with the amounts in some cases being reduced for clothing and other allowances.[20] Rations were similarly small but adequate. In the case of the patriot army in Colombia, individual daily rations in December 1819 amounted to one pound of meat, four ounces of mixed vegetables, and one pound of bread, which could be substituted with plantain, corn, or yucca, while a shortage of vegetables could be made up with an increase in bread or meat. Officers up to the rank of captain received twice as much, while the general of the division received eight times the soldier's ration.[21] For an army of a few thousand, the amount of food would have been substantial. The *porteño* army besieging Montevideo required a long list of supplies, including rice, chickpeas, flour, salt, biscuits, red wine, *aguardiente* (brandy), fat, coffee, sugar, onions, pepper, jerked beef, fresh meat, water, wheat, and *yerba maté*.[22]

The privileges and perquisites associated with a military career provided further incentives to join, for slaves as well as for other sectors of the population. Soldiers in many of the line regiments and disciplined militia units continued to receive the colonial *fuero militar*, although questions were raised whether slave soldiers should be granted it. On one occasion, royalist officials in the north seemed to believe that they did. When two Colombian slaves serving against "the enemies of the king" were accused of several murders, the courts expressed their dilemma on how to deal with them. If they were soldiers, the court believed that they had to be treated like "good Spaniards" and freed from jail, which seems to have been what happened.[23] In view of the continuing slave unrest and racial threats throughout much of the region, this was probably not the type of response that many in the white community supported, but the circumstances demanded concessions if the king's rule was to be maintained. They may also have been uncomfortable with the fact that military service on both sides offered ex-slaves the possibility of social mobility via promotion through the ranks, with those reaching the higher levels even securing the honorific title of "Don," just as their counterparts in the colonial militias had done in the past. Promotion may have been a means of rewarding soldiers in a situation where money was in short supply, as Bolívar admitted at one point, but it was also a recognition of the capabilities of those who were fighting.[24] Among the many former slaves who became noncommissioned officers was the Argentine Miguel Bonifacio Otárola, who had been taken from his owner in 1813 and enrolled in the Seventh Battalion that fought in Upper Peru. Following the dissolution of the battalion, he was assigned to the Ninth Regiment, where he rose to the rank of sergeant. After five years' service, in 1819 he submitted his claim for an absolute discharge, as the law allowed. The authorities had to agree but recommended that quick action be taken to reenlist him in one of the regiments of the line, in order "not to lose a good soldier in the present circumstances."[25] Fewer slaves managed to become officers, but throughout Spanish South America a significant number did. Perhaps the most famous was Páez's loyal "Negro Primero," who became a lieutenant. Another was the Argentine Lorenzo Barcala, who eventually rose to the rank of captain. Born in Mendoza in December 1795, he was freed by assembly decree in 1813, served under San Martín in Cuyo, and later became an instructor. By 1820 he was an ensign and subsequently was promoted to captain.[26] Attaining the same rank was the already-mentioned Andrés Ibáñez, the son of an African prince who was brought to Buenos Aires when he was about sixteen and a few years later joined the Buenos Aires Eighth Battalion. He was with San Martín in Mendoza and subsequently served Miller as his servant as well as a soldier for nearly seven years, winning five medals and a promotion as a result of his bravery.[27]

Drawn by these various and sundry attractions, large numbers of slaves took matters into their own hands. Claiming to be freemen, they tried to enlist. In the Río de la Plata region, that response was evident from the first campaigns, as runaways joined the black units that were heading off for the Banda Oriental. In addition to those already mentioned was Norberto, a slave around twenty years old, valued at 260 pesos, and the property of the dean of the Cathedral of Córdoba. He joined the Second Regiment in the siege of Montevideo and was captured, but somehow he secured his release and then made his way to Buenos Aires, where in 1814 he was serving in the Eighth Battalion. In 1817 several soldiers in the newly formed Cazadores de la Unión Battalion were indicted as runaways, including Santiago Almados, who insisted that he was free; Casimira González's slave Antonio, who had deserted from another unit; and Antonio Hermenegildo, who had fled his owner seven years earlier. Miguel, a mulatto slave who had been bought in 1813 in Buenos Aires for three hundred pesos, ran away and joined the Regiment of Veterans and subsequently served in the Second Battalion of Light Infantry. The Regiment of Veterans also attracted Antonio Bello, who was serving its commander in Santa Fe in 1819 after fleeing the previous year. José Pérez from Montevideo ran away a number of times in order to serve. At the time of the second siege, he was carrying vegetables to the city when he was captured by a squadron of dragoons and compelled to serve in the cavalry under the command of Fernando Otorgués. At some point he left the unit and returned to his owner's wife, but having been advised not to serve as a slave, he rejoined the besieging army. This, too, proved to be of short duration, for he again left the army, this time for the household of the daughter of his now-deceased owner, and accompanied her to Buenos Aires, only to flee once more. In November 1819 he enlisted in the First Regiment in Luján, claiming to be a freeman named José Antonio Moreno.[28]

A factor prompting slaves to flee and enlist was the belief that those in charge would recognize their contribution and support any resulting claim for freedom. In Argentina there was plenty of evidence of such support, as over the years both court officials and military men declared that anyone who had served merited his freedom regardless of the nature of his enlistment. Typical was the comment of Colonel Miguel Estanislao Soler, who in the case of one runaway said that it would be "iniquitous" to return to slavery a soldier who had served almost three years.[29] Court officials were similarly inclined and made decisions benefiting slaves. When Manuela Tadea Pinazo protested that her slave Anselmo had been improperly recruited on the understanding that his owner was Spanish, they commented, "Although the slave that the supplicant reclaims appears to be legitimately her property, because he has passed to the worthy class of freeman by dedicating his energies to the defense of the nation, to reduce him to the painful slavery which he has left would be tyrannical and monstrous." They advised that she should be told that Anselmo had acquired the protection of the government.[30] Even in recognizing that owners enjoyed property rights in their slaves, officials sought compromises that seemed to work to the slaves' advantage. In 1814, when María Mercedes Pont reclaimed her runaway slave, Antonio Lima, after his infirmities had forced him to ask for his release from the military, she recognized that the law prohibited his return. Nevertheless, she argued that since she had not been paid, she deserved him back or his value, as she was responsible for her family. Antonio's commanding officer, Eduardo Holmberg, tried to find a compromise. He wrote, "It does not appear to me to be just that after two and one half years of faithful service, he should return to slavery. But neither should the owner lose her right to her property." His suggestion was that she should receive compensation. The court's decision was that Antonio was free and a member of the Tenth Regiment, but that his owner had a right to choose a replacement slave from the state.[31] More often, however, courts were less inclined to be conciliatory if military service could be proven. When Manuela Matos sought the return of her slave Ventura, who had been legally recruited in January 1815, on the grounds that his injuries had prevented him from completing the required period and had rendered him useless to continue in the military, the court decided that he had "acquired an irrevocable right to his freedom as a consequence of having served under the flags of the fatherland for the time stipulated." Moreover, because his condition was a result of his military service, it denied the request, describing it as "contrary to the dignity and decorum of the government [and] equally in respect to the principles, which it has proclaimed." The court noted the "precious freedom that has been bought with his blood and services," and concluded that his owner should be satisfied with the 280 pesos she had been paid.[32]

The same reasoning was apparent in a case that involved the slave owner José Ignacio Rolón, who in 1817 sought to exchange one of his slaves, Domingo Turiaga, who was serving in the Light Infantry, with another "more suited for the military." Domingo's unsuitability seemed to be linked to a lack of teeth, as the replacement was said to be without any dental problems. The proposal was rejected, as the court found "repugnant" the idea "that someone who once had been declared free should be returned to the state of slavery."[33]

Elsewhere slaves found the same sympathetic response. In New Granada royalist officers came to the defense of Manuel Barrera, a *pardo* slave from Honda who had signed up for eight years in 1816 when he was thirteen or fourteen. Three years later, when he was serving in a light infantry battalion, he was reclaimed by his owner. His commander commented rather caustically that he had served "under the flags of the king" so that "for no reason [could] he be returned to be buried in odious slavery under the dominion of some owners who by the reprehensibility of their acts merit more to be slaves than their own slaves." Stretching the truth, he also claimed that Pablo Morillo had freed all slaves on entering Bogotá.[34] Peruvian owners trying to reclaim their slaves also found themselves challenged by unsympathetic military men. In August 1821 the commander on the south coast sought advice about hacienda slaves in the area who had been freed by the Spanish government in return for military service but had deserted and joined the patriots. Their owners were now reclaiming them on the basis of an edict ordering recent runaways to return to their owners. He wrote because of what he called the "grave inconveniences" that would result from reenslaving those "men who have already enjoyed their freedom, especially when they offered to take up arms."[35]

However, not every decision worked to the benefit of the slaves. Despite the forceful words and frequent favorable decisions, slaves were not certain that military service would lead to freedom. In the Peruvian case, the government provided no clear directive, simply ordering that "all the slaves who had served in the army of the enemy and in that valley and all those who subsequently have appeared after having deserted should be sent as soon as possible to [the] capital at the disposition of the government."[36] The numerous requests by owners for the return of their property indicated that they believed they had a justifiable claim, as they asked not only for runaways but also for donated slaves who had not completed their required period of service as well as others. Antonio Pavón, the Argentine slave who had offered to pay his owner to serve, found how uncertain his status was when his military campaigns and a period of captivity broke his health and forced him to retire, having paid his owner only 130 pesos. The owner claimed that the amount was actually Antonio's wages that were his due, and he now wanted to sell him. Antonio tried to maintain his freedom by asking that his owner be forced to accept the amount as a down payment on his freedom and that the remainder be worked out in terms of a weekly deduction from his wages, but there was no clear resolution.[37] Owners were also reassured by decisions in their favor involving slaves who had served but whose recruitment had not been in accordance with the law. Francisco Agüero was a runaway from Buenos Aires who had enlisted claiming that his owner was a Spaniard when, in fact, he was American born. He was returned to his owner even though the court disagreed, describing Agüero as "a good soldier and cavalryman, filled with integrity and application."[38] In New Granada, the congress refused to recognize the freedom of those slaves whom Nariño had liberated for their military support in 1813, while in Peru owners were demanding the return of their soldier-slaves even before the fighting had ended. José de Pielago wanted his slave, whom he described as belonging to one of the army corps and identifiable by a saber wound in his side. José María Vásquez asked for four of his slaves who were in the Fourth Regiment of Chile, while Josefa Ramírez de Avellano requested the return of slaves from her hacienda who, she said, could be found in the barracks of the Río de la Plata Regiment.[39] José Álvares Calderón went further and asked Bolívar on his arrival in the country for the return of all Peruvian slaves enrolled in the army. Bolívar replied that he would see if the recruiting laws had been applied justly. Subsequently, some slaves who had been taken from their estates for San Martín's army and were found working on the fortifications of Callao were ordered returned to their owners.[40]

Fortunately for many recruits, not all owners wanted their slaves returned, preferring financial compensation instead. Antonio Sánchez was satisfied with 210 pesos for his twenty-four-year-old slave José, who was one of those who joined the *porteño* army as it headed off for Montevideo. Miguel Gorman at first wanted his slave Gregorio returned but eventually agreed to accept 270 pesos. Gregorio, a *pardo* who had been purchased in 1811 when he was seventeen or eighteen, fled in 1813 and joined the army outside Montevideo. Arrested as a deserter, his record was rather hazy, as he claimed to have worked for a shoemaker until joining the elite Regiment of Mounted Grenadiers—although his name did not appear in its list—and later in a sappers' unit. The owner of Lucas Lezica was also prepared to accept compensation, although less willingly. In this case the slave had a more certain military career than had Gregorio, having presented General José Rondeau with a captured musket during the siege of Montevideo and expressing at the time his desire to "follow a military career." He was enlisted and served in Upper Peru, and he claimed he had been wounded and captured at the battle of Sipe-Sipe but managed to avoid execution. Making his way to Buenos Aires, he joined the militia and reestablished contact with his owner, who was now living there as well. Lucas said he had visited his master on several occasions, with nothing said about his status. But when Lucas decided to join a corsair in order to make some money to support his wife and aged mother, his owner had him arrested and reclaimed him. Rondeau testified that he had not been aware that Lucas was a runaway on their first encounter, while another witness claimed that he had not been wounded but had deserted at Sipe-Sipe. His owner eventually indicated that he was willing to sell him if he was prepared to serve in the militia. Lucas was valued at 250 pesos and assigned to the light infantry in March 1817.[41] Another owner satisfied with compensation was Father Francisco Sabastiani, who donated one of his slaves but wanted two hundred pesos for a second, named Gerónimo. The latter was a mulatto trained as a barber who had fled to the Banda Oriental, signed with the Tenth Regiment claiming to be a freeman, served in a number of campaigns, was captured after one battle but managed to escape, and then joined the Eighth Regiment. Josefa Pavón asked for either the return of her slave, then enlisted in the Cazadores de la Unión, or his price, because he had run away and not been "rescued" by the government. Similarly, the College of

Monserrat in Córdoba asked for the return of a number of runaways but indicated a willingness to accept compensation instead. One of the runaways was Blas Villarroel, who had fled to Buenos Aires, enlisted in the Legión Patricia, and served for around four years. The college was prepared to accept 440 pesos for him and another runaway. José Caña put a lower price on his slave, Lorenzo, who had run away and served in the Banda Oriental. On his return to Buenos Aires, he had been arrested, prompting the slave's father to intervene on his behalf and ask for his release or a new master. The owner insisted that he should remain in jail and provide public service, claiming that he could not sell Lorenzo because he was a thief and thus a bad example for other slaves. Nevertheless, he was willing to sell him to the state for one hundred pesos.[42]

Fueling these requests for compensation were the financially ruinous effects of the wars, which left many owners desperate for cash. Teodora and Rosalia Rodríguez, of Buenos Aires, cited their poverty in asking for the return or the value of an unnamed slave who had belonged to a Spaniard, enlisted in 1815, and was sent to Mendoza. Even the prominent were suffering. General Rondeau in 1818 reported that his slave Juan had fled and now appeared under the name Juan José Romero as a soldier in the Third Company of the Battalion of Veterans. He claimed that his reduced circumstances prevented him from making a donation of his slave, but at the same time he did not want "to separate him from the occupation in which he found himself." Therefore, he asked that an evaluation be carried out so that he could ask for compensation.[43] Financial concerns also motivated Vicente Rosas of Guayaquil, who in 1821 faced the prospect of losing his slave as well as one hundred pesos because of the nature of the local manumission law. The slave, whom he had bought as a domestic servant the previous year for four hundred pesos, had fled to the Santander Battalion and now claimed to be free on the basis of this military service. The state was offering only three hundred pesos compensation, causing Rosas to demand either the return of his slave or his full value or restitution from the previous owner.[44]

These and other cases show that the situation was not entirely promising for the slave soldiers, particularly those who were runaways. But in fleeing their owners they had already taken matters into their own hands once, and now, having tasted freedom, they had no intention of giving it up easily. Determined to protect what they had gained, they resorted to a variety of strategies to remain out of the hands of their owners. One simple measure was to change their names to hide their identity and avoid detection. Names were a mutable part of their lives, as few of them, especially those brought from Africa, had any commitment to the names given them.[45] Among the many Argentine runaways who resorted to this was Noberto Funes, who in June 1814 was serving in the Second Regiment as Noberto Aguirre. Another was Antonio Sánchez's slave José, who enlisted in the Eighth Regiment as Josef Mosquiria. By the time that his owner located him and asked for his value of 210 pesos, he was a corporal in the light infantry. Gregorio Gorman adopted the rather odd surname of Ricoman, perhaps mixing Spanish and English to express his hopes, while Tiburcio, one of two slaves who fled from the College of Monserrat, changed his name completely. When the college demanded him back in 1822, an examination of the Tenth Regiment where he was supposedly serving uncovered no one named Tiburcio. However, a Saturnino Espinosa turned out to be the missing slave. He was among those who seemed to believe that a military career was a sure way of maintaining one's freedom, for, from the time of his flight eight years earlier, he had served in the Corps of Veterans, been released with an absolute discharge, reenlisted in the Legión Patricia, and from there passed to the Tenth Regiment.[46] Others also shifted from unit to unit, either to remain hidden from an owner or to build up their record in order to win greater sympathy from officials should the need arise or, for those legally enlisted, to complete their assigned period of service. They might move from a regular unit to the militia or to one of the reserve units of veterans and invalids that proliferated during these years.[47] Manuel Fernando Altolaguirre, on returning to Buenos Aires after the disastrous battle of Sipe-Sipe, asked permission to serve in the Veterans' Battalion "in the quality of *liberto*" to complete his assigned five years. That same desire may explain the request of Pedro Areco, who had been rendered "useless" from a wound suffered at Sipe-Sipe. He asked to be assigned to an urban militia unit "to be useful to the *patria*," but quite possibly to complete his assigned years.[48]

These efforts to remain in the military suggest that while service may have been harsh, to many it was still preferable to slavery. As José Ferreyra explained, he "did not wish to return to the power of his masters, for it was pleasant in the service, and he wished to continue in it." Of the Mina nation, he had been purchased in 1810 for 230 pesos but fled his owner eight years later and in 1819 was serving in the light infantry of the Regiment of Veterans in Buenos Aires, having enlisted under the name Francisco.[49] Another was Patricio Gómez, a slave serving in the Corps of Invalids who, after being jailed on the orders of his owner, asked to be permitted to continue in the military, as it was "his wish to serve in defense of the *patria*" and not return to his owner.[50] Domingo Masariego claimed that after being declared free for his service in the light infantry of the Eighth Regiment, his owners had tricked him into returning to them. He asked that they be ordered to return him to his regiment.[51]

The numerous testimonials and requests by slaves to remain in or return to service give a rather positive picture of military life and undoubtedly aroused others to follow their lead. But many aspects of military service were anything but "pleasant." Whether draftee, recruit, or volunteer, slaves quickly came to realize that fighting for the *patria* or the king left much to be desired, even if it could lead to personal freedom. Put simply, when not tedious and boring, military service could be demanding, brutal, and dangerous. For those in the disciplined units, it first involved weeks or even months of repetitive training. One positive side of this was that it provided opportunities to become settled, mix with the local population, and establish sexual liaisons. However, that idyll ended once the unit was called into action, although campaigning often proved no more stimulating than the tedium of training. The military diary of one Buenos Aires division that included a unit of *pardos* described a campaign into the Banda Oriental between September and November 1811. The send-off was promising, with flags flying and the applause of onlookers. The troops marched from the city, followed by carts carrying the baggage of the officers, munitions, stores, money, and the other necessities of a column on the march. However, a mounted rear guard assigned to frustrate desertions indicated that not every soldier was fully committed to the cause. The column set off each day around eight in the morning and marched until five in the afternoon, covering about five leagues. If no marching took place, the troops underwent further training. On Sundays they first attended church before training or marching. They were permitted to enter local towns to buy provisions under the watchful eyes of their noncommissioned officers. Nonetheless, disorders occurred, usually because the soldiers found their way to the town's taverns. Back on the march, they had to deal with frequent rain and occasional storms, and on this particular campaign these and swollen rivers seem to have been the only dangers encountered. During the two months not a shot was fired in anger, and the enemy was never seen.[52] In fact, campaigning both here and elsewhere seemed to involve more marching than fighting. Daily excitement might come from capturing horses, cattle, mules, and weapons. There would be occasional skirmishes that could result in casualties, but battles were the exception. Yet, campaigning could prove horribly demanding, as the column might advance for days without eating or sleeping, over dreadful roads that quickly destroyed their boots and left them exhausted.[53] General Miller, reporting on San Martín's crossing of the Andes, noted that the troops had to bivouac in the open at temperatures below freezing because they lacked tents. The altitude resulted in *soroche*, mountain sickness "so great that on the march a whole battalion would drop down as if stricken by the wand of a magician."[54] When Bolívar's army crossed the Colombian Andes it faced the same extremes, which explains his desire for soldiers from specific regions, as well as his continuing demands for new recruits.[55]

The realities of campaigning also revealed that most of the immediate attractions of military life were often illusory or short lived. The sought-after uniforms soon wore out, so that many soldiers appeared more like Boves's irregulars than identifiable units. A member of Bolívar's foreign legion described his fellows in Venezuela as "young negroes and mulattoes, most of them mere boys, seemingly not more than thirteen or fourteen years of age, tottering under the weight of their muskets and wearing nothing more than a piece of linen around the loins. Some might wear old military jackets, but would be without pantaloons. Some would be bareheaded, while others might wear straw hats or hairy caps."[56] San Martín, despite his documented concern for his soldiers, was frequently unable to meet their basic needs. In March 1819 he received news that his black recruits were without coats, and that most did not have "even a cloak."[57] Footwear was similarly in short supply. Sucre's troops in June 1823 were described as "for the most part without shoes, and all without stockings. Many had only a piece of cow-hide under their feet, and not a few were even barefooted."[58] The conditions of the royalist troops were no better. Some of the soldiers brought from Spain to Venezuela in 1815 were in the same uniforms three years later and now without footwear.[59] And both sides found that success on the battlefield did not necessarily improve their situation. Sucre wrote to Bolívar in January 1824 that he would like six thousand or eight thousand shirts because they were what the corps most needed and were most difficult to provide. After the battle of Ayacucho he reported that the army was short of all clothing, including trousers, shirts, jackets, and cloaks, and that the officers were "naked."[60]

As a result, soldiers had to make do with whatever they could acquire, including clothing that was stolen, taken from the dead, or bought from fellow soldiers.[61] Their weapons wore out along with the uniforms. In 1813 one Argentine commander, in offering troops to Manuel Belgrano for his invasion of Upper Peru, complained of the lack of arms and mules, as well as workers who could manufacture and maintain the army's weapons, artillery, and cannon supports. O'Higgins wrote to San Martín on numerous occasions pointing to the inadequate arms, uniforms, supplies, money, and food, while one of the obstacles Sucre faced in Peru in 1823 was an insufficient number of muskets and the poor state of those he did have.[62]

At the heart of these shortages was a scarcity of money, as the desperate financial situation of the new countries and the parsimony of the crown meant that funds for the military, along with everything else, were in short supply on both sides.[63] In September 1823 the Ecuadorian government was described as "without the least hope of having funds." The treasury was in deficit and unable to pay the wages of officers and soldiers, the pensions of widows, and other financial obligations. A commentator noted, "Day by day the government is tormented with truly just requests; but it cannot satisfy so many demands because the sources of receipts fall short in a very regrettable way."[64] San Martín's failings in Peru were largely tied to his inability to obtain adequate funding, forcing soldiers in Lima in early 1822 to sell or pawn their uniforms because they were so rarely paid.[65] When Bolívar arrived in northern Peru in March 1824, one of his first tasks was to find money for his troops and the navy, as the latter had not been paid in seventeen months. He raised fifty thousand pesos and obtained new clothing for the army but had to reduce their pay by three-quarters. After the battle of Junín, a report on Bolívar's army of about eight thousand men stated that they "appeared in excellent spirits, were tolerably well clothed, and in very good discipline," but as for their pay, while they were "regularly paid, the last day of each month," both officers and men received only one-quarter what they were owed.[66] Adding to the general economic woes were extraordinary events that also hindered the paying of wages. Among the losses at the battle of Sipe-Sipe were the patriots' records that included the official lists of the names of soldiers, so that no one knew who should be paid and how much they were owed.[67] As a result, the wages that had lured some recruits proved as ephemeral as the uniforms, explaining in part the success of the armies of Boves and Páez, who offered booty as an alternative.

The shortage of funds also translated into a scarcity of food. Rations were often inadequate and when available tended to be monotonous. In June 1818 the situation in Venezuela was so bad that Murillo ordered his troops to cultivate foodstuffs on royalist and unoccupied lands.[68] The patriot forces suffered as well. Tomás de Heres wrote to Bolívar in November 1823 that the Várgas Battalion was "materially dying of hunger." Rations were "short, of bad quality, and incomplete." In addition there was no pay for anyone. "In sum," he lamented, "there is nothing, nothing."[69]

Deprived of the necessities of life, soldiers did what they could to survive. In some cases they turned to crime, which could introduce them to another harsh reality of the service: military justice. Normally, those found guilty for a variety of offenses were flogged through the ranks, which might involve fifty to one hundred blows. In Buenos Aires in 1815, repeat offenders who were also found guilty of theft were flogged two hundred times through the streets and sentenced to ten years of public works, in chains, on the frontier, with the threat of execution if they fled.[70] Punishment by imprisonment, confinement in irons, or extra years of service was common, while execution seems to have been reserved for severe crimes, such as murder and mutiny.

In these circumstances of demanding service, harsh military discipline, constant shortages, and campaigning in unfamiliar environments, other constants in the soldiers' lives were disease and infections. Yellow fever, malaria, typhoid, typhus, measles, and parasites all afflicted the armies. Food poisoning was common, as infected fish, badly cured meat, and improperly prepared vegetables could be part of their diet. Spanish troops seem to have been particularly susceptible in this regard and suffered a high mortality rate because of poor diet and inadequate hospital care.[71] But they were not alone. Bolívar, writing to Santander in June 1820, noted that one of his columns "left with 1,100 men and arrived with 900, of whom only 500 [were] fit for service." He added, "Seventy are near death and the others are in serious condition.... Would you believe that the troop which [Rafael] Urdaneta brought was selected from among the strongest and healthiest, and yet not one recruit reached us in good condition? Would you believe that of 6,000 men whom we sent to the lower Apure [River], scarcely a thousand-odd are left, and that the thousand or more brought by Urdaneta once numbered 6,000 men including their officers?"[72]

For those who survived and remained in the ranks, ultimately there was the fighting, the reason for their recruitment in the first place. With it came the inevitable casualties. Set-piece battles may not have occurred frequently, but there were numerous skirmishes and other types of confrontations. For those killed, burial in a common grave seems to have been almost a luxury, for often the bodies of those who died in battle were burned or left to decompose where they fell. Late in 1817, after the battle of Chacabuco, Samuel Haigh noted "the human bones lying whitening in the wind and sun." The dead from the battle of Maipú were no better attended. The same author recorded that the bodies of the dead were stripped and left naked on the field, fodder for local wildlife.[73] Those who were wounded but survived may have wondered if they were luckier than those who had been killed outright. Many eventually succumbed to their wounds, but thousands of others managed to survive, although with debilitating and crippling injuries. Slaves assigned to noncombat roles were not spared. The previously mentioned Mariano Antonio Rodalleja, who was taken from his New Granada mine work by the royalist army, was crippled as a result of carrying cannons on his shoulders.[74] Those involved in combat suffered shrapnel, bullet, lance, and sword wounds to various parts of the body. They lost fingers, arms, legs, and eyes. Different types of wounds left them coughing blood. An Argentine soldier serving in the Company of Castes was hit in the mouth by two musket balls that severed most of his tongue and entirely destroyed his upper and lower mandibles before exiting from behind his ear. The result was a constantly inflamed mouth and pus-filled cavities that permitted him only to consume liquids, as chewing even soft foods was no longer possible. He was given permission to retire to the Corps of Invalids, as he was considered unfit for service, yet he claimed that he "could serve within this capital [Buenos Aires] in the cavalry in case of enemy invasion."[75] His willingness to continue might be seen as a testament to a patriotism that had developed with the call for self-rule. Alternatively, it may have been a means of obtaining some form of support, since many—perhaps most—of those who were crippled by their wounds were given little or no compensation. Manuel Sánchez, a *liberto* in the Buenos Aires Eighth Grenadiers, in 1817 was removed by his family after a long stay in the military hospital, even though he had not recovered. Two months later he had received nothing to meet his basic necessities, resulting in a request to be transferred to the Battalion of Invalids, where he might at least be fed.[76] Troops serving the king suffered similarly. Soldiers from Coro who had fought under Monteverde and helped defeat Bolívar in April 1814 were released and given nothing, prompting a critic to write that these men who were "so worthy of the national gratitude, are found in Caracas naked and obliged to work as peons in the factories to earn their food."[77]

Soldiers in the field requiring medical care found that services and medicines were limited, if they were available at all. The medical officer of the Army of Peru wrote to Belgrano in November 1812 that he was virtually alone because of a lack of surgeons. The demands on him rose after battles when hospitals had to be set up, but the hospitals were short of staff, lacking a single person for bloodletting. He wrote, "Only the enthusiasm to serve and give relief to the heroes who have sacrificed themselves for sacred liberty can make it bearable."[78] When San Martín's army crossed the Andes he had barely any medical staff, so that "nature" was "the only physician and thought to be, perhaps, the best," an evaluation that was probably true.[79] Morillo wrote to Venezuela's captain general in May 1817 that in Cumaná there was a lack of everything, including medicines. As a result, 250 members of the royalist expedition were in hospital.[80] Medicines such as smallpox vaccine were theoretically available, but frequently they were also the casualty of campaigns. Sucre wrote to Bolívar in February 1824, "Please God that they send us medicines. Our hospitals are short of absolutely everything, and it is a great shame because the hospitals are much reduced." After the battle of Ayacucho he made the same plea and warned that many of the wounded, who numbered more than one thousand, would die unless medicines were provided.[81]

For soldiers unlucky enough to be captured by the enemy, the future was equally uncertain. While the two sides on occasion exchanged prisoners, especially after the Spanish-initiated truce of 1820, officers seem to have been the only ones who benefited.[82] More frequently—although no statistics exist—prisoners were given the opportunity to change sides. In particular, captured American-born royalist soldiers, including slaves, were often conscripted by the patriots into their ranks.[83] Otherwise, they might be released or held as prisoners of war. Among the latter were royalist prisoners, who after the battle of Chacabuco were sent to work as waged peons in Mendoza to replace the slaves recruited from the area.[84] However, execution was far more likely, especially for patriot soldiers who were rebels by definition. Spanish regulations may have presented a fairly short list of those who could be executed, including deserters from the royalist army who fought for the enemy, but the rules were regularly ignored.[85] In Venezuela, at least before 1820, soldiers captured by the royalists and by some patriot leaders were almost invariably executed. In such cases most were shot, but they might be hanged, beheaded, or stabbed with a sword, lance, or knife. When two black soldiers serving under San Martín in southern Peru wandered away from the battalion after disembarking, possibly with the aim of looting, "they were surprised [by royalist troops] and conducted to Tacna where they were shot and their ears cut off and carried away in triumph."[86]

Ex-slaves who were captured by the royalists faced what no other group had to fear, the possibility of reenslavement. Three soldiers of the Sixth Regiment, who were captured in January 1813 while besieging Montevideo, were reported to have been returned to the "hard slavery from which they had fled."[87] In the north, slaves conscripted by the patriots might be sent to Cuba or Panama if they fell into royalist hands, while black soldiers captured at Sipe-Sipe and other battles in Upper Peru were sold by order of the Spanish general to plantations on the southern coast of Peru, giving some credence to the assertion made by San Martín to his black soldiers before his invasion of Chile. In 1821 Miller released about thirty ex-slave prisoners in the Tacna area, all who could be found. They included two who had been promoted to noncommissioned officers because of their good conduct and bravery but who were now so broken by years of renewed enslavement that they were no longer employable.[88]

The attractions of military life, thus, soon lost their allure, and slave recruits, along with others, began to have second thoughts about their decision. A few, given a choice between military service or slavery, opted for the latter. One was Pedro Pérez Blanco, who together with another African-born slave had been brought to Buenos Aires from Rio de Janeiro on the slave ship *Dolores* in 1806 and purchased for 250 pesos. In July 1815 Pedro, along with five other slaves, was taken from his owner, Juana Inéz Pérez, and her Spanish husband and enlisted. Juana protested, claiming that she was not a Spaniard and therefore not subject to expropriations of this sort, and she asked for four of them back. Since they had not been registered as Juana's property, she had to prove to the court that she operated separately from her husband, which she did, and Pedro was ordered returned to her custody. However, his commander, Manuel Dorrego, objected, pointing out "the difficulty of returning to the state of slavery an individual who had been declared free in accordance with a law that says that freedom once ceded can never be taken away." He recommended that she be compensated instead. Pedro's situation, as with many other recruits, was complicated by his domestic situation. He was married and had children who lived with Juana, and she was not prepared to sell them regardless of what was offered. She suggested that he be given the choice of returning or staying in the army, and after repeatedly being asked what he wanted, he selected servitude.[89] Family and security in this case overrode the desire for freedom. A Venezuelan slave named Tomás was similarly inclined. He claimed to have run away in 1816 and then been arrested by the Spaniards as a freeman and drafted. He was subsequently taken prisoner by the patriots, who assigned him to the Battalion of Bravos of Orinoco. In 1821 he appeared before his master, saying that he no longer wanted to serve in the army but instead to return to slavery. His owner was willing but concerned that without the necessary release, "he must be considered a deserter not a slave."[90] When slaves in the Peruvian town of Sayán in 1821 were offered the opportunity to become free by joining the patriot forces, "'they replied that they could not forsake their owners.'"[91]

The declining lure of the military was evident in other ways too. Some Argentine slaves, for example, failed to appear after being recruited. An August 1819 decree in response to the rumored approach of a Spanish expeditionary force ordered slaves over the age of ten to undergo militia training and included a penalty of ten years of military service for those who tried to avoid it. The penalty, however, proved inadequate, for further punishments were introduced in the following February for slaves who failed to participate in the daily exercises and owners who failed to send them.[92] The prospect of having to fight may explain their response, although the fact that by 1819 militia service was no longer a guaranteed route to freedom in Buenos Aires was probably a factor as well.

With the negative aspects of military service increasingly apparent but the desire to be free still incredibly strong, slaves were faced with a conundrum. How could they establish a link to the military and thereby make a claim for their personal freedom, yet avoid serving, which might cost them some horrible injury or worse? Their solution was in keeping with how they dealt with other circumstances that negatively affected them: they tried to manipulate the system to secure some sort of benefit. To take advantage of the tie between military service and personal freedom they cited any type of military service or even military connection as justification for claiming their freedom. In 1813, Domingo Ordoy, an African-born slave who had lived in Montevideo and was now resident in Peru, claimed that he had fought the English at Buenos Aires and asked for his freedom, pointing out that "the other masters of said city freed their slaves so that they could defend the *patria*."[93] The authorities checked with Montevideo and found the claim to be false. Other slaves' links were equally ephemeral, but they laid out these tenuous claims nonetheless. José María Delgado, a slave from Buenos Aires, was taken in the first *rescate* lottery and assigned to the Eighth Regiment. Found medically unfit, he was supposed to be returned to his owner but instead was permitted to live off his own work. Under these circumstances, he was assigned to the militia and almost immediately requested his freedom.[94] Another strategy was to ask for discharge papers after having completed only a portion of the required period of service. The papers were essential, for they were proof of the ex-slave's service and thus a prerequisite to a claim for freedom. Manuel Sado, a soldier from Guayaquil, had served only slightly more than a year out of the two that slaves were supposed to serve when he asked for his papers.[95] A third ploy was to cite illness or some sort of injury to avoid service. Teodoro, a slave of the late Bishop Benito de Lue of Buenos Aires, tried this when he was offered his freedom if he served four years as a soldier. "I would go with pleasure to complete it," he replied, but then added that "it would be a crime to hide my ineptitude." He explained that a fall from his owner's coach had left him in the "shadow of death" for a very long time. He still suffered so that he was unable to throw a stone any distance and at times suffered rheumatism in the same arm. His proposed compromise was to serve as a coach driver, although not in the army.[96] Slaves already in the military likewise cited illness or injury in hopes that this would permit them to leave the army before completing the assigned period. The government of Gran Colombia in 1822 allowed ex-slaves to obtain their absolute discharges in such circumstances, and everywhere slaves made the claim. Another slave of Bishop de Lue, this one sharing his owner's name, was offered his freedom on condition that he serve in the army in the Banda Oriental. Despite the fact that he suffered from a chronic illness, he joined the invading force but because of his infirmities was abandoned on the march. Returning to Buenos Aires, he asked for his unconditional freedom, since he believed that further army service was impossible. Similarly, Manuel Ansuátegui, a native of the Congo nation who served in the Eighth Regiment of the Army of the Andes, claimed that he had been found useless for service in 1819 and asked for his release and the accompanying licence.[97] So, too, did Antonio Sinen, another slave from the Congo nation, who served for six years in the Banda Oriental and after the fall of Montevideo cited a hernia as the reason for his medical incapacity. However, doctors insisted that he was not as unfit as he claimed.[98]

Fabricating an ailment could backfire on the slave, for it could lead to punishment in the form of an additional period of service if discovered. It might also be used by an owner to ask for the return of the slave. When Matías Villoldo, of the Fourth Battalion of the Argentine Brigade, claimed in 1817 to have some sort of chest ailment that had been aggravated such that he could not continue to serve, his owner asked that he be released into her care.[99] Nevertheless, slaves continued to try, citing years of service, advanced age, and concerns for family in their requests. They also often asked for some type of financial assistance that reinforced their claim of decrepitude and might provide vital support if, indeed, they were incapacitated.[100]

When avoiding military service or securing one's early release was not possible or likely, soldiers could still take matters into their own hands and resort to another common option: they could desert. Since many had fled to join the army, fleeing from the army was probably not a difficult decision. Indeed, it may have been easier, for desertion was a fact of life in every military unit during the independence wars, regardless of time, place, race, or conditions. It was a close relative of switching allegiance, which was almost an accepted state of affairs during the independence period that involved not just foot soldiers but even officers and prominent civilian leaders.[101] In response to the shifting fortunes of war, a few made more than one change, with individuals swearing fealty to the king one day and the *patria* the next. Uncertainty also resulted from the changing orientations of the respective governments. Among the patriots there were the divisions between centralists and federalists, while on the Spanish side confusion followed the shifts from absolutism to constitutional monarchy and back again. Thus, what was seen as desertion might have been in some circumstances a desire to follow a consistent political line or a particular leader.[102] Nonetheless, while this confusion may have been a factor in a few desertions, for the ex-slaves it was more likely the abysmal conditions and unwillingness to serve far from home that motivated them.[103]

Desertion plagued all commanders. Even San Martín, despite his close ties to his troops, was not spared. In July 1815 he complained from Mendoza that fewer recruits were arriving than expected. He gave one example of a time when eighty-nine had arrived, out of whom fifty-nine had scaled the walls of the barracks and disappeared. Another complaint in January 1817 produced a request for firm and efficacious measures to capture the deserters.[104] In the north, Bolívar frequently complained of the problem. After his defeat at Ocumare, roughly five hundred men deserted: "all the coastal inhabitants we had recruited," he wrote. In July 1817 he noted, "The rate of desertion is frightful: within two weeks, one hundred Indians in the Batallón de Honor alone have deserted, and the other battalions have lost in proportion."[105] Even an improving military situation failed to stem the flow. In January 1820 his Army of the East had lost five hundred men by desertion, and in January 1824 he reported from Peru, "No sooner are they left to sleep in the open or taken on long marches than they desert to a man."[106]

The royalist commanders had no greater success in holding onto their troops, despite the presence of Spanish veterans. In Venezuela, once Morillo began to suffer reverses whole battalions deserted, including officers; by December 1820, the figure amounted to 1,800 per month.[107] With the royalist ranks being filled with American-born replacements, the likelihood only increased, as the desertion in Peru in 1820 of the entire royalist Numancia Battalion composed of Colombians and Venezuelans revealed.[108] Peru seemed to become a haven for deserters; large numbers from both armies in 1822 collected around Lima, where they engaged in criminal activity, disturbed the peace, and threatened travelers. Some were veterans from the Río de la Plata and Chile regiments, while others were more recent recruits from the Peruvian Legion. Still others had not even been assigned to units. In March 1822 one general complained to the Minister of War and the Navy that of over two hundred recruits, eighty-nine had deserted on the Huaura road because of the "miserable escort" of only a corporal and five men.[109]

The desertion of ex-slaves was, thus, part of a general phenomenon, and there is no indication that they were more or less prone to desertion than any other group. What was different was that their action might be seen as a continuation of an earlier process of running away to enlist, further underlining their desire to have complete control over their lives. Like others, some deserted even before serving, taking advantage of the fact that they were no longer under the watchful eye of their owner. José Exporta Díaz and Gordiano Díaz, slaves of José Díaz of Córdoba, were being evaluated for military service in August 1814 and were both declared unfit, but they ran away anyway, probably to avoid being returned to their owner. A report in June 1815 on the Tenth Battalion of Buenos Aires, which included many slaves, asserted that a lack of vigilance was responsible for the desertions, especially from the hospital but also from the barracks.[110] This may have been true in Chile too, where Miguel Honorario in December 1818 encountered his slave, whom he had donated to the army in February 1817, begging in the streets. Honorario suspected that he had not been guarded properly, and his discovery led to orders that his former property be apprehended.[111]

Some desertions may have been politically motivated, or at least this was the excuse given. Domingo Valera claimed that he had deserted after being donated by his owner to serve in the Peruvian royalist army of Rodil. After deserting he had been recaptured by the royalists and forced to serve with Canterac in the sierra.[112] Also in Peru, slave deserters were among those joining the bands of highwaymen around Lima. They were accused of planning to set up *palenques*, runaway communities that proliferated along the coast and served as bases for assaults on estates.[113]

To prevent desertion, commanders tried various ploys. In Mendoza, San Martín gave instructions that soldiers, including his slave recruits, be kept busy with different carpentry activities, which he believed might also combat the rigors of winter and thereby reduce illness. More often they offered bounties. In 1815 in Buenos Aires the amount was four pesos a head. A more substantial twelve pesos was offered for discovering a plan to desert, with incarceration for those found guilty. Punishments for apprehended deserters varied enormously. They could be relatively mild, as in the case of Buenos Aires, where deserters were usually sentenced to extra service, although the term could be as much as a draconian ten years. One black soldier, Manuel Antonio Mature, was sentenced to four more years for deserting the Sixth Regiment. He had already served four years before deserting, but remained in the military, working as a cook in Artigas's army for a time and then joining the Buenos Aires Second Regiment, when he was arrested. Deserters could also face corporal punishment: in 1810 those from a *pardo* unit from Córdoba received fifty lashes, plus four years of public works.[114] And capital punishment was not uncommon. General José Lara wrote to the Colombian government in December 1822 that in order to stop desertions, they "should shoot at least forty deserters for every one hundred who ha[d] been apprehended."[115] According to a British report, captured deserters taken by the patriots in Peru were shot. However, death sentences were often commuted, possibly because of the uncertainties surrounding the offense. In Ecuador, when two patriot soldiers were found guilty of desertion, one was shot because the penal laws concerning desertion had been read to him, while the other had not and so was sentenced to be flogged three hundred times. In Uruguay six deserters from a *pardo* regiment were let off, even though officers recommended that they be shot. In Argentina death for desertion came to be commuted to six years' imprisonment, while in royalist Peru, the crown's desperate need for soldiers resulted in a royal pardon for deserters on at least one occasion, under the condition that first-time offenders would have to serve six years more, second-time offenders seven, and third-time offenders eight, with no further punishment.[116] For ex-slaves, desertion released the state from its obligations to them and could result in their being returned to their owners. But owners may not have been interested. Hipólito Ochorroso of Buenos Aires sold his slave Antonio, a deserter from the Tenth Regiment, to the state, apparently preferring the money over the slave.[117]

Despite the penalties, slave soldiers continued to desert, as well as to engage in other activities to protect their well-being. They were learning that risking their lives and even suffering injuries were not enough to satisfy some owners, who were far more interested in resuming control of their property than in recognizing their slaves' contribution to the liberation of their homelands. This is evident in the case of Francisco Silva, a *pardo* slave who fled his owner in 1812 and joined the Buenos Aires Regiment of Mounted Grenadiers. He was wounded in battle and, upon his recovery, served without pay in the militia of San Nicolás. Then for nine months he trained twenty-five men, before spending six months in Buenos Aires with the Second Regiment. He subsequently volunteered when he heard of the formation of a squadron to attack Montevideo, and he served on board the schooner *Fortuna* until the end of the siege. Transferred to another ship, the *Trinidad*, he was involved in an attack on Arroyo de la China, where he was wounded again, crippling his right arm. Yet he continued to serve, now on board another vessel. When he eventually decided that he could no longer continue because of his disability, his evaluation of his record—that "he had made voluntary sacrifices for the fatherland"—was a gross understatement. Nevertheless, despite his sacrifices, he was arrested by the police at the request of his owner, taken to jail, and whipped fifty times over two days, causing him additional suffering. Protesting his treatment, he told the court that he was being held in prison until a new owner could be found, but this was unlikely because of his injuries. He asked for help, ideally freedom, for his "one thousand sacrifices."[118]

Similarly treated was José Candido Valenzuela, whose owner had permitted him to enlist. He claimed to have served more than six years in the Argentine Army of Peru, suffering "the calamities of that painful campaign and several actions against the enemy." He had been wounded and as a result was crippled in one arm, permitting him to get his absolute discharge. However, his former owner had seen him working and had him arrested, with the aim of selling him out of the province. In July 1822 he had been in jail for seven months when he asked for his freedom and clarification of his status. But his request remained in doubt, as his commander did not remember him and was unwilling to testify on his behalf.[119] A third slave who suffered arrest at the hands of his old owner was Benito Jiménez, who fled Montevideo to the "flags of the *patria*" at the time of the second siege, fighting in the Tenth Regiment and suffering a musket ball wound. After Montevideo's fall he crossed to Buenos Aires and then returned to the Banda Oriental, where he encountered his owner, who lured him back to his house and then tried to sell him. Benito had resisted, leading to his arrest and then assignment to a bakery and what was described as his new master. He asked the authorities to declare that neither his sale nor his nakedness was justified.[120]

Slaves who had been drafted improperly or illegally added their voices to those appealing for their freedom. Manuel, the Argentine slave of Bautista Garmendia, was taken, along with his owner and his owner's possessions, from the island of Martín García in 1814 by a corsair under the command of Ángel Hubac, despite a prohibition against this type of enslavement. For four years Manuel had been compelled to serve Hubac, oiling cordage. In 1820, now ill and belonging to Hubac's widow, he asked for his freedom.[121]

The personal struggles for freedom, therefore, continued. During the wars, Spanish America's slaves had demonstrated a broad, and on some occasions imaginative, range of resistance strategies. In the process they had challenged the systems of slavery that existed in their respective areas regardless of whether they fought for the crown or the *patria*. This did not mean that slavery was about to disappear. The responses of the owners of Francisco Silva, José Candido Valenzuela, Benito Jiménez, and many others indicated that there was strong opposition to the slaves' demands and a determination to regain control of lost property. Nevertheless, slaves everywhere had demonstrated their willingness to act and to take their struggle into the open. They had clearly shown that if they had ever been a docile sector of the population, this was not the case at the end of the wars of independence. Recruiting had unleashed a veritable wave of slave activism. As a result, slavery may still have been in existence, but it was not the institution that it had been when warfare had erupted.

CHAPTER 7

THE PERSONAL WAR OF
SLAVE WOMEN

 WHEN THE BUENOS AIRES ARMY invaded the Banda Oriental in 1811, one of the slaves whose life was changed forever was a woman by the name of Juliana García. As recounted earlier, she was living at the time with her husband, Miguel, and their two children, Ventura and Mateo, in a town near Montevideo when they heard that the invaders were offering freedom to any slave who joined their ranks. Miguel, like many others, found the offer irresistible and ran away to enlist. Shortly afterwards, Juliana and the children followed him. For the next four years she was part of the Buenos Aires army as it campaigned through the two sieges of Montevideo, invasions of Upper Peru, and the patriot defeat at the battle of Sipe-Sipe in November 1815. In the aftermath of that disaster she managed to make her way, with her children, to Buenos Aires, where she reunited with her husband. Then, on the basis of her experiences, she demanded freedom for herself and for her children.[1]

Juliana's experiences were unique, yet elements of what she went through were familiar to other slave women in Spanish South America during these years. The breakdown of colonial rule, the long years of warfare, and the various offers to the area's slave population affected not just men but also women, and they, like the men, used the changing circumstances to seek improvements in their lives. In some ways the women's responses were the more impressive, for they had to struggle against the triple obstacles of legal status, color, and gender. They also could not assert themselves through military service as men could, although their actions were often mediated through their association with the soldiers. And without some sort of military contribution they seemed to have no legal claim for freedom. Nevertheless, many of them, like Juliana, demanded it, citing a wide range of war-related experiences.

The women's responses were two pronged. Like male slaves, their ultimate goal was personal freedom, but also motivating them was a desire to meet the needs of their families. Their actions indicated a determination to maintain the family unit intact, thereby challenging both the divisiveness that was an inherent part of slavery and the disruptions caused by the independence struggles. During the war years, thus, female slaves became increasingly assertive. They voiced their demands loudly, frequently, and openly. With the successes of the patriots, they recognized the changing balance of power, adopted the language of the time, and appealed to those who promised a brighter future. Not every female slave raised her voice, and those who did were not always successful in achieving their aims. Nonetheless, they made their presence known and in the process added to the pressures that were undermining slavery throughout the continent.

When slave women became involved in the struggles, to some extent they were following a pattern established by elite women committed to the independence cause. Those supporting the royalists probably engaged in similar activities, but existing studies tend to focus on patriot women, particularly those of Venezuela and Colombia, who participated extensively both before and during the wars. Despite concerns raised by republican leaders about female mobilization and its challenge to the traditional patriarchy, women demonstrated their commitment by hosting political gatherings, by supplying money and materiel, and by serving as nurses, spies, and occasionally even soldiers, being accused of using their "feminine wiles" as a military weapon in the process. The royalist general Joaquín de la Pezuela at one point claimed that the Argentine commander Manuel Belgrano was employing women not only to spy but also to seduce royalist officers and troops into deserting. If caught, however, women could not use their gender to avoid punishment, for many lost their property, were forced into exile, and suffered other penalties, including execution.[2]

The contribution of lower-class women, particularly the nonwhite *castas* who constituted the majority of the region's female population, is less well known, yet the existing accounts reveal that they also were a knowledgeable and assertive sector of the population who engaged in some of the same activities. For example, a "seductive" mulatto woman, Carmen Guzmán, was reputed to have played a central role in the desertion of the royalist Numancia Battalion in Peru.[3] Slave women, too, became involved from an early date and contributed in various ways throughout the duration of the wars. They participated as spies, nurses, camp followers, cooks and servants for officers, and even occasionally as soldiers, suffering many privations as a result. In addition, they interceded in other less dramatic but equally assertive ways, such as requesting the wages that their soldier relatives may have assigned to them, asking for charity and other benefits both for themselves and their husbands and sons, and demanding the soldiers' discharge papers that in the case of ex-slaves confirmed their service and consequently their right to freedom. And a small but significant number of slave women took their demands further, citing their involvement and the ideas of the time as justification for demanding their own freedom. These requests, when successful, added to the numbers of slaves being released from bondage.

At the time of the independence wars, female slaves were an important part of Spanish America's slave population. Although during the years of the African slave trade they had constituted approximately one-third of those imported, their numbers had grown with the result that they came to comprise a significant proportion of the New World's slave community. Where natural reproduction had occurred, their numbers equalled and even surpassed those of male creole slaves.[4] In some cities, such as Buenos Aires in the late eighteenth century, that numerical superiority also reflected the migration of male slaves to jobs in the rural sector.[5] As their numbers grew, female slaves came to occupy a variety of roles in the colonies' rural and urban life. They served their owners as domestic servants or made money for them as laundresses, cooks, nursemaids, seamstresses, and street vendors. Some worked in the countryside, again primarily as domestics, but also as laborers on plantations, farms, and vineyards. In common with their male counterparts, they enjoyed certain rights: they could be baptized and receive Catholic indoctrination, marry, live outside the owner's home, collect money in order to purchase their own freedom or that of family members, possess property, make a will, and defend themselves judicially with the assistance of a court-appointed official.[6] As pointed out in Chapter 1, they had a greater chance than males of securing their freedom, at least in Buenos Aires, where studies have shown that women, the elderly, and those who were mulattoes were more likely to be freed by their owners or purchase their own freedom. But the number of freedwomen was still very small. For those who remained in bondage, their rights were often ignored, as they remained property and were treated as such, being sold or punished and suffering the same mistreatment and indignities as male slaves. And more than males, female slaves faced the possibility of sexual abuse at the hands of either their owner or someone else.[7]

With the crisis of 1808 and the resulting political divisions in the colonies, female slaves, like other sectors of the population, found their lives undergoing significant changes. In Buenos Aires, after the May Revolution in 1810 and the creole assumption of power, large numbers of slaveholders who opposed the new regime fled the country, leaving their slaves at the mercy of the new authorities. When Juana Mesagas's owner crossed to royalist Montevideo, she and her two children became the property of the Buenos Aires government, which proceeded to sell them for 350 pesos. Their situation had obviously not improved, except that Juana now knew exactly how much she needed to save to purchase her own freedom and that of her children. According to law, the amount could not be increased, but it was still probably far beyond her means.[8] The outbreak of warfare had even greater repercussions. As the example of Juliana García indicates, when the *porteño* army invaded the Banda Oriental in 1811 and offered freedom to slaves from the city who volunteered their services, the offer struck a chord not only with male slaves but also with women. Several hundred fled their owners to join the invaders and later stayed with the Argentine forces when they withdrew to Buenos Aires. With the second invasion late in 1812 and the renewed offer of freedom, female runaways again appeared among those who flocked to the patriot banners.[9]

The spread of warfare and the extensive recruiting of male slaves drew slave women into the developments in a variety of other ways. Unlike men, there was no expectation that women, regardless of their legal status or race, would fight, since the battlefield was considered a male preserve. Nevertheless, a few seem to have taken up arms. Upper-class women fought in the north, as did some lower-class women. In May 1819, Simón Bolívar's army was reported to have been accompanied by many *"juanas"* serving as nurses and camp followers. According to a commentator, "They were as brave as the men, and when necessary, they even bore arms."[10] How often is not clear, nor is there any indication that any of them was a slave. One of the few references to a female slave who tried to participate as a soldier involved service not with the regular forces but with the patriot guerrillas in Peru. In November 1820, a slave named Josefa Tenorio asked José de San Martín for her freedom—"which is the only thing that I crave," she said—on the basis of her military service. She asserted, "Having heard the rumor that the enemy was trying to reenslave the *patria* once again, I dressed myself as a man and ran at once to the barracks to receive my orders and take up my musket. General [Juan Gregorio de] Las Heras entrusted me with a flag to carry and to defend with honor.... Assigned to the forces of the commander general of guerrillas, Toribio Dávalos, I suffered all the rigors of the campaign. My gender has not impeded me from being useful to my *patria*."[11] Her cross-dressing underlined the fact that fighting was considered a masculine occupation and followed a common pattern in Latin America.[12] However, it failed to convince Las Heras in this case, and his presentation of a flag may have been designed to prevent Josefa from participating in actual combat.

While engaging in armed combat was not common for female slaves, they did perform other activities with a military aspect that provided possible routes to freedom. One such activity was espionage, a role that some have argued was ideal for women because their gender made them less open to suspicion than men.[13] This seemed to be equally true of slaves. An Argentine patriot officer, in a letter to his commanding general in October 1812, reported that he had a man and a woman in Salta whose slave status meant that they could enter and leave the area with ease. He had received the most precise details from them and had offered them their freedom for their services.[14]

A less dangerous way to try to win one's freedom was to denounce enemy activity, an especially appealing action if the person involved happened to be one's owner. Juana de la Patria, a widow living in the Bolivian mining center of Potosí, was ordered to be freed in 1813 by Belgrano for revealing a local band of royalist conspirators who were relaying news of patriot troop movements. Among the conspirators was Juana's mistress, whom she described as "a passionate follower of the present system." She had been writing to her lover, who was an officer in the royalist army, according to Juana's denunciation. Belgrano's order for her freedom, however, proved less than conclusive, as she was still trying to obtain her freedom in Buenos Aires in 1819.[15]

Many slaves, like Juliana García, took a more definite role in military activities by following their men and attaching themselves to the armies as camp followers like Bolívar's *"juanas."* It was an age-old practice associated with armies everywhere in the world, so that the occasional attempts made during the independence wars to eliminate such groups are somewhat surprising. The Uruguayan nationalist José Gervasio Artigas, while welcoming slaves into his army, insisted that their families not accompany them, arguing that they held back his forces and multiplied the difficulties that they faced. Furthermore, he wrote, "It will be impossible to follow us."[16] But despite his wishes, black families became part of Uruguay's military history during this period, just as they did elsewhere, for when slaves ran away to join armies that offered freedom in return for their service, their women followed. Juliana García and her children were only some of the many families that accompanied the Sixth Regiment of Pardos and Morenos, a regiment that attracted camp followers both in Argentina and the Banda Oriental.[17] The Venezuelan *llanero* commander José Antonio Páez mentions in his memoirs the presence of women and children with his forces, some of whom must have been black. Bolívar's vice president, Francisco de Paula Santander, in confirming Páez's recollections, noted that they marched together, were all barefooted, and ate the same roasted beef without salt as the soldiers.[18] Requests by soldiers that their wives be permitted to accompany them indicates that they were an accepted and almost official part of the military.[19] Pezuela claimed that the women accompanying the royalist army in Upper Peru could not be expelled without provoking desertions. Moreover, they filled an important role in providing and preparing food for the men.[20] Nevertheless, like Artigas, others tried to halt the practice. The Argentine authorities issued a decree on December 13, 1819, that prohibited regiments from allowing women to accompany them unless the latter were attached to specific individuals in the regiment. Those women contravening the order were to be arrested immediately.[21] The restriction, however, only gave the women a reason to establish some sort of relationship with the soldiers, and it seems to have been largely unsuccessful, for they continued to participate in this fashion in the warfare that bloodied the region long after independence had been won.[22]

In attaching themselves to an army, some slaves like Juliana joined of their own volition, while others had no control over their actions. When Spanish troops evacuated Bogotá in 1818, they took with them Gerónimo Escobar's slave Manuela, who remained with the army for more than a year, until she was released by the republican forces.[23] Female slaves also accompanied their owners as domestic servants. They may not have suffered the same dangers as Manuela, but they had equally little control over their destinies. Among them was María Demetria Escalada de Soler, a slave of José de San Martín. She was part of his army in 1817 when it made its epic crossing of the Andes.[24] What role María filled and what duties she performed can only be speculated upon. Like other slaves accompanying their masters, she undoubtedly contributed to San Martín's well-being by attending to a variety of his personal daily needs. Thus, her presence in some—however small— way had a direct impact upon him as he made decisions that determined the fate of Chile and ultimately of all Spanish South America. She was part of his army, but unlike others who participated, hers was virtually an unnoticed presence.

Being part of an army could be extremely hazardous to these women, regardless of their background or relationships. In addition to the dangers of marching over unfamiliar terrain for long periods and in all sorts of weather, often with children in tow and no certainty of sustenance or shelter, they faced the possibility of being captured or killed by the enemy. After the battle of Colpayo in Salta, the victorious patriot troops under the Salta caudillo Martín de Güemes counted twelve women among their captives. Royalist casualties at a battle in Chile in 1817 included forty-three soldiers, three officers, and three women. In 1824, royalist forces in Peru killed and captured a number of women, some with their children, who were accompanying patriot troops.[25] Abduction was another possibility. One sergeant in the Buenos Aires Sixth Regiment reported that while he was on the march from Tucumán to attack Salta, he had been robbed of all his clothing, as well as his wife. His complaint may have been well founded, but it is also possible his wife was the thief. In describing his losses, he listed her second after his clothing, suggesting some dissension in their relationship. Clothes were obviously important to him and difficult to obtain, for, as he noted, without them he would be forced to march to Peru naked. In contrast, he seemed to view his wife as replaceable.[26] Captured women also faced the possibility of rape. A British observer reported that royalist troops attacking Salta in April 1817 had stolen food and killed civilians; he added, rather obliquely, "To some females they did something else but not one died that I have heard of." Rape was used as a weapon to terrorize and punish the female population in Venezuela, especially by the Boves forces, while in Peru the viceroy complained to San Martín in January 1821 that insurgents had been committing various atrocities, of which one of the most serious had been to allow black soldiers to rape Spanish women.[27]

The dangers were great, which leads one to ask: why did women take the risk? The reasons varied according to the individual, but two seemed particularly important and were closely intertwined. The first was that accompanying the troops allowed women to remain with their husbands and thereby preserve the family unit. The uncertainties of slave life with the prospect of the family being split apart by sale or inheritance created a profound commitment to marriage and a desire to maintain family ties within the slave community.[28] In the case of slave women in revolutionary Spanish America, remaining with one's husband despite the apparent dangers indicated the depth of the emotional tie. The second reason was to obtain what Joaquina Estrada, another of the slaves from the Banda Oriental who fled with her husband and child to the invading forces, called "beloved freedom."[29] As it was for most male slaves, freedom was their ultimate goal. They "craved" it, as the aspiring soldier Josefa Tenorio stated, and they used their various associations with the military to try to obtain it. One was Francisca Sebastiana de Araujo, a *morena* slave from Montevideo, who was captured by the Buenos Aires forces during the second siege of the city between 1812 and 1814. At the time the invaders under Rondeau were trying to win the backing of male slaves, so they had little interest in female slaves and certainly were not prepared to free them. Francisca was evaluated, put up for sale, and sold for 150 pesos to a lieutenant in the Sixth Regiment named Antonio Parobio, who also seems to have been a *moreno*. Francisca served him throughout the siege, and after Montevideo's fall she accompanied him to Santa Fe, where he freed her in May 1815. Nevertheless, she remained with him and the regiment until the battle of Sipe-Sipe, possibly because their relationship had developed into an intimate one. In the chaos of the battle she somehow lost her manumission papers but managed to obtain a replacement from Güemes in Salta and made her way to Buenos Aires. Here her relationship became known to María Maza, Parobio's wife (or "consort," as she referred to herself), a free *morena*, and to his family, who sought to end the relationship. Francisca's papers disappeared once again—stolen by Parobio's godmother, according to Francisca—and she was reenslaved. In March 1820 she appealed to the courts for her freedom, not only on the basis of the relationship she had had with Parobio but also "for the many services and sacrifices that she had made for him in the campaigns of the Banda Oriental and [Upper] Peru." The basic issue here seems to have been a sexual and not a racial or ownership one, for all the parties were of the same race and during the trial Parobio was accused of "having been unfaithful to the conjugal tie through an illicit commerce with Francisca." But what happened to Francisca remains unknown.[30]

This case indicates that camp following was not a sure route to freedom, as Juliana García also discovered. Having "experienced unspeakable travails and naked poverty" over four years, she and her children made for Buenos Aires after the battle of Sipe-Sipe, while Miguel remained with the Army of Peru. Without food or clothing for herself and her now three children, she was taken into custody by Catalina Rodríguez, the sister-in-law of her former owner. Juliana appealed to the courts for her freedom and that of her children, stating, "I consider myself worthy of being free together with my children, not only because my master has lost all his rights but also because the *patria* owes me for my sufferings of more than four years." The case dragged on for years and through the birth of another child. Lawyers for Juliana argued that the commander of the Buenos Aires forces had offered to free every slave belonging to Spaniards living in Montevideo and that the patriots had confiscated all the property of Spaniards in the city. Rodríguez's lawyers based their argument on property rights, which were supported by the court-appointed protector of slaves, even though he was supposed to be defending the slave's interests. He asserted that the law did not recognize the right of slaves to flee an owner, that generals did not have the authority to dispose of the property of others, and that Juliana could not have been taken by the army, as she was not in Montevideo during the siege. He recognized the spirit of the original decree that recruited slaves, as they could have been of use to the enemy, but he asked, "What services can a woman and two infants provide?" His answer was hardly generous: "None; those of war—the ones that were needed here—cannot be supplied by the claimants because of their sex and their fragile age." The court agreed, finding that the offer of freedom to slaves of Montevideo applied only to those who had fought and those who had fled the city. Juliana had not been living in Montevideo, and her contribution was not considered equal to fighting. As a result, in 1821 she and at least two of her children were returned to slavery.[31]

Nevertheless, as this and other examples indicate, slave women did not docilely accept their situation. They resisted their owners and the system, frequently through their relationships with male relatives who were serving in the military. They seemed to recognize the military's increasing prestige and used it as added leverage. Ana, a slave from Montevideo, was one of those who fled the city to the besieging *porteño* army in 1814. She subsequently returned with a black whom she called her husband, a soldier in the Sixth Regiment, and claimed to be free on the basis of the relationship. Her owner challenged the claim by complaining to the authorities, who responded that all enemy property taken in war passed to the "dominion of the conqueror, having lost the previous quality that it had in the power of the enemy." This may have been true, but it did little to decide Ana's status, which remained unclear.[32] In Peru, San Martín seemed willing to take their relationships with soldiers into account when granting freedom to slave women. One such was Rosa Camenares, a slave who cited the service of her husband, Juan Basurco, in making her claim. She was now a widow, as her husband, a former soldier in the Río de la Plata Regiment, had died of exhaustion while fighting in Peru. Her own service as a laundress and nurse's assistant in hospitals in Huacho, Huaura, and Barranca was also taken into account in San Martín's decision. However, again, her status remained uncertain, as the mother of her former owner tried to reclaim her and her one-year-old daughter.[33]

More often in these circumstances, the male, confident in his military role, was the one who took the initiative. Domingo Miguens, a soldier in the Buenos Aires Third Company of Veterans, asked for custody of his *liberta* daughter, Cresencia, who had accompanied his wife (without Domingo's consent) to a new owner following their master's death. Domingo charged that the new owner had mistreated the girl and failed both to educate her and to provide adequate training as a seamstress.[34] Luis de Larrea was an Argentine sailor who in 1818 asked that his wife's value be reduced from 360 pesos. He wanted it done quickly, as the corsair on which he was serving was about to set sail and he wished to see her free before his departure.[35] Not all of these requests were successful. In 1815, Joaquín Álvares, a soldier in the *porteño* army, pressed the authorities to free his fiancée, Juana Azevedo, so that they could get married. Juana was one of those who had crossed into Argentina with other runaways from Montevideo along with the withdrawing troops. His story was that the pilot of the ship had promised to provide the money if her owner should try to claim her but then had reneged on his promise. Álvares pointed out that other female slaves passing to Argentine territory had been freed. However, he failed to convince the authorities, who insisted that the owner had to be compensated.[36] Also unsuccessful was José Cires, a soldier in the Regiment of Veterans, who tried to free his wife by offering her owner, Father Santiago Rocha, 100 pesos. When his offer was "scornfully" rejected, despite her seven years of good service—probably because she was valued at over 330 pesos—he turned to his superiors to see if they could assist him.[37]

Setbacks, however, failed to stem the flow of requests. José Antonio Albán, a corporal in the Regiment of Civic Free Pardos and Morenos of Buenos Aires, in 1819 asked for and got the value of his wife cut in half from 400 pesos, thereby improving her chances of being freed.[38] Ignacio de los Santos was one of many ex-slaves who tried to win his wife's freedom through the courts. When war broke out he had been living in royalist-controlled Potosí, together with his wife Joaquina, slaves "of an individual" he described as "opposed by nature and opinion to the system of the *país*." In 1811 they fled to Jujuy, where he offered his services to the army and Joaquina found work in the military hospital. He served for six years, until the patriot defeat at Vilcapugio, after which he made his way to Buenos Aires. There Joaquina eventually joined him. He was now a sergeant assigned to the militia, but because of his broken health he wanted an absolute discharge from the military. He also asked for the document confirming his wife's freedom, which, he claimed, Manuel Belgrano had issued to her. She was gravely ill, and his final request was for money to see to her needs.[39] In 1822 José María Martínez, an Argentine soldier in the Second Battalion of Light Infantry, asked that the price of a slave named Juana, who had given her word to marry him more than two years earlier, be reduced from 322 to 230 pesos so that he could buy her freedom and finally exchange vows. He asked for the reduction on the basis of her service and the five children that she had produced, four of whom were females who remained with Juana's owner.[40]

Soldiers in Peru made similar intercessions for female relatives who were slaves. In response to San Martín's antislavery legislation, Domingo García of the Río de la Plata Regiment requested the freedom of his wife, Joaquina Valleja. José Aparicio of the Peruvian Legion did the same in 1822, as much for his past service as for the weakened state in which he found himself. In his case, the general in chief of the army wrote a supporting letter to the minister of War and Navy, commenting, "I believe that this woman and other slave wives of the soldiers of this Army must be given preference in the lottery offered by the Government to benefit this unfortunate caste; for it is only fair that the first fruits of the endeavors of those who fought for freedom should be their families," a view he reiterated on other occasions.[41] In a third case, both spouses appealed on the grounds of the other's contributions to the patriot cause. The appellants were José Jáuregui, another soldier in the Río de la Plata Regiment, and his wife, Mercedes, a slave donated by her owner to the state. In 1822 José asked for Mercedes's freedom, in recognition of her contributions to a series of military campaigns in which she had served officers by washing, cooking, and fulfilling other duties, and for having worked in various hospitals. The request seems to have won San Martín's support, but the following year Mercedes made her own appeal, asking for her own freedom because of the services that her husband had rendered to the liberating army. "Faithful to the *patria*," he had volunteered and was still serving, although now invalided. She noted that San Martín had ordered that she should be freed, but she had lost the document during the campaign that ended with the patriot defeat at Moquegua. As a result, she was asking for new documentation "so that no one will bother me." In this instance, the contribution of her husband seemed to be all important, as it was cited by the authorities in agreeing to her claim.[42]

The examples indicate how this struggle for freedom and change in status had to be negotiated against not only the backdrop of war and military recruitment but also the official commitment to protecting property rights and the interests of slaveholders. As a result, the authorities were not prepared to be overly generous where female slaves were concerned, even to those with a military connection. Nevertheless, many soldiers managed to find ways to assist their family members, often with favorable results. Soldiers commonly assigned a portion of their pay to a spouse or other family member to provide some income while they were in the field.[43] In the case of those with enslaved families, several had the money applied against the slave's purchase price to try to secure her freedom. The well-known black Argentine soldier Domingo Sosa, during the time he was a lieutenant in the Sixth Regiment, directed that part of his pay be used to purchase the freedom of his wife, Pasquala de la Roza. Sosa's fame in his homeland rests on his racial background, his long military career beginning with the English invasions and ending in 1853, and his postmilitary foray into politics. Born in Buenos Aires in 1788, he fought during the independence wars in the first and second sieges of Montevideo, in the campaigns in the Banda Oriental and Upper Peru, and in the battles of Vilcohuma and Sipe-Sipe. In 1816 he was one of the instructors training the newly formed battalion of slaves, and at that time assigned twenty-one pesos per month toward his wife's price of three hundred pesos.[44] A captain in the same regiment, Antonio Pelliza, provided his mother with twenty pesos per month to obtain the freedom of her "legitimate daughter," Benita, while Felipe Malaver, another officer in the regiment, directed that thirty pesos per month be put aside from his wages to purchase the freedom of his wife.[45] She should have been freed in seven months, as she had been valued at two hundred pesos, but Malaver was in the field well over a year before the money was collected and applied. He could not, however, buy her good health. Four years later, in 1819, citing his six years of service in Upper Peru and the Banda Oriental, he successfully pleaded for a house from the state to meet the needs of his wife, who had been prostrate in bed for more than two years.[46]

Requests of this sort did not always originate with the soldier. In several instances women played the principal role in seeking and directing the funds. In December 1815, Malaver's daughter, Mariana Pérez (who was married to a corporal in the Sixth Regiment and sister of Manuel Malaver, a junior officer), asked that the money assigned to her by the state be paid so that she could be "rescued" from slavery.[47] In 1816 María de la Peña, a *morena* slave, requested that the assigned back pay of her husband, Juan Soto, who was then campaigning in Upper Peru, be applied against her value. She wanted it done before her owner, Bernardo O'Higgins, who had been named to collect the funds, departed for Mendoza. She claimed that the state owed 6 pesos per month for twenty-one months, or 126 pesos, leaving 28 pesos of her value outstanding. María Antonia Gauna, the widow of José Bernardino Gauna, a slave who had served for six years in various units and campaigns, ending with his death in January 1820, asked for three years of his assigned wages in order to free herself from slavery. According to her request, they had married in May 1808, six years before he enlisted, and from January 1817 he had assigned two pesos per month to her, which she now sought to use to purchase her freedom.[48] As in other instances, not every request met with success. In 1819, when María Duval, the wife of Joaquín Duval, a soldier who she said was in the Seventh Regiment, asked for eighty pesos to pay off her purchase price, her request was denied, as the regiment had been dissolved and Joaquín's name could not be found on the regimental roster. Nevertheless, requests continued. In that same year, Mariana, the slave of a soldier whom she had not seen for five years and the wife of a soldier in the Army of Peru, sought the money that the latter had assigned to her to obtain her freedom.[49]

These requests reveal the sense of hope that the fight for independence and its attendant antislavery developments had unleashed, but they also point to the uncertainties and the heartbreak that were a part of any warfare. The Argentine records provide numerous cases of women, both slave and free, who lost contact with their soldier relatives and went for years without any news, only to learn eventually that they were gone forever. Their resulting appeals for support of various sorts are as understandable as they are pathetic, for the women had to cope with minimal income while in many cases caring for the needs of the entire family. At the same time, the appeals show that many of these women believed that they were owed something for their loss and were not afraid to make a public demand for compensation. Magdalena Sosa was a *morena* who had been freed "through the generosity of her last owner" and the widow of José Antonio Sosa, a soldier in the Auxiliary Company of Pardos who had served in several campaigns until his death in 1814. In April 1816, she asked for the remainder of the wages that he had assigned to her at the rate of six pesos monthly.[50] The following year Concepción Torres, a "free *parda* and poor," reported that she had been paid the money that her son, Juan José Torres of the Corps of Pardos, had assigned to her until July 1811, but the funds had ended after the battle of Desaguadero, hinting at why the money had stopped.[51] That same year Teresa Caballero asked for the pay owed to her husband Ventura Molina, a "free *moreno*" who had been sold to the Battalion of Veterans. He had previously requested retirement from the service because he was fifty-nine years old and suffered illnesses resulting from a musket ball wound received in the siege of Montevideo. At the time of her request he was experiencing pulmonary problems that were difficult to cure; these had rendered him "unfit" and ultimately proved fatal.[52] In 1818, several women whose relatives had served in the Sixth Regiment of Pardos and paid the ultimate price sought the wages that had been assigned to them. Samora Agueda's son Ambrosio Ruglos had been killed at the battle of Vilcapugio in October 1813, while Ana María Romero's husband, Joaquín, had been captured at the battle of Ayohúma after three years of service and shot a year later by the Spaniards. Francisco Velasco had left Buenos Aires and his wife, Angela Ferreira, on the first campaign against Montevideo and returned safely, but in April 1813, during the second campaign, he was killed in a "guerrilla action" near Montevideo.[53] Numerous others reported on the deaths of sons and husbands and asked for assigned wages or some sort of relief in the form of charity or money for medicines or simply compensation for a loved one killed in action.[54]

Similar appeals were being heard on the royalist side. Isidora Durán, a free *parda* from Montevideo, appealed to the local royalist government for a pension in the form of part of the wages earned by her husband, José Francisco Texeira, a soldier in the Battalion of Volunteers of the Infantry of Montevideo. Having served in "defense of the sacred rights of our monarch," he had "died gloriously at the hands of the insurgents" at the battle of Las Piedras in May 1811.[55] In Peru, María del Carmen Gómez asked for relief in like fashion. She was the widow of Pedro Rosas, who had served in the royalist First Company of Morenos of Lima. Beginning in 1811 he had fought in several battles in Upper Peru and then again from August 1813 to June 1814, when he was killed at the battle of Ilave. Although they had been slaves of the Congo nation when they had married in August 1798, she was referred to as "Doña" in the records, indicating a significant rise in her social status despite her background. She asked for his back wages, which were granted, minus deductions for shirts, four pairs of shoes, socks, money, food, a Lima allowance, a hat, and relief already given.[56]

While the appeals give clear evidence of the close emotional link that existed within families, they also point to the fact that the women were having to cope with a number of practical issues that needed immediate attention. At the most basic level, they were desperate for money for themselves and their families. In some cases, that family now included ex-soldiers who had managed to survive and return home but were so badly injured that productive work was out of the question, at least for the time being. Nevertheless, women sought their return, reaffirming the marital relationships. For a slave woman, regaining a spouse who might eventually find productive work had additional benefits. Her husband was now free and could assist in accumulating the money to pay for her freedom and that of other family members. As a result, in addition to asking for the soldier's back pay, pension, or some other form of relief that they felt he deserved, women sometimes intervened to ask for their husbands' release from service. Among them was María de Concepción Marul, who in 1818 sought the release of her husband, José Ignacio Solis, a former slave who had participated in various campaigns in Upper Peru over a period of five years. Toribia Núñez, who described herself as "*negra*" and was probably a slave, as she did not include the modifier "free," asked for the release of her husband, Silvestre González, a free *moreno* in the Buenos Aires black militia who apparently had been arrested to serve in the Corps of Invalids. She stated that she was confined to bed and described her husband as her only support, "except for heaven." María Rita Montes de Oca, the wife of Manuel Sánchez, a black serving in the Eighth Regiment, asked for his release because of chronic illnesses that prevented him from continuing to serve.[57]

Agitating on their own behalf, as well as in the interests of their families, female slaves everywhere were further aroused into action by the passage of the various antislavery laws, especially the free womb law. It provided a new means for mothers to win freedom for their infant children and in some cases to demand even more. María del Rosario Barvi, a free *morena* from Lima, was one of several Peruvian slaves who cited San Martín's free womb law in asking for the freedom of their children. In November 1823 Domingo Orué, the proslavery landholder and former royalist whose complaints should consequently be viewed with some reservations, charged that women were using the free womb law to refuse to work. According to him, they were justifying their inaction with the claim: "My son is free and I have to care for him." He complained that owners also faced increased costs, for they were having to educate the freed children and meet other expenses.[58]

Orué's charges may have not been entirely unfounded, as some slaves perceived the new laws as tantamount to abolition. María Anselma Vellodas, in asking for the freedom of herself and two children, claimed on the basis of some undefined decree that they were not slaves. Another Peruvian slave, Clara Lavalle, in 1823 referred to the "superior decrees issued in favor of freedom promulgated by edict in this capital" and criticized "those laws contrary to freedom" that were still being applied in Lima. Her owner responded that slaves did not properly understand the laws, which merely permitted slaves to change owners.[59] In fact, they may have understood perfectly but were determined to test the boundaries of the laws and the liberal environment of the times to achieve all that they could.

Additional factors that aroused female slaves at this time were the shifting and uncertain situation regarding their valuations and the resulting new demands that were placed upon them. The end of the African slave trade and the removal of recruited slave males from the workforce created a vacuum that in some areas was expected to be filled by the females. Consequently, their price remained high, especially those who were skilled or "prime" slaves. In Buenos Aires, high prices for individual female slaves were nothing new; in 1808, for example, Juana, a "good nurse" serving as a domestic with cooking, laundering, and ironing skills, had been sold, along with her infant son, for 425 pesos. While average prices for females fell significantly between 1810 and 1821, from 327 to 218 pesos, nevertheless, individual prices could still be very high.[60] In 1814, the owner of another Juana, a twenty-five-year-old domestic slave, accepted 455 pesos for her and her two-year-old son, even though she had sought a price of 600 pesos. That same year, Inés, a slave with a child of six or seven, was sold for 450 pesos, and in 1817, Marta, a slave aged thirty-three and described as "a healthy, robust servant with the best qualities," was offered for 409 pesos.[61]

Slaves such as these continued to be immobilized in their status, unable to change owners or to free themselves through self-purchase. However, their situation was not entirely bleak. As has been shown, money was available through military wages, and some of it was used to purchase the freedom of slave women. Owners may have had reservations about parting with their female slaves because of the abolition of the slave trade and the shortage of males, yet the records show that, at least in Buenos Aires, they were willing to free some, either through self-purchase or by manumission. The numbers were not large, but as the war years passed, women continued to stand a better chance than men of securing their freedom via these routes.[62] And the fact that more and more female slaves were becoming free stimulated others to agitate for the same goal.

In this apparently more liberal environment, slave women in Argentina and elsewhere pressed against the restrictions that continued to bind them. Those who found their goals frustrated by owners who were determined to hold on to their property and unwilling to grant any sort of concessions reacted in various ways. Most notably, they took their demands to the courts. In one case, an Ecuadorian slave, Victoria Gonzales, protested that she had paid for herself, yet her owner claimed that she still owed fifty pesos and demanded that she be returned. In her defense Victoria revealed a sophisticated political awareness, referring to the recent developments that had resulted in "the transformation of all the peoples of America," and in particular to the "progressive and political methods that the Most Excellent Superior Government had dictated to protect the unfortunates of said class whose freedom had been taken away so barbarously by the Spaniards."[63] Her words seemed a deliberate attempt to blame slavery on the colonizer in the hope that the new republican leaders and citizens would divorce themselves from this colonial inheritance just as they were rejecting other aspects of colonial rule. A Venezuelan slave, María Josefa Ramírez, also cited the changing political landscape as she sought recognition of the freedom that she, her husband, and their two children had won by fleeing from royalist to republican territory after the battle of Carabobo. The son of their old owner claimed that they were runaways and donated them to the state, specifically enlisting María's husband in his place in the light infantry of the Apure Battalion. María consequently appealed to the intendant to restore their freedom, noting, "Señor, the poor and the unfortunate are regularly the plaything of the powerful, because the former can only with difficulty demonstrate to those who govern the latter's ... insults." She claimed her previous owner had treated her husband "as an animal" for being a patriot, harshly punishing him in various ways. After Carabobo he had fled to republican territory and served the patriots as a spy on numerous occasions, for which he had won his freedom. The intendant accepted all her facts and declared them free because they had supported the patriots' "just cause" and because, "having taken refuge in the free territory of the Republic, they [could not] be reduced again to servitude."[64]

Claims like these were part of the new awareness and increased assertiveness that were apparent among the slaves of Ecuador, according to the historian Camilla Townsend, and were also evident elsewhere. As Townsend points out in her examination of the life of one slave, Angela Batallas, they were not afraid to appeal to or to challenge the most powerful individuals in the new states. Angela sought the personal intercession of Simón Bolívar in her fight for freedom on the grounds of sexual intimacy with her owner, drawing a parallel between her personal freedom and the freedom of the country.[65] And Angela was not a solitary figure, for others expressed their wishes as openly and eloquently, and in at least one case also approached Bolívar. María del Carmen Sarria was a Peruvian slave who appealed directly to the Liberator for his assistance in improving her situation. Bought in 1818 for 400 pesos for the purposes of domestic work, she had been sent to a bakery after marrying a soldier from the Río de la Plata Regiment. Bad treatment and diseases, described as pulmonary illnesses and bleeding from her mouth, prompted her to flee. Her godmother said that she was unfit as a result of her illnesses, while her owner claimed she had been a nuisance since her marriage, as she wanted to be free; indeed, he said, she had acted as if she were free. He offered to reduce her price by 150 pesos, but within a stipulated period, and unfortunately for María—and unlike Ángela, who did obtain her freedom—the offer was not taken up in the allotted time.[66]

A third case, this time in Buenos Aires, also involved a prominent independence figure, although not as a potential savior but rather as a target of attack from a mother who was trying to protect her son. When Bernardino Rivadavia in 1814 tried to sell a family slave, Lucas Rivadavia, to the state for military service, Lucas's mother, María Dolores Rivadavia, resisted the move, accusing the family of having mistreated her son. Bernardino Rivadavia's wife challenged the claim. Echoing the owner of María del Carmen Sarria and adding to the impression that owners were losing control of their slaves, she charged that her husband's frequent absences had been exploited by Lucas, during which time he acted as if he were free. The case continued, with Lucas's mother, who was also a slave, first asking that her son be assigned to the house of her own mistress and then that he be sold and his price reduced to two hundred pesos. Eventually, to end what was becoming an increasingly embarrassing affair, Rivadavia's wife agreed to a reduction in Lucas's value, which permitted him to buy his freedom or find a new owner.[67]

Actions such as these show that the independence era served as a watershed for slave women. Unknown numbers participated directly in the events of the period, from those who accompanied their masters on military expeditions, to the wives who chose to follow their husbands on campaigns, to those who acted on their own as spies and informers, to the women who stayed at home maintaining the family, collecting money, purchasing their freedom, and seeking the return of their loved ones. The lives of many changed as a result. In common with male slaves, they became a much more active sector of the population, so that as the wars came to an end, slaves throughout Spanish South America were attracting attention for their aggressive behavior. Owners may have complained that slaves were acting as if they were free, but in many cases they were simply defending the rights that they had managed to secure during the war years or were demanding the rights that they believed were now theirs. Their actions were not sufficient to end the system of slavery in the region, but they did assist in severely weakening it. The first and very significant steps on the road to complete abolition had been taken, and slave women had been an important part of that process.

CHAPTER 8

THE SURVIVAL OF SLAVERY

 THE COUNTRIES OF SPANISH South America had finally
won their independence, and slaves throughout the region had played
a vital role in achieving that goal. In doing so they had also weakened
some of the pillars of colonial authority, including centralized absolutism, the church, and, of course, slavery. The last of these appeared
on the brink of collapse at war's end because of the wartime challenges and other antislavery pressures of the time. Further attacks on
the institution seemed likely, as critics of slavery had assumed leadership of the new nations, liberal values remained in vogue, and ex-slave
soldiers were available to press the issue. Having risked their lives to
win their countries' independence, they had some justification for ex-
pecting additional legislation to assist those who had not been freed.
They had already used their status and links to assist family members
who were in bondage, they were trained veterans who numbered in
the thousands, they were part of the now-influential military apparatus, and they were armed. Slavery, as a result, seemed doomed.

Yet the institution managed to survive almost everywhere for another generation. It survived because its roots in the area were extremely deep and because various elements combined to prevent its
collapse. First and foremost was the fact that the wars had not been
fought to end slavery. They were wars of independence, not wars of
abolition, and the accompanying antislavery initiatives had largely
been a necessary but not always desirable by-product to attract slave

support. Even the slaves who fought claimed their reason for serving was for the *patria* or for the king. It was not to end slavery, although many must have hoped that this would be the eventual outcome. In addition, slavery was still too important an institution and the slaveholders too powerful a group for it to be abolished in the 1820s. Few of the national leaders, including critics of slavery, were prepared to challenge the slaveholders, for their immediate goal was to end the divisions that wracked their new nations. Within the black community, those who might have pressed the issue, especially slaves and ex-slaves who had been recruited and seemed to have the capabilities for spearheading the final assault on the institution, failed to provide the necessary leadership. Thousands had fought on the understanding that their reward would be personal freedom, but those experiences did not transform them into campaigners for abolition, even though many still had relatives who were slaves. Coping with the demands of the postwar world occupied much of their time and attention. Moreover, a significant number of the ex-slave soldiers found themselves trying to protect their recently won freedom against former owners. And since slavery already seemed about to expire on its own without their intervention, they had little reason to mobilize and confront it directly. As a result, this pillar of the colonial era may have been severely shaken, but almost everywhere it weathered the storm and remained in place for another thirty years.

At the end of the wars this seemed an unlikely scenario, as all signs pointed to a renewed attack on the institution. Liberal ideas that emphasized equality and the rights of the individual, along with the desire to eliminate the relics of Spanish rule, were widely held and frequently enunciated. In the case of Chile, this led to a short, if somewhat bumpy, road to abolition. Bernardo O'Higgins, as Supreme Director, tried promulgating it in late October 1822 but fell from power before it could be implemented. His opponents claimed that it was unnecessary, since Chilean slaves were "benignly treated" by their owners, who fed, clothed, educated, and cared for them when they were ill. The new executive shared these views and also expressed the need to defend slave owners' property rights. The country's senators, however, were less tied to the past, and on July 24, 1823, they passed an abolition law that was subsequently incorporated into the country's constitution. With only four thousand slaves remaining in bondage, mostly women and the elderly who had been unable to take up arms, Chile might be considered something of an exceptional case. Nevertheless, its abolition decree established a precedent that had repercussions beyond the country's borders. In neighboring Mendoza, for example, slaves heard of the legislation and began crossing to Chilean territory to try to take advantage of it, until a law in April 1824 stopped the migration.[1]

Antislavery pressure was coming from other quarters, too. Great Britain insisted that compliance with its crusade against the slave trade was a condition for formal recognition of the new states, and the leaders of those states seemed likely to fall in line in order to curry British favor.[2] Slavery also remained a target of the Liberator, Simón Bolívar, whose calls for abolition, heard first at the Congress of Angostura in 1819, showed no signs of abating. The constitution that he wrote for Bolivia in 1826 included an abolition clause, and he hoped to extend it to all the countries that he had liberated.[3] Bolívar's voice was the most insistent on the subject, but his was not alone. Military commanders and civilian courts that had already condemned attempts to reenslave those who had risked their lives for the *patria* in the ranks of the patriot armies continued to be heard after independence. Among them was Colonel Francisco de Buenza of Lima, who in 1828 emulated Bolivarian language in commenting on one such attempt. "This is a crime," he wrote, "in which the masters try to enslave those unfortunates who have been disabled by their heroic actions, spilling their blood on the Champ de Mars for the freedom and independence that, it is said, the American people enjoy." He believed that the owners in this case had no right to reclaim their slave, especially since he had been "rendered unfit in the campaign." Rather, he fully merited his freedom.[4] Civilians such as the Peruvian Manuel Lorenzo de Vidaurre, who had called for reforms to protect slaves even before his country had been liberated, were also pressing the issue.[5]

What drove these gestures may in some cases have been deeply felt humanitarian beliefs and a commitment to equality. At the same time, they reflected pragmatic concerns, as the new rulers sought to avoid conflict with a slave population that had already revealed its potential for violence and had not been completely pacified. In the aftermath of the war, many slaves found themselves on their own because of the death or flight of their owners and the absence of any alternative authority. A report in 1826 on the situation in Ecuador could have been applied much more widely. It stated that local slaves had been without masters and temporal or spiritual aid for more than fourteen years, and they continued to be without these, as well as food and clothing.[6] Lacking sustenance and overseers, the slaves had every reason to believe that slavery had ended and that they were as free as their new nations. In Ecuador and elsewhere, owners and officials complained of the loss of slaves, the hostility and resistance of those who remained, and the resulting harm done to the economy. One commentator wrote to the Venezuelan vice president in January 1822 that he was "unable to let pass in silence the evils that [he had] observed affecting so much the inhabitants of this Valley" because of the slaves' military service. "I say so myself," he continued, "that since they entered into military service, one half (no lie) of the haciendas that compose this pueblo have deteriorated."[7] In Peru similar complaints had been voiced almost from the time of San Martín's invasion. Owners of sugar estates and vineyards charged that they had been ruined by the loss of their slaves, "the best suited to be soldiers," and the refusal of the rest to work. Estate owners from the Ica Valley south of Lima protested to William Miller that their slaves "desire to be free [and] refuse absolutely to comply with their obligations"; consequently, the harvest had been lost. They called on him to do something to contain the slaves' "libertinage." The same was true of estates closer to the capital, where owners claimed that "slaves, abusing the political freedom, were applying it to the individual." They refused to recognize any dominion, producing fears that they might make attempts on the lives of the slaveholders.[8] The situation had not improved in 1826, when the British consul wrote from Lima about the dispersal of estate slaves, many of whom had been "engaged in the different armies," while others had "fled into the interior." They had not been recovered, and since no alternative labor force had been found, production remained "considerably diminished."[9]

Attempts by landowners and officials to reassert their authority often provoked new violence. Venezuela, with its still-unsatisfied black population, was particularly affected, as different parts of the country experienced unrest, occasionally stirred by royalist sympathizers. The administrator of the Obra Pía de Chuao estate in March 1822 complained that its slaves, under the misapprehension that "it was the time of freedom," were stealing, refusing to work, selling stolen produce, running away, attacking people, and influencing others.[10] The Zope estate was reported to be paralyzed because of its slaves' refusal to obey. When the foreman remonstrated, they claimed to be free. In August 1823, after another owner tried to make an inventory of his hacienda slaves, they all rose up, and, "insulting [him] with words and actions," forced him to flee. Black guerrillas also remained active. Near Puerto Cabello, one group prompted the authorities to mobilize one hundred soldiers to try to suppress it. In June 1822, another band of what were described as black "agitators" invaded the town of Canoavo. In the ensuing confrontation one of its leaders, a woman, was killed, while another nine women and two children were captured.[11] Even the capital was threatened. In 1825, after a letter from his sister describing Caracas as a city that had become "uninhabitable because of the excesses and threats of domination by the people of color," Bolívar urged Santander to send four thousand men to control the situation.[12]

Other regions experienced similar agitation at the end of the wars. In Colombia there were reports of slave unrest and flight. Those in Barbacoas rose up in 1822, charging that the government had decreed abolition but that the cabildo had suppressed it. In Ecuador, deserters trying to avoid capture were responsible for some of the instability. A report on the area around Palenque claimed, "Most of them are *libertos*, but they live in the *montañas* and are well armed." They refused to surrender, and the authorities lacked the weapons to capture them, perhaps explaining why the coastal region remained unsettled with further uprisings in 1825 and 1827.[13] In Peru, runaways continued to join the bands of highwaymen and guerrillas that infested the countryside, disrupted coastal communications and commerce, and threatened political stability. Even in Buenos Aires, with its long history of slave tranquility, fear of possible unrest among those who were living and working on their own led to a law in 1822 that compelled them to carry their registration papers at all times.[14]

Most slaves were not prone to violence, but even the more quiescent were aware of the circumstances and realized that the era's rhetoric of equality had only limited application as far as the nonwhite populations were concerned.[15] Those who had fought and been freed could now claim citizenship in the new republics, but they quickly learned that being a citizen brought few rewards. Denied what they believed they deserved, slaves who had acquired a sense of their rights were prepared to enunciate and defend them. But rather than resorting to violence, they turned to the courts, just as others had been doing in recent years. In Peru, female slaves were particularly prominent in making their voices heard in this manner, asking for their freedom, new evaluations, or a change of owner. Among them was Isabel Verano, who in 1825 challenged her owner and was even prepared to appeal directly to the government if her demands were not met. She sought to obtain a new owner after a quarrel with her master, the mayor of the coastal town of Huaura, had resulted in her being whipped for her temerity. In court she insisted, "We are constituted in republics and enjoying all that liberty provides, and it is not just that you deny the miserable slave the only freedom that the law grants him, of [changing owners]."[16]

However, although actions and pressures such as these aroused fears, provoked criticism, and further challenged slavery, they were not sufficient to overcome those sectors of society who were determined to see the institution survive. The proslavery forces were diverse, determined, and prepared to do whatever they could to reestablish and maintain the system. Except for Chile, no country in South America passed an abolition law at this time, while defenders of slavery staunchly resisted their opponents. In the forefront were the slaveholders; their numbers may have declined during the wars, as many had been killed, others had fled, and even more had lost their property, but as a group they had not disappeared. In some areas, such as the gold-producing region of Colombia, they had hardly been affected at all and remained very influential. Elsewhere, slaveholders had managed to hold on to their slaves and convince governments to rescind or reduce the impact of antislavery legislation. In Buenos Aires, for example, recruiting laws after 1816 were less clear about offering slaves freedom in return for a defined period of military service. In postwar Colombia, congressional representatives successfully resisted Bolívar's call for abolition. In Peru, slaveholders undermined San Martín's recruiting laws by hiding their slaves and having the resulting legislation that threatened to punish them reversed. They managed to recover some of their slaves and won further concessions following the arrival of Bolívar, who, despite his declared commitment to abolition, seemed to pander to their interests. In 1825 he established rules for rural slaves that included ordering the arrest of those without proper documentation and prohibiting them from carrying arms, machetes, axes, or knives. In November, a further law, which claimed that it was designed to prevent ex-slave soldiers from being reenslaved by their owners, also acted against slave interests by narrowly defining which recruits had the right to freedom. Only those who had enlisted before November 5, 1824, and were still in the army, as well as those who had been invalided out of the service, could claim it. The rest were to be returned to their owners.

As the political leaders' commitment apparently weakened, the slaveholders' resistance rigidified. They sought workers to restore their economic activities, criticized antislavery laws as an unjust challenge to property rights, and in some areas even managed to reestablish a slave trade.[17] Their successes reflected the end of the liberalism that had marked the independence era and the beginning of a more conservative period in which groups promoting traditional values and institutions became politically dominant.

While the slaveholders flexed their muscles, the abolitionist forces, if they could be called such, were almost invisible. One problem was that they had no real leaders. Although Bolívar was the obvious choice, and he continued to espouse the cause of abolition, he was a lonely figure in a vast area, and his true feelings were never entirely clear. He seemed suspicious and fearful of blacks even as he called for their liberation, and his legislation was not always in the slaves' interest. Antagonized by black unrest and conspiracies, he still spoke of the "natural enmity of the people of colour" and considered a black revolt "a thousand times worse than a Spanish invasion."[18] Other recognized political leaders were even less supportive, and the black community was unable or unwilling to fill the vacuum, in part because "their most active members with a potential for leadership" had been lost.[19] The execution of Manuel Piar in 1817 had removed one possibility. Another *pardo*, Admiral José Padilla, who had fought at Trafalgar, then served the republican forces in Venezuela as head of the navy and established his fame in the capture of Maracaibo in 1823, was executed in 1828 when he chose to side with the Santander forces against the implementation of Bolívar's conservative constitution. The stated reason for his execution was sedition, but his race and his relationship with the *pardos* of the Caribbean coast have been cited as the real factors that prompted the still suspicious Bolívar to act.[20] Other recognized black leaders, such as the heads of some of the Peruvian guerrilla groups, did little to push the cause of abolition and were basically regional figures. None of the blacks who had served in San Martín's Army of the Andes emerged as a potential leader. Only a small percentage of the army ever returned home, perhaps 150 of those who had been recruited.[21] How many of these were former slaves or even black is unknown. Not all the rest were dead, as many had deserted during the wars, while others chose to remain in Peru or Chile or were assigned elsewhere. But few of the survivors were capable of providing leadership. Some who had fought were so badly wounded that they were incapable of any type of activity, except to live off the support of families or public charity. Among the many describing themselves as unfit was Juan Ortega, a free *moreno* who had joined the Argentine Sixth Regiment in Montevideo, served in the Army of Peru, and fought at the battle of

Ayohúma, where he had been captured. He somehow managed to avoid being executed but was taken to Lima as a prisoner, eventually to be freed when San Martín occupied the city. He then rejoined the army, only to suffer two musket-ball wounds at the battle of Pasco, one in the right leg and the other in the face that severely damaged his lower jaw. On recovering, he worked his way back to Buenos Aires as a cook for some officers but now had to figure out how to make a living.[22]

Despite their disabilities, many still felt responsible for the welfare of their families. One blinded soldier in Buenos Aires, for example, had a mother for whom he was caring. But what were they to do? The African prince Andrés Ibáñez opened a *pulpería* on returning to Buenos Aires, but he was an exception. Far more were left with nothing. Ex-soldiers in Venezuela and Colombia who were promised grants of land found the offer largely a fiction as their commanders appropriated whatever became available.[23] As a result, many were reduced to begging. The "old African" from Buenos Aires who had fought at the battle of Chacabuco and secured the rather grotesque souvenir of a Spanish soldier's moustache was encountered selling candles in the streets of Lima in the 1840s.[24] Still others, not limited by injuries, sought employment where they could. A few, in their desperation, even tried to return to their former masters.[25] The veterans' aims were consequently quite simple: survive, make some money if possible, and care for their families as they settled down and married.[26] They had no time or inclination to play a role in the political life of their new nations.

The changing demographics of the slave population also had an impact on possible black agitation. Wartime developments, such as the abolition of the African slave trade, the free womb laws, the freeing of recruits, civilian losses, and deaths in battle had reduced the number of slaves significantly. In the most bitterly contested area, the province of Caracas, the slave population was estimated to be one-third of what it had been before the wars.[27] Even in Buenos Aires, where there had been virtually no fighting, the decline was noticeable. A British observer wrote in 1824, "The number of Negroes . . . is at present extremely small, never having been considerable, and having been reduced since the Revolution by the prohibition of the Slave Trade and by giving liberty to Slaves on condition of serving in the armies, which have been repeatedly recruited in this manner, the state indemnifying the owner."[28] In Lima, too, the absence of males attracted attention. "Youths from 12 to 20 are not much seen of any colour in Lima," a British commentator reported in

1824.[29] And those blacks who remained were predominantly free. Thousands had been liberated for their military contribution, with many others manumitted by their owners for good service or by purchasing their own freedom. Some, as has been shown, were also using their military wages to free family members, while in Gran Colombia, the manumission juntas were collecting funds to free slaves in accordance with the law of July 19, 1821. In Guayaquil, for example, thirty-five slaves were freed by August 1823, and money was available to free a few more.[30] In addition, special occasions were marked by freeing groups of slaves. In 1821, San Martín had ordered twenty-five Lima slaves to be freed annually in recognition of their defense of the city against the royalist army, while in 1822 a number of Venezuelan slaves were manumitted to celebrate the national holiday.[31] Existing antislavery legislation was also being applied. In Lima, Timoteo de la Vega, the slave of a Spaniard who had fled upon San Martín's entry into the city, claimed his freedom on the basis of the November 1821 law that freed all slaves belonging to Spaniards or Americans who had left the country. His owner had tried to transfer ownership to local relatives, but his efforts failed and the court supported Timoteo's claim.[32] Decisions of this sort were further evidence of the antislavery environment and proof that even those who had not served in the military were securing their freedom in the newly independent states. As a result, the ratio of slave to free shifted dramatically in some areas. In Buenos Aires, 77.4 percent of blacks and mulattoes had been slaves in 1810, but by 1827 the figure had dropped to somewhere between 36.6 and 45.2 percent.[33]

Another demographic effect of recruiting and wider access to freedom was a preponderance of female over male slaves in some areas. In the case of Buenos Aires, where female slaves had predominated since the late colonial period, the wartime developments increased the ratio markedly. By 1827 there were 100 women for every 58 men, a pattern that was replicated in other parts of Argentina and in Montevideo.[34] The same also seems to have been true in the north. A survey of postwar sales in Bogotá reveals a heavy weighting in favor of female slaves. According to one notary's records, the number of sales of males and females for the years 1824 to 1828 was consistently in the latter's favor, and by substantial amounts: 125 females as opposed to 35 males over the five-year period.[35] One result was that many slave women were now heads of household and had to deal with the various responsibilities that this entailed. Their increased obligations may explain some of the antagonism and alienation that led to postwar appeals to the courts, but for most of the aggrieved, work and household demands left little time to agitate. Moreover, while they may have acquired a certain status as head of the household, this did not translate into leadership positions within the black community as a whole. Paternalism continued to dominate postcolonial Latin America, so that while individual females were prepared to challenge masters and draw attention to the continuing inequities and inhumanity of the slavery system, no slave woman emerged as a recognized figure in the call for abolition.

In any event, with the doors to freedom apparently opening wider and wider, there was less incentive for the black population, whether male or female, to try to push the antislavery issue in any forceful way. Slavery seemed to be weakening, even if the situation was far from perfect. Members of the community recognized that the decrees and laws freeing slaves were not always being followed, the odds of actually obtaining one's freedom were still very long, some juntas of manumission were moribund because of a shortage of funds, and in Uruguay the percentage of slaves was rising, not falling.[36] Nevertheless, antislavery legislation was on the books, and freedom appeared to be available. So why should slaves and ex-slaves adopt a more aggressive stance along the lines of the Haitian example? Some slaves may have supported greater activism, as the continuing slave unrest in Venezuela, Ecuador, Peru, and elsewhere showed, but many did not. This further weakened the postwar struggle against slavery and points to another of the factors that was having the same effect: divisions within the black community.

In common with almost every other sector of the population, Spanish America's blacks and mulattoes were unable to present a unified front. That lack of unity had been evident from the day fighting began. Slaves and free blacks had served in the armies of both sides, directing their weapons against one another on numerous occasions. Some of those who had supported the crown out of loyalty and in the belief that this was the most promising route to freedom were appropriately rewarded by the royalist authorities, but once independence was declared, this door was firmly closed. Indeed, "having loved the King of Spain" was cited among other reasons for denying three Ecuadorian female slaves their request for freedom.[37] A few royalist supporters even found themselves being prosecuted for their actions. One Ecuadorian ex-slave, Manuel Facundo, was tried in 1824 for murder and theft and found guilty, despite the weakness of the case against him. The crimes had been committed when he had been serving as a corporal in the royalist forces, but he insisted that he had not committed any murders and that he was simply following orders. He used that same excuse when justifying the theft of cattle and horses from the hacienda of his former owner. The court-appointed defender of slaves asserted that any accusations leveled by his owner had to be discounted: "If his master has surrendered the dominion that he once had, then he [Facundo] must remain free and not be subjected to conditions at the former's pleasure, especially since our just, charitable, and liberal government strongly protects the freedom of slaves." But the court was unmoved, and even though Manuel had already suffered a long imprisonment, he was sentenced to a further period of service in the army.[38] Blacks on the patriot side seemed unlikely to intervene on behalf of those who had fought against them. Furthermore, long-standing divisions between blacks and *pardos*, which had been particularly evident in the north, remained unresolved, as *pardos* tried to maintain a position of racial superiority, despite the new republics' supposed commitment to greater equality.[39]

Other fissures were also apparent, usually along national lines. In 1818 Admiral Bowles, in his description of San Martín's army in Chile, had commented on the animosities that existed between the local troops and those brought from Argentina.[40] Following Bolívar's entry into Peru, similar divisions occasionally degenerated beyond animosities. In March 1824, Colombian and Peruvian troops in Trujillo came to blows, resulting in a number of casualties.[41] The end of the wars did not resolve the differences. The British representative in Bogotá, reporting on the situation in Lima in 1826, noted that "a great jealousy appears always to have existed on the part of the auxiliary army of Buenos Ayres in Peru, against the Colombians by whom they conceived their glory eclipsed in that country."[42] Emerging nationalism seems to have produced a greater sense of unity among the troops than their racial background.

Bolívar viewed this growing sense of national identity among the troops with some misgivings and after the wars sought to reduce it by reorganizing the soldiers and relocating them away from their homelands. He seemed to believe that this might reduce the number of desertions that had frustrated him throughout the independence struggles and also prevent the creation of personal armies by military caudillos that could be used for political ends. He still recognized the importance of environmental issues in repositioning the soldiers and tried to ensure that those who were recruited from warmer climes served on the coast, while highlanders were stationed at higher elevations or were at least first acclimatized. Before moving the Bogotá battalion in 1826 from Potosí to Venezuela, he instructed Sucre to send them to the warmer Cochabamba, "so that these men can accustom themselves to the hot coastal climate and forget the frosts of Potosí." He planned to discharge the troops from Venezuela, Magdalena, and Panama and replace them with Peruvians, explaining, "My intention is to bring to Venezuela a body of troops foreign to all parties and to all troublemaking and to leave in the south only native Colombians who can render fine service here but who might do much harm there."[43] Already he had ordered that the Junín battalion that comprised 1,400 Peruvians, including slave recruits, along with two hundred grenadiers, be sent to Venezuela. This was to be followed by the Callao battalion of 1,200 men, along with a company of grenadiers, once the royalist-held fortresses in Callao fell.[44] To facilitate the movement of the troops, instructions were sent to arrange shipping along the way so that they would "arrive at their destination as fast as possible and in the best state of health."[45] The possibility of war with Brazil in the south and with Spain over Cuba briefly interrupted these plans, but the relocation of units soon resumed.[46]

In addition to preventing "troublemaking" and desertions, Bolívar's army reorganization had the explicit goal of controlling the black population, raising once again questions about the Liberator's true feelings toward them. In January 1826, the British consul in Cartagena reported that 1,600 men had recently arrived in the city under the command of Colombian officers, "composed of Indians from the provinces of Upper Peru, who speak only their native tongue." They were part of the much larger force that Bolívar was drawing from Bolivia "to keep in check the coloured population of Columbia on the coasts of the Atlantick." The consul went on to note that the black officers from Colombia who were sent to Peru had "nearly all been detained in the South" and replaced by creole officers. He referred to the continuing prejudices of the new nation against "the coloured population, or, more distinctly speaking, the descendants of African negroes" that had not been eliminated by independence. His own prejudices were evident in his concluding comment that "the mass of the military force of Columbia is composed of Indians, of mestizos, and of creoles and the present policy of government seems wisely to be to purge it wholly of African blood."[47]

The relocation came to a definitive halt in 1827, largely because of the reaction of the soldiers whose nationalistic feelings had been further inflamed. Early in the year, Colombian troops stationed in Lima, who were disgruntled with the prospect of being mobilized to end Spanish rule in Cuba and further aggrieved by the *limeños'* clear hostility to their presence, responded to pressure from local creoles who were opposed to Bolívar, and perhaps from Chilean and Argentine agitators, by arresting their superior officers and sending some of them to Colombia. The mutineers numbered about three thousand, one-third of whom were Peruvian-born recruits who had been assigned to replace Colombian casualties. They were described as having been "debauched and enervated" by their long stay in Lima. Many had local wives and children, leading to frequent desertions and disciplinary action. In March, in the aftermath of the mutiny and to prevent further problems, about two thousand of the participants were loaded onto transports for transfer north. However, the small size of the ships assigned to transport the mutineers raised concerns about the spread of disease and even suffocation because of overcrowding. Adding to the crush were "wives and other females [who] were allowed to embark to the number of about four or five hundred, but the major part of them were subsequently forced ashore." Along with the women, about seven hundred Peruvian recruits, deserters, and invalids were left behind.[48]

Many of the ex-slaves who remained in Peru and elsewhere found themselves engaged in a different type of struggle, as they sought to retain the freedom that they had fought so hard to win. As the comments and actions of Bolívar and others indicate, numerous attempts were made to reenslave them. Owners who had grudgingly accepted recruitment responded to the end of hostilities by challenging the antislavery legislation and attempting to regain control of their former property. While they particularly targeted runaways who had joined the military, they also aggressively reclaimed those who had been recruited under the various laws and decrees. Their goal was usually to regain ownership of the slave's person, but they were prepared to accept some sort of compensation if the slave was beyond their grasp. In either case, black veterans everywhere spent long periods in the courts defending themselves against these threats to their freedom.

In Peru, both owners and slaves began approaching the authorities about their rights almost immediately after the battle of Ayacucho. From early in 1825 there were "continuous claims" from slaves enrolled in the forces asking for advice, and owners requesting their return. In one, an owner insisted that his slave, who had served with the guerrillas, "now no longer wishe[d] to belong to them but to his owner." The authorities referred to a vague time of enlistment to determine whether slaves should be returned or not, but no one seemed certain if this should be accepted. To end the confusion, Bolívar issued a law in November 1825 that set November of the previous year as the crucial date.[49] However, even this proved less than definitive, as troops and workers were still required for the siege of the royalist-controlled fortresses of Callao, and slaves were used for both, despite complaints about their declining numbers. At least one who was conscripted as a laborer was killed by cannon fire, and others were injured.[50] With the end of the siege in January 1826, owners again asked for the return of their property. Those enrolled after the November 1824 date were now ordered returned, while the others were declared "free of all servitude."[51] But their situation was still not resolved. Both recruits and some officials objected to returning the ex-soldiers to slavery and recommended, as was done in similar situations elsewhere, that the owners be indemnified instead. Reiterating what was now a familiar refrain, one commander noted, "It does not seem the most judicious ... that those who have sacrificed themselves to break the chains of their homeland and have suffered the rigors of the siege remain condemned to perpetual servitude."[52] And in at least one case, the courts agreed. Manuel del Castillo, who had been forcibly drafted to serve in the siege of Callao after November 5, 1824, asked for his freedom when his former owner's widow claimed him. The court decided that she should be paid one hundred pesos, noting that he had risked his life "for the liberty of the Republic" for eleven months and thus had "the right not to be returned to servitude and slavery."[53] Nevertheless, many of the recent recruits feared the worst and resorted to a common expedient that should have surprised no one: they deserted.[54] Their future remained uncertain, which was true also of the slaves who had fought with the royalists in the fortress. At first glance, their situation seemed clear, for they were ordered returned to their legitimate owners at the end of the siege. However, this contravened Spanish law, which declared that those once freed could not be reenslaved.[55] But were the republican authorities in independent Peru prepared to recognize the laws of the now-discredited mother country? The sources are silent on the point, which suggests that the order returning the slaves to their owners was probably implemented.

In Gran Colombia, the status of the ex-slave soldiers was complicated by the existence of the manumission fund. It may have aroused the hopes of those who were still enslaved, but it also drew many ex-slaves into the courts as owners reclaimed them in the hope of securing if not their person, at least some compensation from the fund. Owners also pursued their former property because the law paid only for those who had enlisted after October 1821.

To try to increase their returns, they labeled slaves who had signed up before the date as runaways and demanded their return.[56] But the latter resisted, arguing that owners had no right to reclaim slaves who had served on behalf of the *patria*. It was an argument made frequently in Venezuela, where owners continued to assert their rights despite negative court decisions. In one case involving a reclaimed slave who was serving in the Orinoco Battalion, the authorities decided that "no slave enlisted by his Excellency General Bermúdez who has contributed to the campaign on this capital [Caracas] can be returned." His commander had testified that the soldier's "conduct has been the best," and his valor had been equally meritorious.[57]

Behind the owners' efforts was their desire to restore their estates and other enterprises now that the fighting had ended, and they saw slaves as essential to their plans. That desire was the real reason why Antonio Montes de Oca sought to reclaim his slave José Felipe, even though he based his argument on the fact that José should not have been recruited because he was only thirteen and unable to handle a musket and other equipment. However, his claim failed, as José's enlistment was declared legal, and he had to be satisfied with compensation.[58] Many owners were willing to do so because the amount—three hundred pesos—was fairly generous and it was assured. This seemed to be the thinking of the grandson of María Josefa Velez Cossio, whose slave Juan Antonio had enlisted with others from the Capaya hacienda and subsequently claimed to be free on the basis of his military service. María had disputed the claim and argued that he should be treated as a criminal, because he had run away to enlist. María's death and Juan Antonio's unknown location probably convinced her grandson that compensation from the manumission fund was his only option. Rosa Pérez also accepted compensation but had to wait longer to get her three hundred pesos from the fund in exchange for her parents' slave, Cirilo Pérez, who had been donated to the military, served in the dragoons, and in 1826 was in the Corps of Invalids. The authorities initially decided that compensation was not warranted, because Cirilo had been enlisted before the issuance of the 1821 law, but eventually in 1830 agreed that his service had in fact begun afterwards. In another case, the widow of Francisco Ignacio Serrano had a better claim for compensation, as her slave had volunteered in the militia with his owner's knowledge after the passage of the law.[59] She was awarded three hundred pesos in 1831. However, she may not have received the money, for by the early 1830s the manumission funds had run out.[60]

In Ecuador, the manumission juntas had to deal with the same issues. A number of ex-slave soldiers who had served in the area of Guayaquil, for example, found themselves having to defend their freedom following complaints about slaves wandering the city and the surrounding villages. A directive from Bolívar declared that slaves who did not wish to serve would be returned to their masters. Some preferred to remain in the military, and their wishes were respected, while others cited their military record to resist (often successfully) being reenslaved by their old owners. One was Alejandro Campusano, the slave who had been drawn by "the sweet voice of the patria" to fight. He had served for a year under Sucre and then been given his absolute discharge and his freedom because of illnesses contracted while he was a soldier. His fortunes continued to decline. He lost his manumission papers, resulting in his reenslavement, and in December 1826, when he asked for preferential treatment from the manumission funds that were distributed at Christmastime, he described himself as a "miserable slave" who was supporting his ancient mother. The authorities ordered him freed and his owner compensated according to his present value.[61] Alejandro's claim was validated, but the decision indicated that past grants of freedom to runaways were no longer certain and that satisfying the interests of slave owners was now more important than respecting the contribution of those who had fought for independence.

Owners in Ecuador, like those elsewhere, were of two minds with regard to their former property. Some were content with compensation. José María de Arteta had "spontaneously" donated a slave, Juan Enrique Mosquera, for service in the cavalry late in the wars in 1824. Enrique, who served in the Pasto campaign in southern Colombia, had become an "excellent soldier," according to his commander. But Arteta now faced paying taxes on his hacienda and asked for four hundred pesos from the manumission fund. He was given three hundred.[62] Other owners seemed more determined to recover their slaves, demanding in some cases a strict interpretation of the recruiting law. In a case that eventually was sent to the courts to decide, Teodoro Zamora's owner claimed that he had not complied with the law's provisos that he defend the patria with loyalty and honor for two years. Rather, having been recruited to protect Guayaquil, he had served until Bolívar declared the area's independence and then had deserted to avoid accompanying the battalion to Peru. He had subsequently reenlisted and fought in the second Pasto campaign, but again deserted and returned to Guayaquil, where his owner had encountered him begging in the streets. Pointing out that other owners had recovered slaves who had served, he charged, possibly with some validity, that Teodoro's military service had "not been out of love for the republic's independence but for the specific goal of securing his own emancipation without any risk while gaining all the advantages that were reported to be enjoyed by those who served with distinction."[63] The same argument was made by the representative of the owner of José Antonio Quiñones—that he had not satisfied the requirements of serving "the Republic with faithfulness and love." José Antonio had been recruited in Cartagena, served until 1822, and was living in Guayaquil in 1824 when his owner reclaimed him. The ex-soldier asked for his freedom and the *fuero* of a retired soldier. In this case, his owner was prepared to accept compensation, pointing out that, according to the manumission law, owners in his situation were supposed to receive preferential treatment.[64] A third owner who made the same argument recovered his slave, even though he had already received compensation. Jacinto Santos's owner claimed that Jacinto had been sold to the state for military service, but he had served only briefly and "suffered no danger by not having to fight." Instead, he had taken to the streets, "serving neither the state nor his owner" until illness caused him to return to his owner's house. Given a choice, Jacinto decided to remain with his master, who repaid the three hundred pesos given him by the state. But the court was not entirely satisfied and continued to consider the case.[65]

In addition to slaves who had not strictly fulfilled the recruiting legislation, those who had been drafted and clearly promised freedom in return for their service found, with the end of the fighting, that the promises amounted to little and that their status was in doubt. Among them were the veterans of the failed Nariño campaign in southern Colombia. Andrés Lino Mosquera was one of fifty-two slaves bought in Popayán to serve as laborers for the expedition. He had managed to escape after Nariño's defeat but was captured with the relief column and then sold to an estate, where his treatment, in his words, was "inhumane." He had either escaped or been released, for he subsequently rejoined the army. In 1824, now living in Ecuador, he asked for his freedom. He was aware of the manumission fund but refused to appeal to it on the grounds that by law he was already free, both for having enlisted and for suffering injuries on a campaign. The courts agreed, granting him freedom and even awarding back pay from November 1816 to October 1824, yet his owner continued to challenge the decision and once again attempted to gain control over him. Another veteran of the 1813 expedition was Francisco Gerónimo Cicero, who in 1822 asked for his freedom in Colombia through the protector of slaves. He was now broken in health and unfit for work as a result of his service in the campaign that had involved hauling cannons. He had returned to the Saldaña estate where, despite a promise of freedom, he was still in service in 1822.[66]

Similar stories of reenslavement and denied freedom were heard in Argentina. José Aguiar joined the Tenth Regiment after fleeing Montevideo and served in Upper Peru, where he had been completely incapacitated, and he was forced to turn to charity to survive. In 1824, after enjoying freedom for four years, he was claimed by someone who said he was his owner and held in jail while his case was resolved.[67] Antonio Garrido had served in the Sixth Regiment in the siege of Montevideo as "one of its brave ones" and in the process had "contributed service to the country in the militia, spilling his blood in its defense and liberty." But he had been reclaimed and reenslaved by his former master. Taking his case to court, he heard the prosecutor declare that in instances of this sort the courts should follow the law of June 21, 1812, which protected property rights, and return the slave to the owner. However, the court decided that Antonio had acquired his right to freedom through his service to the *patria*, so that the owner had to be satisfied with his value according to the decree of February 6, 1821. Yet it still assigned him to four more years of military service.[68]

While these examples indicate that owners' claims were often denied, the situation of the ex-slaves remained far from settled. And the passage of time did not clarify their status, as former owners tried to regain dominion of their property years after the wars had ended. Ancelmo Zagal found himself in court in 1828, six years after he had left the service of the Corps of Slaves in Lima to work as a wage laborer south of the capital in the Cañete Valley. He cited his possession of money as a reason for refusing to recognize his owner's rights when he returned to Lima but claimed his freedom on the basis of his earlier military service.[69] Peruvian owners became so importunate in seeking the return of their former property that a law was passed in December 15, 1829, in an attempt to control their demands, but without much effect.[70] Francisco Paniso was an ex-soldier whose owner reclaimed him in 1831. He had obtained his freedom in 1822 after joining a *montonero* group the previous year and participating in a number of battles. In 1823 he moved to Trujillo, then returned to Lima in 1826, where he worked as a servant, suffering some sort of mental breakdown during this period as well as mislaying his papers. His former owner, a hacendado whose wartime losses had been extensive, wanted compensation and made the novel claim that the law freeing slaves did not apply to those who had belonged to *montonero* groups. Witnesses at Francisco's trial disagreed, pointing out that his owner's husband had already been compensated, but the case continued until December 1833.[71] In Venezuela, claims by owners kept the courts particularly active between 1828 and 1830. One involved the ex-slave José Ambrosio Surarregui, whose defense was a familiar one: that "a man who defends this sacred right [the freedom of his country] with his blood and with his life could not be a slave."[72] Here, too, decisions could drag on for years. Two Venezuelan slaves taken from a mill in 1821 for military service and reclaimed almost immediately were still awaiting resolution of their request in 1840, in large part because of the lack of manumission funds.[73] And at least one Venezuelan slave, Toribio Gascue, was still asking for his freedom on the basis of his military career in November 1854, eight months after abolition. According to his story, at the age of seven he had been bought and taken into the service of a man named Pablo Gascue. In 1814, then thirteen, he was incorporated into the patriot forces of José Félix Ribas as a *carabinero* (rifleman) and later a cavalryman. He fought with Bolívar and Ribas at the battle of Urica, was gravely wounded, hid until he recovered, and then joined the army of General Pedro Zaraza, in which he served until 1818. Taken prisoner, he managed to escape to Caracas, where he hid in the house of his owner and then accompanied him to Puerto Rico in 1820. In 1821 he found himself back in Venezuela and joined the army of Bermúdez, but shortly afterwards he was returned to his owner and then sold twice. He began claiming his freedom for his military service in 1845 but still had not received it nine years later, perhaps because of the bankruptcy of the manumission funds or perhaps because of inconsistencies in his story.[74] Whatever the reason, his case once again illustrates the difficulties faced by the former soldiers in their efforts to secure and protect their freedom.

In these situations, most of the ex-slaves were left in a legal limbo. This uncertainty and threats to their status may account for some of the agitation that marked this period, but more often those threatened were probably inclined to avoid attention. It had been a wise strategy during the wars and seemed equally advisable now. When that strategy failed and they were brought to public attention, in many cases because they sincerely believed they were free and had no reason to dissemble or hide, their actions and their words indicated that they had a clear understanding of their status and the declining force of slavery. In the process they may have influenced others; they certainly helped to keep the issue of slavery and its inequities alive, and they may even have weakened slavery further. But the overall effect of slaveholder efforts to regain control of their former slaves was to convince the latter to stay out of the public eye. They had managed to win their freedom at great cost to themselves, and they had no desire to lose it, even for a brief time, to a vindictive or grasping owner. Attacking the institution of slavery on a broader front might have ended these challenges, but it was not a gamble the ex-slaves were willing to risk. They were acutely aware that they were operating in a hostile environment. Despite their role in the independence struggles, they were still viewed largely in racist and derogatory ways. In 1830, an article in a Lima newspaper entitled "Freedom of Slaves" repeated the charges that had been used frequently before the wars to prevent arming slaves. In rejecting abolition, it charged that slaves would not know what to do if they became their own masters and that those "of a ferocious spirit, of which this caste is replete, [would] turn to pillage and murder" to meet their needs.[75] The wartime sacrifices of the slaves seemed all but forgotten.

Threatened by former owners, divided by nationalism, assigned to strange locales, criticized by civilian leaders, married to local women, the black veterans of the independence wars were pulled in a multitude of directions that often had little to do with the issue of slavery. Moreover, many of them were soon fighting once again, as the divisiveness of the wars split not only the black population but also the new leaders of the former colonies, leading almost immediately to wars both within the new states and between them.[76] In Argentina, civil wars broke out even before the royalists had been defeated, with provinces confronting both the national government and one another. To meet military needs, recruiters once again turned to the black population. The numbers were substantial and undoubtedly included many of those taken in the past. In 1820 the British naval commander in the area reported on a battle in June between the Argentine centralists under General Miguel Soler and the governor of Santa Fe, Estanislao López, who headed the federalist forces. López was victorious, capturing four hundred of what were described as "the best Black Troops."[77] The region was also bloodied by warfare between Argentina and Brazil (1825–1828) over the status of the Banda Oriental. It was a war that involved some of the remaining veterans of the independence wars, as well as untested slaves. Call-ups in 1826 that sought troops for the defense of Buenos Aires included "all slaves capable of bearing arms."[78] In the northern part of the continent, continuing warfare was also the order of the day, as Peru's new leaders in 1828 sought to destroy the influence of Bolívar and his Gran Colombia. Both sides used slaves, offering them their freedom if they served for the duration of the campaign, with the Gran Colombian owners being compensated from the manumission fund.[79] However, while this new recruiting effort highlighted the reputation slaves had achieved as soldiers, never again would they assume the military importance they had during the independence era. Moreover, being drawn back into the military added to the factors diverting the attention of the black community away from racial issues. It also further divided them, as once more warfare pitted slave against slave. Divisiveness was the order of the day, and the achievement of independence had not overcome that fact. Slavery continued, and most of the racial barriers established during the colonial period remained firmly in place, despite the sacrifice of thousands of slaves.

In a way, then, the story of the slaves who served in the wars of independence can be seen in the bones of those dead heroes of the battle of Chacabuco that Samuel Haigh observed shortly after it was fought. They represented but a handful of the soldiers who had served throughout the continent and whose contributions had helped to win the independence of Spanish America. But their names were largely unknown, as were their backgrounds. There was certainly no marker to indicate their race. The bones of the ex-slaves were mixed with those of fellow soldiers drawn from every racial group in Latin America. Together their remains gradually decayed into dust. In this natural and inevitable process, men who had suffered under slavery and then won their freedom in exchange for their skills in the art of war became one with the soil of the nations that they, as well as their predecessors, had helped to create in so many different and fundamental ways. They had fought and died under the flags of freedom, and Spanish South America was now free, thanks in no small part to their involvement. Many of those who survived—probably the majority—were now personally free, even though slavery remained a force in their new nations. Yet their actions during the wars had also begun the process of dismantling that institution. It would not be completed in most of the new states for at least another generation, but it had begun. Slave soldiers might not battle for abolition as they had for *patria* or for king, but by their actions they had helped to unleash the process. Unfortunately for them, that role would remain largely unrecognized, much like their contribution to the independence struggles. They had fought for freedom, their efforts had been crowned by national independence and personal liberty, and abolition would eventually follow. These were indeed impressive accomplishments, and they serve as a fitting memorial for Spanish America's slave soldiers.

NOTES

LIST OF ABBREVIATIONS

AA-C: Archivo Arzobispal, Caracas

AA-L: Archivo Arzobispal, Lima

AANH-C: Archivo de la Academia Nacional de la Historia, Caracas

ADM: Public Record Office, London, Admiralty files

AGI: Archivo General de Indias, Seville

AGN-B: Archivo General de la Nación, Bogotá

AGN-BA: Archivo General de la Nación, Buenos Aires

AGN-C: Archivo General de la Nación, Caracas

AGN-L: Archivo General de la Nación, Lima

AHG G: Archivo Histórico de Guayas, Guayaquil

AHM-G: Archivo Histórico Municipal "Camilo Destruge," Guayaquil

AHM-L: Archivo Histórico Militar, Lima

AHPBA-LP: Archivo Histórico de la Provincia de Buenos Aires, La Plata

ANC-S: Archivo Nacional de Chile, Santiago

ANE-Q: Archivo Nacional del Ecuador, Quito

BN-B: Biblioteca Nacional, Bogotá

BN-L: Biblioteca Nacional, Lima

FO: Public Record Office, London, Foreign Office files

CHAPTER 1: A HISTORICAL TRADITION

1. "Expediente formado por el negro Francisco, esclavo de Don José Alberto Caisena y Echevarria: Reclamando su libertad," 1813, AGN-BA, Administrativos (hereafter cited as Admin.), leg. 29, exp. 984, IX–23–8–3.

2. George Reid Andrews, *The Afro-Argentines of Buenos Aires, 1800–1900* (Madison: University of Wisconsin Press, 1980); Núria Sales de Bohigas, *Sobre esclavos, reclutas y mer-*

caderes de quintos (Barcelona: Editorial Ariel, 1974); Peter M. Voelz, *Slave and Soldier: The Military Impact of Blacks in the Colonial Americas* (New York: Garland, 1993). For a study of slave soldiers in different parts of the world through history, see the chapters in Christopher Leslie Brown and Philip D. Morgan, eds., *Arming Slaves from Classical Times to the Modern Age* (New Haven: Yale University Press, 2006).

3. One version of Mitre's Falucho story can be found in Bartolomé Mitre, *Historia de San Martín y de la emancipación sudamericana* (Buenos Aires: Editorial Universitaria de Buenos Aires, 1968), 3:350.

4. Sales de Bohigas, *Sobre esclavos*, 102.

5. John Lynch, *The Spanish American Revolutions 1808–1826*, 2nd ed. (New York: W. W. Norton, 1986), 272; José Semprún and Alfonso Bullón de Mendoza, *El ejército realista en la independencia americana* (Madrid: Editorial MAPFRE, 1992), 146.

6. *Cartas Santander-Bolívar* (Bogotá: Biblioteca de la Presidencia de la República, 1988), vol. 3, *Cartas 1820–1822*, 61.

7. Rebecca A. Earle, *Spain and the Independence of Colombia 1810–1825* (Exeter: University of Exeter Press, 2000), 30–31. See Semprún and Bullón de Mendoza, *El ejército realista*, 112, 113, 118, 154–55, 156, and 159, for a regional breakdown of the troops shipped from Spain.

8. John K. Thornton, "African Soldiers in the Haitian Revolution," *Journal of Caribbean History* 25, nos. 1 and 2 (1991): 65–66.

9. Compelling recruits to serve beyond their native province was a problem for all recruiters. For gaucho regional loyalty in Argentina and their unwillingness to sacrifice themselves for some distant political leader, see Richard W. Slatta, *Gauchos and the Vanishing Frontier* (Lincoln: University of Nebraska Press, 1992), 127. See also Clément Thibaud, *Repúblicas en armas: Los ejércitos bolivarianos en la guerra de independencia en Colombia y Venezuela* (Bogotá: Planeta, 2003), 455.

10. For a discussion of the wars of independence as social movements, see Brian R. Hamnett, "Process and Pattern: A Re-examination of the Ibero-American Independence Movements, 1808–1826," *Journal of Latin American Studies* 29, no. 2 (1997): 279–328.

11. Aguirre is referring to slave actions in Peru during the early republican period, but the phrase seems equally applicable to this earlier period. See Carlos Aguirre, *Agentes de su propia libertad: Los esclavos de Lima y la desintegración de la esclavitud 1821–1854* (Lima: Pontificia Universidad Católica del Perú, Fonda Editorial, 1993).

12. John V. Lombardi, *The Decline and Abolition of Negro Slavery in Venezuela, 1820–1854* (Westport, CT: Greenwood, 1971), 46.

13. Lynch, *Spanish American Revolutions*, 348.

14. Philip D. Curtin, *The Atlantic Slave Trade: A Census* (Madison: University of Wisconsin Press, 1969), 21–36.

15. Frederick P. Bowser, *The African Slave in Colonial Peru, 1524–1650* (Stanford: Stanford University Press, 1974), 100; David Bushnell, *Simón Bolívar: Liberation and Disappointment* (New York: Pearson Longman, 2004), 6; Tulio Halperín-Donghi, *Politics, Economics and Society in Argentina in the Revolutionary Period*, trans. Richard Southern (Cambridge: Cambridge University Press, 1975), 40–41, 43–44, 49.

16. For details of slave life in colonial Spanish America, see George Reid Andrews, *Afro–Latin America, 1800–2000* (New York: Oxford University Press, 2004), chap. 1; Bowser, *African Slave;* María Eugenia Chaves, *María Chiquinquirá Díaz, una esclava del siglo XVIII: Acerca de las identidades de amo y esclavo en el puerto colonial de Guayaquil* (Guayaquil: Archivo Histórico del Guayas, 1998); Nicholas Cushner, *Lords of the Land: Sugar, Wine, and Jesuit Estates of Coastal Peru, 1600–1767* (Albany: State University of New York Press, 1980); Alberto Flores Galindo S., *Aristocracia y plebe: Lima, 1760–1830 (estructura de clases y sociedad colonial)* (Lima: Mosca Azul Editores, 1984), 108–9, 121; Marta B. Goldberg and Silvia C. Mallo, "La población africana en Buenos Aires y su campaña: Formas de vida y de subsistencia (1750–1850)," *Temas de África y Asia* 2 (1993): 36, 37, 39, 46; Michael McKinley, *Pre-Revolutionary Caracas: Politics, Economy and Society, 1777–1811* (Cambridge: Cambridge University Press, 1985), 9–11, 22–23, 46–51, 55–57, 115–25; Colin A. Palmer, *Slaves of the White God: Blacks in Mexico, 1570–1650* (Cambridge, MA: Harvard University Press, 1976); Leslie B. Rout Jr., *The African Experience in Spanish America: 1502 to the Present Day* (Cambridge: Cambridge University Press, 1976), chap. 3; William Frederick Sharp, *Slavery on the Spanish Frontier: The Colombian Chocó, 1680–1810* (Norman: University of Oklahoma Press, 1976), esp. chap. 7; John Hoyt Williams, "Observations on Blacks and Bondage in Uruguay, 1800–1836," *The Americas* 43, no. 4 (1987): 415, 421.

17. Flores Galindo, *Aristocracia,* 105–6, 110–12, 117–19, 128–32.

18. ANE-Q, Esclavos, caja 21, 1811–18, exp. 1.

19. Andrews, *Afro-Argentines,* 39, 41, 95.

20. Lyman L. Johnson, "Manumission in Colonial Buenos Aires, 1776–1810," *Hispanic American Historical Review* 59, no. 2 (1979): 260n4.

21. Paulo de Carvalho Neto, *El negro uruguayo (hasta la abolición)* (Quito: Editorial Universitaria, 1965), 25–26, 29, 38, 48–49; Ildefonso Pereda Valdés, *El negro en el Uruguay: Pasado y presente* (Montevideo: n.p., 1965), 45, 46, 244–48.

22. Christina Ana Mazzeo, *El comercio libre en el Perú: Las estrategias de un comerciante criollo, José Antonio de Lavalle y Cortés, 1777–1815* (Lima: Pontificia Universidad Católica del Perú, 1994); *El Peruano* (Lima), Dec. 16, 1826. John Fisher has provided a different picture of Peru, writing that only small numbers were imported in the late colony despite various plans and pressures to increase the flow. See John Fisher, *Government and Society in Colonial Peru: The Intendant System, 1784–1814* (London: The Athlone Press, 1970), 148–49.

23. Federico Brito Figueroa, *La estructura económica de Venezuela colonial* (Caracas: Instituto de Investigaciones, Facultad de Economía, Universidad Central de Venezuela, 1963), pp. 134, 136–137; Miguel Izard, *El miedo a la revolución: La lucha por la libertad en Venezuela (1777–1830)* (Madrid: Editorial Tecnos, 1979), 55–57.

24. There is no agreement with regard to slave numbers. For Río de la Plata, see John Lynch, *Argentine Dictator: Juan Manuel de Rosas, 1829–1852* (Oxford: Clarendon Press, 1981), 119; Williams, "Observations," 414. For New Granada, see Allan J. Kuethe, *Military Reform and Society in New Granada, 1773–1808* (Gainesville: University Press of Florida, 1978), 29. For Venezuela, see Brito Figueroa, *La estructura,* 58; Stephen K. Stoan, *Pablo Morillo and Venezuela, 1815–1820* (Columbus: Ohio State University Press, 1974), 10. For

Ecuador, see Fernando Jurado Noboa, "Algunas reflexiones sobre la tenencia de los esclavos en la colonia: 1536–1826," *Boletín del Archivo Nacional* (Quito) 22 (1992): 99–100; Manuel Lucena Salmoral, *Sangre sobre piel negra: La esclavitud quiteña en el contexto del reformismo borbónico* (Quito. Ediciones Abya-Yala, 1994), 59. Por Perú, see Timothy Anna, *The Fall of the Royal Government in Peru* (Lincoln: University of Nebraska Press, 1979), 17. For Chile, see Guillermo Feliú Cruz, *La abolición de la esclavitud en Chile: Estudio histórico y social,* 2nd ed. (Santiago: Editorial Universitaria, 1973), 32, 33. See also Robin Blackburn, *The Overthrow of Colonial Slavery, 1776–1848* (London: Verso, 1988), 334–35.

25. In the case of Lima, for every two slaves who purchased their own freedom, one was freed by his or her owner. See Carlos Aguirre, *Breve historia de la esclavitud en el Perú: Una herida que no deja de sangrar* (Lima: Fondo Editorial del Congreso del Perú, 2005), 129–30.

26. "Expediente promovido por Manuel Domingo Arechederra sobre su libertad," 1808, AA-C, Justiciales, leg. 132; "Don José Francisco Visbal contra Don Domingo Alvarez, sobre que este le pague de los bienes de Doña Isabel Ramos el valor de un esclavo que le vendió," 1809, AA-C, Justiciales, leg. 133; "Don Francisco de Paula Ramiro, sobre que Doña María Petrona Montero lleva la esclaba llamada Juana, que le vendió," AGN-BA, Admin., 1808, leg. 22, exp. 713, IX–23–7–3; Brito Figueroa, *La estructura,* 363–68, 379–85; Flores Galindo, *Aristocracia,* 103; Christine Hünefeldt, *Paying the Price of Freedom: Family and Labor among Lima's Slaves 1800–1854* (Berkeley: University of California Press, 1994), 117, 169–70; Johnson, "Manumission," 260–62, 270, 273–77, 279; McKinley, *Pre-Revolutionary Caracas,* 23–24.

27. Rout, *African Experience,* chap. 4.

28. Andrews, *Afro–Latin America,* 20–22, 24–25; Carmen Bernand, "La población negra de Buenos Aires (1777–1862)," in Mónica Quijada, Carmen Bernand, and Arnd Schneider, *Homogeneidad y nación con un estudio de caso: Argentina, siglos XIX y XX* (Madrid: Consejo Superior de Investigaciones Científica, 2000), 120; John Thornton, *Africa and Africans in the Making of the Atlantic World, 1400–1800,* 2nd ed. (Cambridge: Cambridge University Press, 1998), 328.

29. Andrews, *Afro-Argentines,* 138–42; Bowser, *African Slave,* 247–51; Matt D. Childs, *The 1812 Aponte Rebellion in Cuba and the Struggle against Atlantic Slavery* (Chapel Hill: University of North Carolina Press, 2006), chap. 3; Hünefeldt, *Paying,* 100–105.

30. Andrews, *Afro-Argentines,* 95.

31. Scarlett O'Phelan Godoy, *Rebellions and Revolts in Eighteenth Century Peru and Upper Peru* (Cologne: Böhlau, 1985), 229, 255.

32. Ildefonso Gutiérrez Azopardo, *Historia del negro en Colombia ¿Sumisión o rebeldia?* 4th ed. (Bogotá: Editorial Nueva América, 1994), 71–73; John Leddy Phelan, *The People and the King: The Comunero Revolution in Colombia, 1781* (Madison: University of Wisconsin Press, 1978), 110–11, 153, 195.

33. Brito Figueroa, *La estructura,* 373–74; Childs, *Aponte,* 35–37; David Patrick Geggus, "Slave Resistance in the Spanish Caribbean in the Mid-1790s," in *A Turbulent Time: The French Revolution and the Greater Caribbean,* ed. David Barry Gaspar and David Patrick Geg-

gus (Bloomington: Indiana University Press, 1997), 132–33, 136; Aline Helg, *Liberty and Equality in Caribbean Colombia 1770–1835* (Chapel Hill: University of North Carolina Press, 2004), 108–18; Lucena Salmoral, *Sangre sobre piel negra*, chaps. 1, 2, and 6; McKinley, *Pre-Revolutionary Caracas*, 122, 125; Stoan, *Pablo Morillo*, 17–18.

34. For the classic work on the Haitian Revolution, see C. L. R. James, *The Black Jacobins: Toussaint L'Ouverture and the San Domingo Revolution*, 2nd ed. (New York: Vintage Books, 1963). On the revolutionary potential of slaves in America, see Eugene D. Genovese, *From Rebellion to Revolution: Afro-American Slave Revolts in the Making of the Modern World* (Baton Rouge: Louisiana State University Press, 1979), 18–19; Voelz, *Slave and Soldier*, 275, 277.

35. Among those who argue that the French and Haitian Revolutions had an impact on Spanish American slaves are Carvalho Neto, *El negro uruguayo*, 95; Carlos M. Rama, "The Passing of the Afro-Uruguayans from Caste Society into Class Society," in *Race and Class in Latin America*, ed. Magnus Mörner (New York: Columbia University Press, 1970), 33–34; José Marcial Ramos Guédez, "La insurrección de los esclavos negros de Coro en 1795: Algunas ideas en torno a posibles influencias de la revolución francesa," *Revista Universitaria de Ciencias del Hombre . . . Universidad José María Vargas* 2, no. 2 (1989): 103–16; and Winthrop R. Wright, *Café con Leche: Race, Class, and National Image in Venezuela* (Austin: University of Texas Press, 1990), 25–26. For a somewhat more critical view, see the articles in Gaspar and Geggus, *Turbulent Time*, especially Geggus, "Slavery, War, and Revolution." For an indication of slaveholder fears of slaves and slave revolt following the Haitian Revolution, see Matt D. Childs, "'A Black French General Arrived to Conquer the Island': Images of the Haitian Revolution in Cuba's 1812 Aponte Rebellion," in *The Impact of the Haitian Revolution in the Atlantic World*, ed. David Geggus (Columbia: University of South Carolina Press, 2001), 135–56.

36. Andrews, *Afro–Latin America*, 37–40, 59; Jorge I. Domínguez, *Insurrection or Loyalty: The Breakdown of the Spanish American Empire* (Cambridge, MA: Harvard University Press, 1980), 56–57, 151, 157–60; Flores Galindo, *Aristocracia*, 116–17; Lynch, *Spanish American Revolutions*, 194; Judith Prieto de Zegarra, *Mujer, poder, y desarrollo en el Perú* (Lima: Editorial DORHCA, 1980), 2:26–28.

37. Brito Figueroa, *La estructura*, 355–59; Domínguez, *Insurrection*, 47; Sales de Bohigas, *Sobre esclavos*, 96–97n45.

38. Rama, "The Passing," 33–34.

39. See, for example, Aguirre, *Breve historia*, 218; Bowser, *African Slave*, 154–56; Sherwin K. Bryant, "Enslaved Rebels, Fugitives, and Litigants: The Resistance Continuum in Colonial Quito," *Colonial Latin American Review* 13, no. 1 (2004): 16; Carvalho Neto, *El negro uruguayo*, 96; Carlos Eduardo Valencia Villa, *Alma en boca y huesos en costal: Una aproximación a los contrastes socio-económicos de la esclavitud. Santafé, Mariquita y Mompox 1610–1660* (Bogotá: Instituto Colombiano de Antropología e Historia, 2003), 179–80.

40. Carvalho Neto, *El negro uruguayo*, 96; Domínguez, *Insurrection*, 99; Lynch, *Spanish American Revolutions*, 193; Ramos Guédez, "La insurrección," 103–16.

41. Voelz, *Slave and Soldier*, 29, 31.

42. Seth Meisel, "War, Economy, and Society in Post-Independence Córdoba, Argentina" (PhD diss., Stanford University, 1998), 46–47; Stoan, *Pablo Morillo*, 13.

43. Camprún and Bullón de Mendoza, *El ejército realista*, 44–46; Voelz, *Slave and Soldier*, 118–21. For the Bourbon military reforms, see Christon I. Archer, *The Army in Bourbon Mexico, 1760–1810* (Albuquerque: University of New Mexico Press, 1977); Leon G. Campbell, *The Military and Society in Colonial Peru, 1750–1810* (Philadelphia: American Philosophical Society, 1978); Herbert S. Klein, "The Colored Militia of Cuba: 1568–1868," *Caribbean Studies* 6, no. 2 (1966): 17–22; Allan J. Kuethe, *Cuba, 1753–1815: Crown, Military, and Society* (Knoxville: University of Tennessee Press, 1986); Kuethe, *Military Reform;* Jane Landers, *Black Society in Spanish Florida* (Urbana: University of Illinois Press, 1999), chap. 9; Lyle N. McAlister, *The "Fuero Militar" in New Spain, 1764–1800* (Gainesville: University of Florida Press, 1957); Ben Vinson III, *Bearing Arms for His Majesty: The Free-Colored Militia in Colonial Mexico* (Stanford: Stanford University Press, 2001), 37–41.

44. AGN-B, Colonia, Milicias y Marina, tomo 14, 82–83, 730, tomo 17, 1054–58, tomo 27, 199–259, tomo 45, 443–45; AGN-L, Real Hacienda, Ejército, 1820–21, leg. 8; Andrews, *Afro-Argentines*, 115, 118; Andrews, *Afro–Latin America*, 46; Juan Beverina, *El virreinato de las provincias del Río de la Plata, su organización militar: Contribución a la "historia del ejército argentino,"* 2nd ed. (Buenos Aires: Circulo Militar, 1992), 310, 311, 337–39, 352; Leon G. Campbell, "The Army of Peru and the Túpac Amaru Revolt, 1780–1783," *Hispanic American Historical Review* 56, no. 1 (1979): 45–46; Helg, *Liberty*, 100–105; Kuethe, *Military Reform*, 29–30, 178; Homero Martínez Montero, "El Soldado Negro," in Carvalho Neto, *El negro uruguayo*, 272; Alfonso Múnera, *El fracaso de la nación: Región, clase y raza en el Caribe colombiano (1717–1821)* (Bogotá: El Áncora Editores, 1998), 83, 94–96; Stoan, *Pablo Morillo*, 17; Thibaud, *República en armas*, 28.

45. Childs, *Aponte*, 87.

46. Bowser, *African Slave*, 3–4, 8–10; Matthew Restall, "Black Conquistadors: Armed Africans in Early Spanish America," *The Americas* 57, no. 2 (2000): 167–205.

47. Bowser, *African Slave*, 97–98, 196–97; Jane Landers, "Transforming Bondsmen into Vassals: Arming the Slaves in Colonial Spanish America," in Brown and Morgan, *Arming Slaves*, 120–45.

48. Klein, "The Colored Militia," 20; Jane Landers, "Africans in the Spanish Colonies," *Historical Archaeology* 31, no. 1 (1997): 89; Landers, *Black Society*, 206–7. The situation in the Spanish Caribbean and the northern borderlands with regard to using slaves in the military may have been different from Spanish South America.

49. AGN-B, Colonia, Milicias y Marina, tomo 13, 201–3; Sales de Bohigas, *Sobre esclavos*, 134.

50. Childs, *Aponte*, 24–25.

51. Halperín-Donghi, *Politics*, 132.

52. "Razón de las cantidades que ha suplido el cabildo de los fondos públicos por el valor de 25 esclavos," AGN-BA, Hacienda, leg. 141, exp. 3623, IX–34–8–3; Andrews, *Afro-Argentines*, 43, 94–95; Bernand, "La población negra," 123; Carvalho Neto, *El negro uru-*

guayo, 146–52; Klaus Gallo, *Great Britain and Argentina: From Invasion to Recognition, 1806–26* (Basingstoke, U.K.: Palgrave, 2001); Halperín-Donghi, *Politics*, 132; Martínez Montero, "El soldado negro," 273; Sales de Bohigas, *Sobre esclavos*, 132–34.

53. Sales de Bohigas, *Sobre esclavos*, 134.

54. Marixa Lasso, "Haiti as an Image of Popular Republicanism in Caribbean Colombia: Cartagena Province (1811–1828)," in Geggus, *The Impact of the Haitian Revolution*, 187.

CHAPTER 2: SERVING THE KING IN VENEZUELA AND NEW GRANADA

1. For the concept of loyalty to the "father king," see Timothy E. Anna, "Spain and the Breakdown of the Imperial Ethos: The Problem of Equality," *Hispanic American Historical Review* 62, no. 2 (1982): 254–55, 267–68, 271.

2. The term comes, of course, from Benedict Anderson, *Imagined Communities: Reflections on the Origin and Spread of Nationalism*, 2nd ed. (London: Verso, 1991).

3. "Causa criminal mandada seguir por el Sr. Governador al Sargento Mayor de Infanteria contra unos pardos que se atumultuaron en una pulpería, 1811," AHG-G, no. 3357; "Nombramiento de escribano hecho a favor del sargento 1° Garzón Antonio Tesillo, a fin de que actue como tal en la sumaria ejecutada contra los soldados del batallón Pardos, José Aguirre, Basilio Lozano, Francisco Santana Elizondo, 1815," AHG-G, no. 6688; ANE-Q, Milicias, caja 5, 1810–14, exp. 8; AGN-B, Archivo Restrepo, caja 6, fondo 1, vol. 10, fol. 341; Jaime E. Rodríguez O., *The Independence of Spanish America* (Cambridge: Cambridge University Press, 1998), 144–46.

4. Lynch, *Spanish American Revolutions*, 236–37, 239–40. Clément Thibaud refers to this first stage of the revolutionary wars as a "war between cities." See Thibaud, *Repúblicas en armas*, 104.

5. Brian R. Hamnett, "Popular Insurrection and Royalist Reaction: Colombian Regions, 1810–1823," in *Reform and Insurrection in Bourbon New Granada and Peru*, ed. John R. Fisher, Allan J. Kuethe, and Anthony McFarlane (Baton Rouge: Louisiana State University Press, 1990), 303; Helg, *Liberty*, chap. 4; Aline Helg, "The Limits of Equality: Free People of Colour and Slaves during the First Independence of Cartagena, Colombia, 1810–15," *Slavery and Abolition* 20, no. 2 (1999): 8, 19–20, 22; Múnera, *El fracaso*, 173–78, 183–86, 193–201, 209–10; Rodríguez, *Independence*, 155.

6. AGN-B, Colonia, Negros y esclavos, Cundinamarca, tomo 11, 385–93.

7. Fernando Jurado Noboa, *Esclavitud en la costa pacífica: Iscuandé, Tumaco, Barbacoas y Esmeraldas, siglos XVI al XIX* (Quito: Ediciones Abya-Yala, 1990), 379.

8. Thibaud, *Repúblicas en armas*, 48–50.

9. Lynch, *Spanish American Revolutions*, 195–96; McKinley, *Pre-Revolutionary Caracas*, 151–53, 159–61; Stoan, *Pablo Morillo*, 31.

10. Domínguez, *Insurrection*, 157–60, 174, 238; Lynch, *Spanish American Revolutions*, 196–98; Stoan, *Pablo Morillo*, 32. Patriots in Cartagena also continued to support slavery, not viewing abolition as a necessary step on the road to democracy. See Helg, *Liberty*, 140.

11. Domínguez, *Insurrection*, 176–77; Stoan, *Pablo Morillo*, 36.

12. Quoted in Rodríguez, *Independence*, 85.

13. BN-B, libro 223, no. 727, 1–7, and libro 435, no. 1498, 43–54; Anna, "Spain and the Breakdown," 256–58, 260; José U. Martínez Carreras, "España y la abolición de la esclavitud durante el siglo XIX," in *Estudios sobre la abolición de la esclavitud*, ed. Francisco de Solano (Madrid: Consejo Superior de Investigaciones Científicas, 1986), 172; James F. King, "The Colored Castes and American Representation in the Cortes of Cádiz," *Hispanic American Historical Review* 33, no. 1 (1953): 33–64; Rodríguez, *Independence*, 83, 85–87.

14. Domínguez, *Insurrection*, 75, 174–76; John V. Lombardi, "Los esclavos negros en las guerras venezolanas de la independencia," *Cultura Universitaria* 93 (Oct.–Dec. 1966): 155; Stoan, *Pablo Morillo*, 36.

15. To the governor of Guayana, Sept. 28, 1813, AGI, Caracas 385.

16. Lombardi, "Los esclavos negros," 157.

17. ANE-Q, Esclavos, caja 21, 1811–18, exp. 4; AGN-B, Archivo Restrepo, caja 6, fondo 1, vol. 10, fols. 48–50; "Criminales contra los negros del Chaparral por insubordinación a sus amos," AGB-B, Archivo Anexo, Esclavos, tomo 2, 287–91; Germán Colmenares, "Popayán: Continuidad y discontinuidad regionales en la época de la independencia," in *América Latina en la época de Simón Bolívar: La formación de las economías nacionales y los intereses económicas europeos 1800–1850*, ed. Reinhard Liehr (Berlin: Colloquium Verlar, 1989), 160; Hamnett, "Popular Insurrection," 304, 307.

18. Quoted in Hamnet, "Popular Insurrection," 313.

19. For details of the slave unrest in New Granada, see Cabildo of Barbacoas to viceroy, Feb. 5, 1812, AGN-B, Archivo Restrepo, caja 6, fondo 1, vol. 10, fol. 168; letter of Francisco Gregorio de Angulo, Fernando de Angulo, and Nicolás Montestruque, May 10, 1812, AGN-B, Archivo Restrepo, caja 6, fondo 1, vol. 10, fols. 185–87; letter to viceroy, Apr. 13, 1813, AGN-B, Archivo Restrepo, caja 6, fondo 1, vol. 10, fols. 215–17; Juan de Samano to Toribio Montes, Feb. 7, 1813, AGN-B, Archivo Restrepo, caja 9, fondo 1, vol. 25, fols. 393–95; Hamnett, "Popular Insurrection," 308, 312–13, 325; Jurado Noboa, *Esclavitud en la costa pacífica*, 380.

20. AGN-C, Revolución y Gran Colombia, Ilustres Próceres, José Antonio Andújar, letra A, tomo 4, fol. 287; "Francisco Rodrigues Illada reclamando un esclavo alistado en el batallón milicias," AANH-C, Civiles-Esclavos, tomo 1812-RV, exp. 3.

21. Aline Helg has written that slaves were drafted in "limited" numbers in Caribbean New Granada. See Helg, *Liberty*, 153.

22. AGN-C, Revolución y Gran Colombia, Ilustres Próceres, Capt. Fernando Suárez, letra S, tomo 79, fol. 269; AGN-C, Revolución y Gran Colombia, Ilustres Próceres, Julián Carreño, letra C, tomo 16, fol. 313; AGN-C, Revolución y Gran Colombia, Ilustres Próceres, Juan Escalona, letra E, tomo 25, fol. 264.

23. John V. Lombardi, "Los esclavos en la legislación republicana de Venezuela," *Boletín Histórico, Federación John Boulton* 13 (Jan. 1962): 47–48; Lombardi, "Los esclavos negros," 155–57; Stoan, *Pablo Morillo*, 38; Thibaud, *Repúblicas en armas*, 97–99.

24. Manuel Vicente Magallanes, *Historia política de Venezuela*, 7th ed. (Caracas: Univer-

sidad Central de Venezuela, Ediciones de la Biblioteca, 1990), 213–14; Stoan, *Pablo Morillo*, 38–39.

25. Monteverde to Ministro de Gracia y Justicia, no. 11, Oct. 24, 1812, AGI, Caracas 459.

26. "Informe del Ayuntamiento de Caracas," Oct. 3, 1812, AGI, Caracas 62; see also "Escrito sobre el sistema de libertad e independencia de las Provincias de Venezuela," AGI, Caracas 823.

27. See, for example, "Exposición de Simona Nadal al Capitán General solicitando esclavo que le fué reclutado por las fuerzas reales," San Carlos, Feb. 5, 1813, AGN-C, La Colonia, Gobernación y Capitanía General (hereafter cited as Gob. y Cap. Gen.), tomo 232, fol. 320.

28. "Representación de varios hacendados," La Guaira, Aug. 4, 1812, AGN-C, La Colonia, Gob. y Cap. Gen., tomo 220, fol. 100; "Oficio de José Bernardo Pérez, para Domingo Monteverde," San Mateo, Aug. 10, 1812, AGN-C, La Colonia, Gob. y Cap. Gen, fol. 152; "Comunicación de Francisco Zerberis para el Comandante General," La Guaira, Aug. 28, 1812, AGN-C, La Colonia, Gob. y Cap. Gen., tomo 221, fol. 67; "Sobre conato de alzamiento de negros en la costa de Choroní," Caracas, Mar. 12, 1813, AGN-C, La Colonia, Gob. y Cap. Gen., tomo 235, fol. 111; "Informe del atentado que hubo al sublevarse veinte negros esclavos del valle de Choroní, los cuales fueron aplacados por la tropa," Caracas, Mar. 31, 1813, AGN-C, La Colonia, Gob. y Cap. Gen., tomo 236, fol. 309; Lynch, *Spanish American Revolutions*, 198.

29. José Francisco Heredia to Sec. de Estado y del Despacho Universal de Gracia y Justicia, Feb. 26, 1813, AGI, Caracas 62. See also Domínguez, *Insurrection*, 177; Lynch, *Spanish American Revolutions*, 200; Stoan, *Pablo Morillo*, 43–44.

30. Magallanes, *Historia política*, 238; John Lynch, *Simón Bolívar: A Life* (New Haven: Yale University Press, 2006), chap. 4; Lynch, *Spanish American Revolutions*, 203–4.

31. Quoted in Lynch, *Spanish American Revolutions*, 198.

32. Ibid., 204–5.

33. AGN-C, Revolución y Gran Colombia, Ilustres Próceres, José Antonio Mújica, letra M, tomo 58, fol. 149; Thibaud, *Repúblicas en armas*, 137.

34. Letters of the governor of Maracaibo, Don Pedro Ruiz de Porras, May 22 and June 18, 1812, AGI, Caracas 62; solicitations of Agustín Amaya, June 10, 1813, Isidro Araujo, Dec. 3, 1812, and José Fermin Sola, Oct. 23, 1813, AGI, Caracas 385.

35. Thibaud, *Repúblicas en armas*, 169–73.

36. Richard Graham, *Independence in Latin America*, 2nd ed. (New York: McGraw-Hill, 1994), 92; Lynch, *Spanish American Revolutions*, 206; Thibaud, *Repúblicas en armas*, 169–73; Stoan, *Pablo Morillo*, 51–57.

37. "Testimonio de la instancia de D. Juan Bautista Mendía, sobre que se le abonen dos criados que murieron en la Guerra, veinte y ocho mulas, y tres juntas de bueyes que franqueo para el servicio," AANH-C, Civiles-Esclavos, tomo 1815-LM, exp. 5.

38. "Expediente obrado a instancia de D. Juan de la Cruz Mena reclamando de la Reales cajas el valor de 27 esclavos de su propiedad . . . ," AANH-C, Civiles-Esclavos, tomo 1816-LM, exp. 11.

39. "El Señor Candelario Espinosa cobrando al Estado el valor de su esclavo, Silvestre,

que tomó las armas en defensa de la República," AANH-C, Civiles-Esclavos, tomo 1829-ACEF, exp. 3.

40. Tomás Pérez Tenreiro, *José Tomás Boves: Primera lanza del rey* (Caracas: La Oficina Técnica del Ministerio de la Defensa, 1969), 25.

41. Gutiérrez Azopardo, *Historia del negro*, 76.

42. Juan Vicente González, *José Félix Ribas: Biografía* (Buenos Aires: Ministerio de Educación Nacional de Venezuela, 1946), 85–87, 94–96; Lester D. Langley, *The Americas in the Age of Revolution, 1750–1850* (New Haven: Yale University Press, 1996), 188–89; Stoan, *Pablo Morillo*, 53. For Boves's excesses, see also Daniel Florencio O'Leary, *Bolívar and the War of Independence*, trans. and ed. Robert F. McNerney Jr. (Austin: University of Texas Press, 1970), 59–60, 63, 69–70.

43. Level de Goda to Sec° de Estado y del Despacho de la Gobernación de Ultramar, Feb. 2, 1814, AGI, Caracas 459; Ayuntamiento de Caracas, Sept. 19, 1814, AGI, Caracas 62.

44. Ayuntamiento de Caracas, Sept. 19, 1814, AGI, Caracas 62; letter of Antonio Sainz, May 12, 1814, AGI, Caracas 136.

45. Morillo to Sec^to de Estado y del Desp° Universal de Indias, May 23, 1815, AGI, Caracas 109.

46. "Sumaria información promovida contra Juan Izaguirre por propagar ideas de rebeldía entre los esclavos," Maracay, Apr. 19, 1815, AGN-C, Archivo de Aragua, tomo 75, 1815, fol. 78.

47. Morillo to Sec^to de Estado y del Desp° Universal de Indias; "Expediente obrado a instancia de D. Juan de la Cruz Mena reclamando de la Reales Cajas el valor de 27 esclavos de su propiedad"; Stoan, *Pablo Morillo*, 75, 112.

48. Manifesto of Antonio Sainz to the European Spaniards, May 12, 1814, AGI, Caracas 136; Request for Medal, 1814, AGI, Caracas 386.

49. "Juan José Ledesma, esclavo de Don Pedro Ledesma, solicitando se le de la libertad por haber militado en el Ejército de Su Majes.," 1815-LM, AANH-C, Civiles-Esclavos, exp. 1; "José Geronimo Ramires, esclavo de doña María Carreño, solicitando se le de la libertad ofrecida por haber militado en el ejército de Su Majestad," AANH-C, Civiles-Esclavos, 1815-R, leg. 19, no. 23, exp. 3.

50. "Libertad de Ramón Piñero, esclavo de Dr. D. Juan de Roxas," AANH-C, Civiles-Esclavos, tomo 1815-OP, exp. 5.

51. Mariano Antonio Rodallega, June/July 1816, ANE-Q, Esclavos, caja 21, 1811–18, exp. 10; Salmoral, *Sangre*, 191–92n223.

52. "D. Manuel García, Capitan de la compañía de Cazadores del Regimiento de Sagunto pretendiendo la libertad del esclavo Juan Nepomuceno de los bienes de Conde de Tovar," AANH-C, Civiles-Esclavos, tomo 1815-GHI, exp. 2; "Juan José Ledesma, esclavo de Don Pedro Ledesma, solicitando se le de la libertad"; "José Geronimo Ramires, esclavo de Doña María Carreño, solicitando se le de la libertad."

53. AGN-B, Archivo Anexo, Esclavos, tomo 3, 187–89.

54. Request for royal protection by Santiago Sanse, Aug. 12, 1814, AGI, Caracas 386; case of José Belem, Oct. 31, 1814, AGI, Caracas 386; letter of José Manuel Fernández to Captain General of Cuba, May 2, 1815, AGI, Caracas 825.

55. Complaints about Morillo, AGI, 1815, Caracas 19.

56. "Don Mateo Montiel reclamando un esclavo de su propiedad que se había profugado de su poder y se haya en el Real Servicio," AANH-C, Civiles-Esclavos, tomo 1816-LM, exp. 8.

57. Lynch, *Spanish American Revolutions,* 207–9; Stoan, *Pablo Morillo,* 66–68, 71–72, 74, 81–83.

58. Jurado Noboa, *Esclavitud en la costa pacífica,* 385–86.

59. Emeterio Ureña to Gov. of Trinidad, Jan. 20, 1813, AGI, Caracas 122; Stoan, *Pablo Morillo,* 50, 73.

60. "El C° Sindico Procurado General solicita la libertad de varios esclavos . . . , 1815," BN-B, tomo 331, no. 987, 114–25; Francisco Gerónimo Cicero, slave of Hacienda Saldaña, BN-B, tomo 329, no. 962, 103–6; see also Lynch, *Spanish American Revolutions,* 241.

61. Relación of Juan del Corral, AGN-B, Archivo Restrepo, caja 4, fondo 1, vol. 7, fols. 368–71, 377–425, 430–31; Hamnett, "Popular Insurrection," 309–10.

62. Lynch, *Spanish American Revolutions,* 224.

63. *Boletín de Cartagena,* Apr. 18, 1815; "Lino Rodrigues, sargento pide se le declare libre de servidumbre por sus servicios puestados a la República," AANH-C, Civiles-Esclavos, tomo 1825-BCGJMPRT, exp. 7; AGN-C, Revolución y Gran Colombia, Ilustres Próceres, Félix Bastardo, letra B, tomo 9, fol. 101.

64. José Cevallos to Secret de Estado y del Dept Universal de Indias, July 22, 1815, AGI, Caracas 109.

65. "Plan descriptivo de seguridad para el Istmo de Panamá que propone el Dr. D. Juan José Cabarcas, June 2, 1814," AGI, Santa Fe 668.

66. Harold A. Bierck Jr., "The Struggle for Abolition in Gran Colombia," *Hispanic American Historical Review* 33, no. 3 (1953): 365.

CHAPTER 3: FIGHTING FOR THE *PATRIA* IN THE RÍO DE LA PLATA

1. AGN-BA, Solicitudes Militares (hereafter cited as Sol. Mil.), 1815, X–8–7–4.

2. "Lorenzo Villanueva, pardo esclavo de Don Juan Antonio de Sta. Coloma, solicitando que se le otorgue papel de venta," 1812, AGN-BA, Admin., leg. 29, exp. 997, IX–23–8–3.

3. Lynch, *Spanish American Revolutions,* 42–46, 49–58.

4. José María Salazar to Gabriel de Ciscar, no. 76, June 30, 1810, AGI, Buenos Aires 156.

5. In the records, the words "battalion" and "regiment" were used interchangeably, which, together with the different names used for the same unit, creates some confusion.

6. AGN-BA, Contaduría, 1810–1813, caja 22, III-4–2–7; AGN-BA, Lista de Revista, no. 22, III-44–2–7; AGN-BA, Guerra, Ejército Auxiliar del Perú, 1812, X–3–10–3 and X–3–10–4; AGN-BA, Sol. Mil., 1812, X–6–5–7; copy of letter enclosed with Elío to Ministerio de Estado, Feb. 18, 1812, AGI, Buenos Aires 317; Argentina, Senado de la Nación, *Biblioteca de mayo: Colección de obras y documentos para la historia Argentina. Guerra de la*

independencia (Buenos Aires: Imprenta del Congreso de la Nación, 1963), 14:12927. Information about the activities of the free black units can also be found in Andrews, *Afro-Argentines*, 118–20; Bernand, "La población negra," 125; Halperín-Donghi, *Politics*, 8, 156–57; Francisco Morrone, "La participacion del negro en el ejército," in *El negro en la Argentina: Presencia y negación*, ed. Dina V. Picotti (Buenos Aires: Editores de América Latina, 2001), 357; *Cronología militar argentina 1806–1980* (Buenos Aires: Editorial CLIO, S.A., 1983), 23, 24, 31.

7. *Gaceta de Buenos Aires*, July 19, 1810; AGN-BA, Sol. Mil, 1810–13, X–35–7–6.

8. Halperín-Donghi, *Politics*, 95, 156, 167, 188, 190–226, 262.

9. AGN-BA, Representantes de la Junta, Castelli y Belgrano, Ejército del Norte y Banda Oriental, X–3–2–4; AGN-BA, Guerra, Ejército Sitiador B. Oriental, 1812–14, X–7–9–7.

10. "La morena Juliana García, esclava que fué de Don Pedro García, reclamando su libertad," 1818, AGN-BA, Admin., leg. 33, exp. 1179, IX–23–8–7.

11. AHPBA-LP, Trib. de Cuentas, Civiles y Militares, 1817 and 1818, 14–1–8–1022; AGN-BA, Guerra, Sol. Mil., 1812, X–6–5–7; copy of letter enclosed with Elío to Ministerio de Estado.

12. Argentina, *Biblioteca de mayo*, 14:12658.

13. José María Salazar to Gabriel de Ciscar, nos. 127, 93, 109, and 128, July 16, July 22, Aug. 5, and Aug. 17, 1810, AGI, Buenos Aires 156; Salazar to Secret° de Estado y del Despacho Universal de Marina, nos. 183, 52, 63, and 128, Nov. 3, 1810, Mar. 8, 1811, Mar. 12, 1811, and May 19, 1811, AGI, Buenos Aires 156; Salazar to Ministerio de Marina, no. 28, Sept. 18, 1811, AGI, Estado 79; Oficio of José María Salazar, no. 37, May 22, 1811, AGI, Estado 87; AGN-BA, Representantes de la Junta, Castelli y Belgrano, Ejército del Norte y Banda Oriental, X–3–2–4; AGN-BA, Guerra, Sol. Civiles y Mil., 1813, X–6–9–1.

14. Salazar to Naval Ministry, no. 31, Nov. 19, 1811, AGI, Estado 79; "Memoria del Sr. General D. Nicolás de Vedia," *Boletín Histórico, Estado Mayor General del Ejército* (Montevideo) 96–97 (1963): 106–7.

15. AGN-BA, Sol. Mil., 1820, X–11–9–2; "La morena Juliana García, esclava que fué de Don Pedro García, reclamanado su libertad."

16. Vigodet to Junta Gubernativa of Buenos Aires, Nov. 28, 1811, Gobierno to Vigodet, Dec. 28, 1811, AGN-BA, Gobierno, Correspondencia del Gobierno de B° Aˢ con Elío y Vigodet, 1810–1814, X–1–5–10; Elío to Doña Carlota Joaquina de Borbón, Aug. 1811, AGI, Buenos Aires 98; *Suplemento a la Gaceta de Buenos Aires*, Jan. 31, 1812; *Gaceta Extraordinaria de Buenos Aires*, Feb. 15, 1812; José Oscar Frigerio, "Con sangre de negros se edificó nuestra independencia," *Todo Es Historia* 250 (1988): 55; "República Oriental del Uruguay, Estado Mayor General del Ejército, Sección 'Historia y Archivo,'" *Boletín Histórico, Estado Mayor General del Ejército*, 100–103 (1964): 63.

17. AGN-BA, Gobierno, Feb. 1812, X–6–7–5.

18. Artigas to Supreme Government of the United Provinces, Mar. 13, 1812, AGN-BA, Guerra, Sol. Mil., 1812, X–6–5–6; Lynch, *Spanish American Revolutions*, 96–97.

19. AGN-BA, Guerra, Ejército Sitiador B. Oriental, 1812–14, X–7–9–7. Francisco Acuña de Figueroa's diary includes a long poem that makes several references to Soler's black soldiers during the second siege of Montevideo. Acuña de Figeroa, "Diario histórico

del sitio de Montevideo en los años 1812–13 y 14," Colección de Manuscritos Pablo Blanco Acevedo, Casa de Lavalleja, Montevideo, Uruguay.

20. Carranza to governing junta, Jan. 2, 1812, AGN-BA, Guerra, Sol. Mil., 1812, X–6–5–7; "Doña Luisa Bossorino reclamando al negro José Pérez," 1822, AGN-BA, Admin., leg. 34, exp. 1223, IX–23–9–1.

21. AGN-BA, Guerra, Rescate de Esclavos, 1813–17, X–43–6–7; AGN-BA, Sol. Mil., 1812, X–6–5–7; AGN-BA, Sol. Civiles y Mil., 1812, X–6–6–13.

22. AGN-BA, Guerra, Sol. Mil., 1812, X–6–5–6.

23. Rondeau to executive, Dec. 14, 1813, AGN-BA, Guerra, Sol. Civiles y Mil., 1813, X–6–9–1.

24. AGN-BA, Sol. Mil., 1815, X–8–7–6.

25. AGN-BA, Sol. Mil., 1817, X–9–7–10. See also Ayuntamiento to Regency, no. 75, Oct. 30, 1813, AGI, Estado 79; "Sitio de Montevideo, 1° de enero a 21 de agosto, 1813," AGN-BA, Guerra, X–23–2–5, 1811–16; Argentina, Biblioteca de mayo, XIV: 14:12737, 12739, 12740.

26. AGN-BA, Sol. Civiles y Mil., 1812, X–6–6–12; AGN-BA, Guerra, Sol. Mil., 1812, X–6–5–7.

27. "Sitio de Montevideo, octubre a abril, 1812–1813," AGN-BA, Guerra, X–23–2–5; "Relación que hace el Tte. Coronel Miguel E. Soler de la parte que le cupo al Regimiento de su mando (no. 6) en la toma de Cerrito," Jan. 16, 1813, AGN-BA, Guerra, X–23–2–5; "Refutación de Rondeau al parte del Tnte. Coronel M.E. Soler, Jefe de Regimiento no. 6," Jan. 26, 1813, AGN-BA, Guerra, X–23–2–5; "Memorias de Dámaso de Uriburu," in Argentina, Biblioteca de mayo, 1:679; Gaceta Ministerial del Gobierno de Buenos Ayres, June 30, 1813; Cronología militar, 37; Vicente Osvaldo Cutolo, Nuevo diccionario biográfico argentino (1750–1930) (Buenos Aires: Editorial ELCHE, 1985), 7:604–5; Pereda Valdés, El negro, 108–9; Ildefonso Pereda Valdés, Negros esclavos y negro libres: Esquema de una sociedad esclavista y aporte del negro en nuestra formación nacional (Montevideo: Imprenta "Gaceta Comercial," 1941), 120.

28. Halperín-Donghi, Politics, 166, 193, 248, and chap. 4. A critical view of the governments of the period and their policies toward slaves can be found in Maïté Klachko, "Le processus de destruction du système esclavagiste á Buenos Aires 1810–1860" (Master's thesis, Université de Paris X, Nanterre, 1996–97).

29. Argentina, Registro oficial de la república Argentina que comprende los documentos expedidos desde 1810 hasta 1872 (Buenos Aires: "La República," 1879), 1:168; Suplemento a la Gaceta Ministerial, May 29, 1812; Rafael M. Castellano Sáenz Cavia, "La abolición de la esclavitud en las Provincias Unidas del Río de la Plata (1810–1860)," Revista de Historia del Derecho (Buenos Aires) 9 (1981): 57, 85.

30. Argentina, Registro oficial, 1:171.

31. AGN-BA, Cuerpo de libertos, Compra de esclavos por el estado, 1812–14, III-37-3–22.

32. Argentina, Registro oficial, 1:179.

33. Argentina, Registro oficial, 1:194, 213, 253–54; Gazeta Ministerial del Gobierno de Buenos Aires, Dec. 29, 1813; Cutolo, Nuevo diccionario, 1:323–24.

34. AGN-BA, Guerra, Rescate de Esclavos, 1813–17, X–43–6–7; Argentina, *Registro oficial*, 1:221; Castellano Sáenz Cavia, "La abolición," 90–95; Frigerio, "Con sangre," 57–60.

35. *Cronología militar*, 40–41; Bowles to Dixon, Nov. 18, 1813, enclosure with Dixon to Croker, no. 117, Dec. 1, 1813, ADM 1/22.

36. Argentina, *Registro oficial*, 1:249–50; AGN-BA, Guerra, Rescate de Esclavos, 1813–17, X–43–6–7; Castellano Sáenz Cavia, "La abolición," 97–98.

37. AGN-BA, Guerra, Rescate de Esclavos, 1813–17, X–43–6–7; Castellano Sáenz Cavia, "La abolición," 99–102; Klachko, "Le processus," 108.

38. AGN-BA, Policía, Ordenes Superiores, no. 137, tomo 1, X–32–10–1.

39. Argentina, *Registro oficial*, 1:328.

40. AGN-BA, Guerra, Rescate de Esclavos, 1813–17, X–43–6–7.

41. Argentina, *Registro oficial*, 1:378–79, 382, 383; Castellano Sáenz Cavia, "La abolición," 104–5, 107.

42. Argentina, *Registro oficial*, 1:390–92; Castellano Sáenz Cavia, "La abolición," 107–8.

43. Argentina, *Biblioteca de mayo*, 14:12421–23; Argentina, *Registro oficial*, 1:393–94.

44. Argentina, *Biblioteca de mayo*, 14:12431–33; Castellano Sáenz Cavia, "La abolición," 108.

45. AGN-BA, Guerra, 1811–16, X–3–2–3; AGN-BA, Sol. Civiles y Mil., 1813, X–6–9–1; AGN-BA, Rescate de Esclavos, 1813–17, X–43–6–7; "Manuel Garmendia, moreno esclavo sobre su libertad," AGN-BA, Admin., leg. 33, exp. 1142, IX–23–8–7; Liliana M. Crespi, "Negros apresados en operaciones de corso durante la guerra con el Brasil (1825–1828)," *Temas de África y Asia* 2 (1993): 112–13.

46. AGN-BA, Contaduria, 1810–13, caja 22, III–44–2–7; AGN-BA, Guerra, Rescate de Esclavos, 1813–17, X–43–6–7; AGN-BA, Guerra, Rescate de Esclavos Certificados, 1813–17, X–43–6–8; AGN-BA, Protocolos, Escribano Juan Cortés, registro 7, 1813, Escribano Narciso de Iranzuaga, registro 4, 1813, Escribano Ignocensio Agrelo, 1813–14, 51–52; *Gazeta Ministerial del Gobierno de Buenos-Ayres*, June 30, 1813.

47. *Gazeta Ministerial del Gobierno de Buenos Ayres*, Sept. 29, 1813; AGN-BA, Guerra, Sol. Civiles y Mil., 1813, X–6–9–2; Andrews, *Afro-Argentines*, 116.

48. "1816–1817, Contribución de fincas, Comprobantes de pago," AGN-BA, Contribución Directa, 1813–17, III–35–4–5; AGN-BA, Guerra, Rescate de Esclavos, 1813–17, X–43–6–7; AGN-BA, Sol. Civiles y Mil., 1816, X–9–2–4.

49. AGN-BA, Guerra, Rescate de Esclavos, 1813–17, X–43–6–7.

50. AGN-BA, Sol. Mil., 1815, X–8–7–4.

51. See below, 61.

52. AGN-BA, Guerra, Rescate de Esclavos Certificados, 1813–17, X–43–6–8.

53. AGN-BA, Guerra, Rescate de Esclavos, 1813–17, X–43–6–7; AGN-BA, Solicitudes, Protección de Esclavos, 1816, X–22–1–2.

54. For a list of slaves taken and the application of part of their value to various taxes, see AGN-BA, Contribución Directa, 1813–17, III–35–4–5.

55. "Instancias: Sobre esclavos mandados presentar por el ultimo bando de la materia," AGN-BA, Hacienda, leg. 146, exp. 3831, IX–34–8–8; "Dª Manuela Tadea Pinazo solicitando la entrega de los esclavos europeos," AGN-BA, Admin., 1816–1817, leg. 32, exp. 1123,

IX–23–8–6; "Doña Clemencia Fernández solicitando la entrega de un esclavo," AGN-BA, Admin., 1814–1815, leg. 31, exp. 1064, IX–23–8–5; AGN-BA, Sol. Mil, 1815, X–8–7–6; AGN-BA, Sol. Mil., 1817, X–9–7–10.

56. AGN-BA, Sol. Mil., 1815, X–8–7–6.

57. AGN-BA, Guerra, Rescate de Esclavos, 1813–17, X–43–6–7; AGN-BA, Guerra, 1811–16, X–3–2–3; AGN-BA, Sol. Mil., 1815, X–8–7–4.

58. AGN-BA, Guerra, Rescate de Esclavos, 1813–17, X–43–6–7; AGN-BA, Guerra, Rescate de Esclavos Certificados, 1813–17, X–43–6–8; AGN-BA, Rescate de Esclavos, Listas y Ordenes del Pago, 1816–17, X–43–6–9; AGN-BA, Tribunal de Cuentas, Tomas de Razón, Esclavos Rescatados, Boletos, 1813–17, X–41–4–5; AGN-BA, Contribución Directa, 1813–17, III–35–4–5; AGN-BA, Guerra, Sol. Civiles y Mil., 1813, X–6–9–2; AGN-BA, Sol. Mil., 1820, X–11–9–2; *Gazeta Ministerial del Gobierno de Buenos Ayres*, Sept. 7, 1814.

59. AGN-BA, Guerra, Rescate de Esclavos, 1813–17, X–43–6–7; AGN-BA, Solicitudes, Protección de Esclavos, 1816, X–22–1–2.

60. AHPBA-LP, Tribunal de Cuentas, 1813, Civiles y Militares, 14–1–4–1018.

61. Bowles to Rear Admiral Dixon, Sept. 14, 1813, enclosure with Dixon to Croker, no. 111, ADM 1/22.

62. AGN-BA, Guerra, Sol. Civiles y Mil., 1813, X–6–9–2.

63. AGN-BA, Guerra, Sol. Civiles y Mil., 1813, X–6–9–2; AGN-BA, Sol. Civiles y Mil., 1816, X–9–2–4; Holmberg to Viara, Sept. 28, 1814, AGN-BA, Guerra, 1811–16, X–3–2–3.

64. Argentina, Comisión Nacional del Centenario, *Documentos del Archivo de San Martín* (Buenos Aires: Imprenta de Coni Hermanos, 1910), 2:28.

65. Salazar to Secretario de Estado y del Despacho Universal de Marina, no. 292, Dec. 12, 1811, AGI, Buenos Aires, 156.

66. Viana to S.P.E. of the United Provinces of Río de la Plata, AGN-BA, Guerra, Sol. Civiles y Mil., 1813, X–6–9–2.

67. AGN-BA, Sol. Mil., 1818, X–35–7–9, and 1824, X–13–4–8; *Cronología militar*, 50; Lynch, *Spanish American Revolutions*, 122, 123.

68. AGN-BA, Sol. Mil. 1815, X–8–7–5.

69. Andrews, *Afro-Argentines*, 126–27.

70. Quoted in José Luis Masini, *La esclavitud negra en Mendoza: Época independiente* (Mendoza: Talleres Gráficos d'Accurzio, 1962), 18–19. See also Argentina, *Documentos*, 1:539; "Antecedentes y organización del Ejército de los Andes," in Argentina, *Biblioteca de mayo*, 16, part 1: 14215.

71. John Miller, *Memoirs of General Miller, in the Service of the Republic of Peru*, 2nd ed. (London: Longman, Rees, Orme, Brown, and Green, 1829), 2:427; Bernand, "La población negra," 129.

72. Lynch, *Spanish American Revolutions*, 138–40; Irene S. Ricoy, "San Martín y la formación de batallones de negros en el Ejército de los Andes," *Boletín Informativo, Dirección de Estudios Históricos, Comando General del Ejército* (Buenos Aires) 7–8 (1973): 120–22.

73. Argentina, *Documentos*, 2:232–34; AGN-BA, Guerra, 1811–16, X–3–2–3; San Martín to Viana, Feb. 4, 1815, AGN-BA, Ejército de los Andes, 1814–15, X–4–2–5; Masini, *La esclavitud*, 12–13, 18–20; Ricoy, "San Martín," 123.

74. San Martín to Balcarce, July 6 and Dec. 11, 1815, and San Martín to Director Supremo de Estado, Sept. 27, 1815, AGN-BA, Ejército de los Andes, 1814–15, X–4–2–5; San Martín to Sec. de Guerra, Feb. 13, 1816, AGN-BA, Ejército de los Andes, 1816, X–4–2–6; Masini, *La esclavitud*, 29–31, 44; "Antecedentes y organización del Ejército de los Andes," in Argentina, *Biblioteca de mayo*, 16, part 1: 14215.

75. Lynch, *Spanish American Revolutions*, 61, 68–69.

76. Gerónimo Espejo, "El paso de los Andes: Crónica histórica de las operaciones del Ejército de los Andes para la restauración de Chile in 1817," in Argentina, *Biblioteca de mayo*, 16, part 1: 14017–18; Víctor Barrionuevo Imposti, *Los esclavos de San Luis en el Ejército de los Andes y otros documentos sanmartinianos* (Villa Dolores: Tallares Gráficos "Democracia," 1947), [p. 4]; Frigerio, "Con sangre," 63–66; Masini, *La esclavitud*, 21, 25.

77. Barrionuevo Imposti, *Los esclavos*, [5–6].

78. O'Higgins to Sec. de Estado en Depto de Guerra, Sept. 14, 1816, AGN-BA, Ejército de los Andes, 1816, X–4–2–7; Argentina, *Documentos*, 4:520, 527, 539; Masini, *La esclavitud*, 21–22, 24; Ricoy, "San Martín," 125–26.

79. Quoted in Masini, *La esclavitud*, 30.

80. Argentina, *Documentos*, 2:206–7, 211.

81. "Antecedentes y organización del Ejército de los Andes," in Argentina, *Biblioteca de mayo*, 16, part 1: 14222–23, 14229; San Martín to Sec. de Estado, November 9 and 14, 1816, AGN-BA, Ejército de los Andes, 1816, X–4–2–7.

82. Castellano Sáenz Cavia gives slightly different figures: Mendoza supplied 264 recruited and 6 donated slaves worth a total of 62,875 pesos, while San Juan provided 233 slaves worth 73,426 pesos. See Castellano Sáenz Cavia, "La abolición," 103. For the names, owners, and values of the slaves taken in San Luis, see Barrionuevo Imposti, *Los esclavos*, [7–9].

83. San Martín to Sec. de Estado, Nov. 9, 1816, AGN-BA, Ejército de los Andes, 1816, X–4–2–7; Argentina, *Documentos*, 2:543–44; Andrews, *Afro-Argentines*, 117; Masini, *La esclavitud*, 23–28, 32–34.

84. Barrionuevo Imposti, *Los esclavos*, [4].

85. The sources differ as to the supposed punishment for captured slaves. See Espejo, "El paso," 14038; Sales de Bohigas, *Sobre esclavos*, 76.

86. Bowles to Croker, Secret no. 21, Jan. 10, 1817, ADM 1/23; Morrone, "La participación," 356.

CHAPTER 4: CHANGING LOYALTIES IN THE NORTH

1. José Antonio Páez, *Autobiografía del General José Antonio Páez* (Caracas: Petróleos de Venezuela, 1990), 1:208–10; AGN-C, Revolución y Gran Colombia, Ilustres Próceres, Letra C, Pedro Camejo, tomo 15, fol. 81; Vicente Dávila, *Diccionario biográfico de ilustres próceres de la independencia suramericana* (Caracas: Imprenta Bolívar, 1924–26), 1:62.

2. Rebecca Earle, "Popular Participation in the Wars of Independence in New Granada," in *Independence and Revolution in Spanish America: Perspectives and Problems*, ed. Anthony McFarlane and Eduardo Posada-Carbó (London: Institute of Latin American Studies, 1999), 88–89, 90–101; Lynch, *Spanish American Revolutions*, 212.

3. AGN-B, Colonia, Negros y Esclavos, Magdalena, tomo 1, 233–35; AGN-B, Archivo Anexo, Guerra y Marina, tomo 152, fol. 141; "Demanda promovida por José Manuel García contra Manuel Rizo para que le entregue siete esclavos," Maracay, Mar. 29, 1816, AGN-C, Archivo de Aragua, tomo 77, 1816, fol. 217; "Folio suelto sobre un decreto relacionado con el esclavo Ignacio García," AGN-C, Archivo de Aragua, tomo 78, 1816, fol. 308; "Justificación evacuada por Don Marcelo Feo," Turmero, May 14, 1819, AGN-C, Archivo de Aragua, tomo 83, 1819, fol. 26.

4. Quoted in J. L. Salcedo-Bastardo, *Bolívar: A Continent and its Destiny*, ed. and trans. Annella McDermott (Atlantic Highlands, NJ: Humanities Press International, 1977), 104.

5. Quoted in Rodríguez, *Independence*, 185–86. See also Gerhard Masur, *Simon Bolivar*, revised ed. (Albuquerque: University of New Mexico Press, 1969), 197–98.

6. Bolívar's animosity may have had a personal element. While in Jamaica, one of his slaves (who had been bribed by Spanish agents) tried to assassinate him. Lynch, *Simón Bolívar*, 96–97.

7. Vicente Lecuna, comp., and Harold A. Bierck Jr., ed., *Selected Writings of Bolívar*, trans. Lewis Bertrand (New York: The Colonial Press, 1951), 1:131.

8. "Francisco Cortés para el Capitán General," Puerto Cabello, July 24, 1817, AGN-C, La Colonia, Gob. y Cap. Gen. , tomo 294, fol. 253; Domínguez, *Insurrection*, 198; Lombardi, "Los esclavos en la legislación," 51; Lynch, *Spanish American Revolutions*, 213.

9. Thibaud, *Repúblicas en armas*, chap. 5, 338–40.

10. Charles Stuart Cochrane, *Journal of a Residence and Travels in Colombia, during the years 1823 and 1824* (London: Henry Colburn, 1825), 1:367; Earle, *Spain*, 107.

11. "Borrador para el Administrador de la Obra Pía de Chuao," La Guaira, Caracas, Apr. 13, 1817, AGN-C, La Colonia, Gob. y Cap. Gen., tomo 286, fol. 222; Juan Bautista Pardo, Sept. 21, 1817, AGN-B, Archivo Restrepo, caja 13, fondo 1, vol. 31, fol. 238.

12. AGN-B, Archivo Restrepo, caja 13, fondo 1, vol. 31, fol. 217; O'Leary, *Bolívar*, 102; Thibaud, *Repúblicas en armas*, 274–75.

13. "Remigio María Bobadilla para el Capitán General," La Guayra, Jan. 21, 1817, AGN-C, La Colonia, Gob. y Cap. Gen., tomo 280, fol. 233; "Borrador para el Comandante de Artillería," Caracas, Jan. 23, 1817, AGN-C, La Colonia, Gob. y Gen., tomo 280, fol. 288; Zambrano to viceroy, Mar. 15, 1817, AGN-B, Archivo Restrepo, caja 2, fondo 1, vol. 6, fol. 332; AGN-BA, Archivo Anexo, Guerra y Marina, tomo 153, fols. 44, 537.

14. ANE-Q, Esclavos, caja 21, 1811–1818, exp. 20.

15. AGN-B, Archivo Anexo, Solicitudes, tomo 5, 45–103.

16. AGN-B, Archivo Anexo, Solicitudes, tomo 13, 618–36; Earle, *Spain*, 93–94, 113, 114–15.

17. AGN-B, Archivo Anexo, Esclavos, tomo 3, 391–403.

18. Oficio of the Council of the Indies, May 28, 1819, AGI, Santa Fe, 549; AGN-B, Archivo Anexo, Particulares, tomo 9, Oct. 15, 1817, 171–73.

19. "Estebán Cambreleng para el Capitán General," Apr. 26, 1817, Caracas, AGN-C, La Colonia, Gob. y Cap. Gen., tomo 287, fol. 209; "Borrador para el Intendente," Caracas, Apr. 27, 1817, AGN-C, La Colonia, Gob. y Cap. Gen., tomo 287, fol. 216; "Borrador para el Alcalde de Primera Elección," Caracas, July 9, 1817, AGN-C, La Colonia, Gob. y Cap. Gen., tomo 293, 1817, fol. 41.

20. "Instrucciones para el general en jefe de la expedición," AGN-B, Archivo Restrepo, caja 98, fondo 1, vol. 22, fol. 63.

21. "Expediente obrado a instancia de D. Juan de la Cruz Mena reclamando de la Reales Cajas el valor de 27 esclavos de su propiedad que se hallan empleados en el servicio de las tropas del mando del Sr Brigadier D. Francisco Tomás Morales, 1816," AANH-C, Civiles-Esclavos, tomo 1816-LM, exp. 11.

22. Morillo order, Cura, Mar. 1, 1818, AGN-B, Archivo Restrepo, caja 9, fondo 1, vol. 21, fol. 146; "María Bernarda Rada para el Gobernador y Capitán General," Caracas, Nov. 5, 1818, AGN-C, La Colonia, Gob. y Cap. Gen., tomo 313, fol. 330.

23. Stoan, *Pablo Morillo*, 213.

24. *Correo del Orinoco* (Angostura), Oct. 28, 1818; Izard, *El miedo*, 61; Hernán Segundo Montiel, "Historia parabólica: Los negros en la independencia," *El Nacional* (Caracas), Jan. 15, 1993, 4. The audiencia was the highest court of the captaincy and had significant political clout.

25. AGN-B, Archivo Anexo, Esclavos, tomo 3, 613.

26. Lecuna and Bierck, *Selected Writings*, 1:135, 142.

27. Quoted in Masur, *Simon Bolivar*, 234.

28. Lecuna and Bierck, *Selected Writings*, 1:163; Stoan, *Pablo Morillo*, 207.

29. Alfred Hasbrouck, *Foreign Legionaries in the Liberation of Spanish South America* (New York: Columbia University Press, 1928), 97; Masur, *Simon Bolivar*, 240. See also Matthew Brown, *Adventuring through Spanish Colonies: Simón Bolívar, Foreign Mercenaries and the Birth of New Nations* (Liverpool: Liverpool University Press, 2006).

30. "Expediente seguido por José Ambrosio Surarregui reclamando su libertad por haber servido a los tropas de la República," 1829, AANH-C, Civiles-Esclavos, tomo 1829-LRST, exp. 6.

31. Paéz, *Autobiografía*, 1:140.

32. Morillo to Juan Bautista Pardo, June 11, 1818, AGN-B, Archivo Restrepo, caja 9, fondo 1, vol. 21, fol. 195.

33. Quoted in Lynch, *Simón Bolívar*, 105.

34. Stoan, *Pablo Morillo*, 212.

35. Domínguez, *Insurrection*, 225; Lynch, *Simón Bolívar*, 102–7; Lynch, *Spanish American Revolutions*, 211–12. Ramos Pérez argues that Piar's plans threatened British support because of the possibility of both racial and social warfare. He failed when Mariño refused to support him. See Demetrio Ramos Pérez, *España en la independencia de América* (Madrid: MAPFRE, 1996), 432.

36. Lynch, *Spanish American Revolutions*, 213, 215.

37. *Cartas Santander-Bolívar*, vol. 1, *Cartas 1813–1820*, 186; Lecuna and Bierck, *Selected Writings*, 1:208; Domínguez, *Insurrection*, 225.

38. Earle, *Spain*, chap. 7; Lynch, *Spanish American Revolutions*, 216–18.

39. *Cartas Santander-Bolívar*, vol. 1, *Cartas 1813–1820*, 149–51.

40. *Cartas Santander-Bolívar*, vol. 2, *Cartas 1820*, 1–2, 50, 153–54, 183.

41. For the dramatic increase in the size of the patriot army after Boyacá, that was largely dependent on forced recruitment, see Thibaud, *Repúblicas en armas*, 452–57.

42. Sales de Bohigas, *Sobre esclavos*, 94–95.

43. Thibaud, *Repúblicas en armas*, 465–66.

44. For this transformation of the patriot army, see ibid., 392–94, chap. 8.

45. *Cartas Santander-Bolívar*, vol. 2, *Cartas 1820*, 87–88.

46. Italics in the original. Ibid., 225.

47. Ibid., 82.

48. Ibid., 242.

49. Ibid., 137.

50. Ibid., 87–88; Lecuna and Bierck, *Selected Writings*, 1:222–23.

51. Thibaud, *Repúblicas en armas*, 462.

52. *Cartas Santander-Bolívar*, vol. 2, *Cartas 1820*, 152–55.

53. Ibid., 64–66, 85–86, 87–88, 145.

54. Lecuna and Bierck, *Selected Writings*, 1:241; "Campaña Libertadora de 1820–22," AHM-G, Listas de Revistas y Estados, Hojas de Servicio, Junta y Consejo de Guerra, no. 1569, fol. 59.

55. *Cartas Santander-Bolívar*, vol. 2, *Cartas 1820*, 219–20, 282, 311; Colmenares, "Popayán," 161–63.

56. Sales de Bohigas, *Sobre esclavos*, 98.

57. *Cartas Santander-Bolívar*, vol. 2, *Cartas 1820*, 321–22, and vol. 3, *Cartas 1820–1822*, 15, 19.

58. *Cartas Santander-Bolívar*, vol. 2, *Cartas 1820*, 123, 138, 211–12; Thibaud, *Repúblicas en armas*, 455–56.

59. "Copiador de oficios de la Comandancia General de la Columna de Retaguardia del Ejército Libertador, a cargo del Coronel Manuel Manrique," Nov. 22, 1820, AGN-C, Gran Colombia, Papeles de Guerra y Marina, tomo 1, 1820–21, fol. 48.

60. AGN-B, Archivo Restrepo, caja 11, fondo 1, vol. 24, fol. 131; *Cartas Santander-Bolívar*, vol. 2, *Cartas 1820*, 2153–54. See also the accusations against three runaways in Ecuador, ANE-Q, Criminales, caja 226, 1820, exp. 21.

61. Brown, *Adventuring*, 140.

62. Earle, *Spain*, chap. 8; Lynch, *Spanish American Revolutions*, 218–19; Thibaud, *Repúblicas en armas*, 472–73, 479–82; Margaret L. Woodward, "The Spanish Army and the Loss of America, 1810–1824," *Hispanic American Historical Review* 48, no. 4 (1968): 594–99.

63. Gómez to Morillo, Dec. 5, 1820, included in La Torre to Ultramar, no. 6, Jan. 22, 1821, AGI, Caracas 55; La Torre to Ultramar, no. 25, May 28, 1821, AGI, Caracas 55.

64. Morillo letter, August 6, 1820, AGI, Caracas 387. Stoan claims that the decree was withdrawn because of audiencia opposition. See Stoan, *Pablo Morillo*, 225.

65. See "Francisco del Pino para el Jefe Superior Político, Caracas, Aug. 23, 1820," AGN-C, La Colonia, Gob. y Cap. Gen., tomo 335, fol. 56; "Comunicación de Francisco del Castillo al Jefe Superior Político," Sabana de Ocumare, Apr. 7, 1821, AGN-C, La Colonia, Gob. y Cap. Gen., tomo 345, fol. 105; "Fernando Machado to the Jefe Superior Político," Santa Teresa, Apr. 7, 1821, AGN-C, La Colonia, Gob. y Cap. Gen., tomo 345, fol. 121.

66. "Carta firmada por el Licenciado don Luis Martín Ramírez Presbítero, y don Fran-

cisco Ríos," Valencia, Feb. 20, 1820, AGN-C, La Colonia, Gob. y Cap. Gen., tomo 329, fol. 211; "Oficio que firma José María Hernández de Monagas," Valencia, Feb. 29, 1820, AGN-C, La Colonia, Gob. y Cap. Gen., tomo 329, fol. 266; Colmenares, "Popayán," 161.

67. "Comunicación de Francisco Jiménez para el Capitán General," Sabana de Ocumare, Aug. 6, 1820, AGN-C, La Colonia, Gob. y Cap Gen., tomo 334, fol. 65; "Comunicación de José Justo Romero para el Jefe Superior Político," Caruao, Sept. 30, 1820, AGN-C, La Colonia, Gob. y Cap. Gen., tomo 337, fol. 168; "Oficio firmado por Bernabé Planas para el Jefe Superior Político," Barquisimeto, Oct. 31, 1820, AGN-C, La Colonia, Gob. y Cap. Gen., tomo 338, fol. 301; "Minuta al Intendente," Caracas, Nov. 9, 1820, AGN-C, La Colonia, Gob. y Cap. Gen., tomo 339, fol. 156; "Borrador de comunicación para el alcalde de Santa Lucía," Caracas, Jan. 4, 1820 [sic 1821], AGN-C, La Colonia, Gob. y Cap. Gen., tomo 328, fol. 26; Correo del Orinoco, Dec. 9, 1820.

68. "José de Jesús Malpica, esclavo de los herederos de Melchor Carnivel, sobre su libertad," 1827, AANH-C, Civiles-Esclavos, tomo 1827-CMPR, exp. 2.

69. "Solicitud que hace Narciso Ochoa, para que le abone el precio de dos esclavos de su propiedad que fueron enrolados al servicio de las armas a la entrada de las tropas del General Bermúdes a esta capital," Caracas, May 19, 1821, AGN-C, La Colonia, Gob. y Cap. Gen., tomo 347, fol. 164; "El Señor Candelario Espinosa cobrando al Estado el valor de su esclavo, Silvestre, que tomó las armas en defensa de la República," 1829, AANH-C, Civiles-Esclavos, tomo 1829-ACEF, exp. 3.

70. Del Pino to Señor Ministro de la Guerra, Jan. 1, 1821, AGI, Caracas 55.

71. Sterling quoted in Ramos, España y la independencia, 430.

72. Report of Gonzalez de Linares and Mixares, June 26, 1821, AGI-S, Caracas 55.

73. De la Torre to Sec^to de Estado y del Despacho de la Gobernación de Ultramar, Jan. 15, 1821, no. 29, June 15, 1821, AGI, Caracas 55; "Reglamento ... al reclutamiento ... del ejército, 1821," AGI, Caracas 498; Bushnell, Simón Bolívar, 117.

74. Correo del Orinoco, Feb. 5, 1820.

75. Lecuna and Bierck, Selected Writings, 1:274.

76. Correo del Orinoco, Oct. 13, 1821; Gaceta del Gobierno de Lima, July 28, 1825; Domínguez, Insurrection, 225; Helg, Liberty, 163.

77. Hamilton to Canning, no. 7, Feb. 8, 1825, FO, 18/12; Lombardi, "Los esclavos," 55–58; Lynch, Spanish American Revolutions, 225; Sales de Bohigas, Sobre esclavos, 99.

78. José Marcial Ramos Guédez, "Simón Bolívar y la abolición de la esclavitud en Venezuela," Ultimas Noticias, Suplemento Cultural (Caracas), July 31, 1994, 7.

79. "El Señor Procurador Municipal en defensa de Antonio Quiñones sobre se le declare libre en atención a los servicios hechos a la República," 1826, AHG-G, no. 6207; Luís Horacio López Domínguez, comp., De Boyacá a Cúcuta: Memoria administrativa 1819–1821 (Bogotá: Biblioteca de la Presidencia de la República, 1990), 375; Sales de Bohigas, Sobre esclavos, 101.

80. Cartas Santander-Bolívar, vol. 3, Cartas 1820–1822, 181.

81. AHM-G, Oficios al Intendente, 1822, no. 47, fol. 65.

82. "Juan Bautista Eraso hace diligencias para que se le satisfaga el valor de esclavos manumitidos y que prestaron servicios en el ejército," AGN-C, Gran Colombia, Intenden-

cia de Venezuela (hereafter cited as Int.-Ven.), La Guaira, Sept. 19, 1821, tomo 40, fol. 392; "Servicio de dos esclavos," Caracas, Aug. 18, 1823, AGN-C, Gran Colombia, Int.-Ven., tomo 9, fol. 44; "Representación del ciudadano Cristóbal Ortega al Intendente," Caracas, Sept. 2, 1823, AGN-C, Gran Colombia, Int.-Ven., tomo 9, fol. 73; "La Señora Rosa Ramona Perez cobrando trescientos pesos contra los fondos centrales de manumisión por valor de su esclavo José Cirilo que tomó servicio en los ejércitos de la República," AGN-C, República, Secretaria del Interior y Justicia, 1830, tomo 1, fol. 169; "La Señora Manuela Suárez de Urbina reclamando el valor de un esclavo de su propiedad que tomó servicio en los ejércitos de la República," AGN-C, República, Secretaria del Interior y Justicia, 1831, 23, fol. 142.

83. "Diligencias de pago por el erario nacional a Teresa Serrano del valor de un esclavo que sirve en el Batallón de Orinoco," Caracas, Oct. 11, 1821, AGN-C, Gran Colombia, Int.-Ven., tomo 44, fol. 257; "De H. Avendaño para el Intendente," AGN-C, La Guaira, Sept. 1, 1821, tomo 308, fol. 163.

84. "Solicitud que hace Narciso Ochoa, para que le abone el precio de dos esclavos de su propiedad que fueron enrolados al servicio de las armas a la entrada de las tropas del General Bermúdes a esta capital," Caracas, May 19, 1821, AGN-C, La Colonia, Gob. y Cap. Gen., tomo 347, fol. 164; Director General de Rentas, Fernando Peñalver, to Ministro de Cajas de la Capital, Caracas, Oct. 23, 1821, AGN-C, Gran Colombia, Int.-Ven., tomo 46, fol. 179.

85. Document relating to slaves seeking freedom in republican territory, Naguanagua, July 5, 1823, AGN-C, Gran Colombia, Int.-Ven., tomo 9, fol. 87; "De José María Pérez al intendente," Caracas, Aug. 27, 1823, AGN-C, Gran Colombia, Int.-Ven., tomo 149, fol. 224.

86. Hasbrouck, *Foreign Legionaries*, 266.

87. Páez, *Autobiografía*, 223.

88. AGN-B, Notaria, 2a, Cayo Ángel, 228, fol. 103; "Don Juan Pablo Ayala para el Intendente: Solicita se le devuelvan dos esclavos pertenecientes a su hermano, que fueron empleados para el servicio de las armas," Caracas, Sept. 6, 1822, AGN-C, Gran Colombia, Int.-Ven., tomo 104, fol. 16; "Representación del Señor Juan José Lander al Intendente," Caracas, May 6, 1822, AGN-C, Gran Colombia, Int.-Ven., tomo 4, fol. 338.

89. Morales to Aymerich, Feb. 17, 1822, ANE-Q, Fondo Especial, caja 240, 1822, vol. 3, no. 90; copy of letter from *marqués* de San José, Mar. 4, 1822, ANE-Q, Fondo Especial, caja 240, 1822, vol. 4, no. 44; letter of Juan de Burbano, Mar. 4, 1822, ANE-Q, Fondo Especial, caja 240, 1822, vol. 4, no. 50; Valdez to viceroy, Mar. 5, 1822, ANE-Q, Fondo Especial, caja 240, 1822, vol. 4, no. 54.

90. AGN-B, Archivo Restrepo, caja 11, fondo 1, vol. 24, fol. 202; Report of José Acosta y Albuquerque, Mar. 13, 1822, ANE-Q, Fondo Especial, caja 240, 1822, vol. 4, no. 115; Lista de negros, March 16, 1822, ANE-Q, vol. 4, no. 140.

91. AHM-G, Diversos Funcionarios, 1821, vol. 1, no. 43, fol. 111, vol. 2, fols. 44, 128, 130, 141, and 1823, and vol. 1, no. 51, fols. 72, 74.

92. "El ciudadano Vicente Rosas, reclamando su esclavo Joaquín Mosquera o su valor," AHG-G, 1821, no. 1427.

93. "El Señor Procurador Municipal, por le esclavo Jacinto Santos, sobre se le declare libre por el servicio hecho de soldado en la República," 1826, AHG-G, no. 6007; "El Señor

Procurador Municipal en defensa de Diego Penedo, sobre se le declare libre," AHG-G, no. 6196. See also AHM-G, Diversos Funcionarios, 1823, vol. 1, no. 51, fol. 72, for other slave recruiting in Ecuador.

94. ANE-Q, Fondo Especial, caja 240, 1822, vol. 5, no. 106.

95. "El Señor Procurador Municipal en defenza de Alexandro Campusano, esclavo, sobre se le declare exento del servicio de esclavitud," 1826, AHG-G, no. 5996.

96. Lecuna and Bierck, *Selected Writings*, 1:352–53; Lynch, *Spanish American Revolutions*, 248–49.

97. Pimentel to Junta Superior del Gobierno, Apr. 18, 1822, AHM-G, Diversos Ministerios, 1822, no. 46, fols. 94–95.

98. "Oficio de Soublette to General Páez," Caracas, Mar. 1, 1823, AGN-C, Gran Colombia, Guerra y Marina, tomo 53, 1823, fol. 16.

99. Documents referring to the service of a slave, José Luciano López, in the Batallón Restaurador, Cumaná, May 25, 1822, to Sept. 12, 1829, AGN-C, Gran Colombia, Int.-Ven., tomo 9, fols. 24–43.

CHAPTER 5: CONTROLLING SLAVE RECRUITMENT IN CHILE AND PERU

1. Anna, *Fall*, 202.

2. Stephen Clissold, *Bernardo O'Higgins and the Independence of Chile* (London: Rupert Hart-Davis, 1968), chaps. 9–12; Simon Collier and William F. Sater, *A History of Chile, 1808–1994* (Cambridge: Cambridge University Press, 1996), 32–37; Lynch, *Spanish American Revolutions*, 132–38.

3. Miller, *Memoirs*, 1:112; Feliú Cruz, *La abolición*, 38–40, 42, 43, 48, 50.

4. Quoted in William F. Sater, "The Black Experience in Chile," in *Slavery and Race Relations in Latin America*, ed. Robert Brent Toplin (Westport, CT: Greenwood Press, 1974), 49n103.

5. "Expediente formado por D^n José Antonio Ovalle Soto sobre la libertad de su esclavo, Francisco," 1814, ANC-S, Capitanía General, Causas Particulares, vol. 109, no. 1940, fol. 398; Feliú Cruz, *La abolición*, 50–54, 127–28; Sater, "The Black Experience," 35, 48n102, 49n103.

6. Sepúlveda shared the classical philosopher's ideas of a natural aristocracy and natural servitude. He is probably best remembered for his debate with Bartolomé de Las Casas in Valladolid in 1550 regarding the right of the Spaniards to enslave the indigenous peoples of the Americas. See J. H. Parry, *The Spanish Seaborne Empire* (London: Hutchinson, 1977), 146–49.

7. *Gaceta de Buenos Aires*, May 1, 1811.

8. Feliú Cruz, *La abolición*, 54, chap. 10.

9. Ovalle y Vivanco to Supreme Director, Santiago, Sept. 5, 1817, and Urrutia y Mendiburu to Junta Delegada, Dec. 13, 1817, ANC-S, Ministerio de Guerra, Provincia de Santiago i sus Dep^{tos}, 1817–28, tomo 18; Troncosa to Supreme Director of the State, Rancagua, July 15, 1817, ANC-S, Ministerio de Guerra, Correspondencia de Santiago, Casablanca, Meli-

pilla, y Rancagua, 1817–18, tomo 17; Intendencia to Director Delegado, no. 29, July 3, 1817, and Intendencia to Director Delegado, no. 12, Aug. 16, 1817, ANC-S, Intendencia, Santiago, vol. 1, 1817–25; Feliú Cruz, *La abolición*, 56–57; Sales de Bohigas, *Sobre esclavos*, 76.

10. Italics in the original. A rough translation would be, "I don't want suga'. Take your suga' and shove it." Espejo, "El paso de los Andes," 14105.

11. Feliú Cruz, *La abolición*, 147; Sales de Bohigas, *Sobre esclavos*, 76; Sater, "The Black Experience," 36.

12. Samuel Haigh, *Sketches of Buenos Ayres, Chile, and Peru* (London: Effingham Wilson, 1831), 225, 235.

13. Bowles to Croker, Most Secret, no. 59, Feb. 14, 1818, ADM 1/23.

14. Bowles to Croker, Secret, no. 113, Oct. 3, 1818, ADM 1/23.

15. Bowles to Croker, Secret, no. 165, Feb. 27, 1819, ADM 1/24; Clissold, *Bernardo O'Higgins*, 179–81; Lynch, *Spanish American Revolutions*, 173–74.

16. José María Aguirre, "Compendio de las campañas del Ejército de los Andes," in Comisión Nacional del Centenario, *Documentos del archivo de San Martín* (Buenos Aires: Imprenta de Coni Hermanos, 1910–11), 10:223.

17. To Alcalde Benito Vargas, no. 41, 1818, to Dirc[n] Supremo, no. 98, Sept. 7, 1819, to Dirc[n] Supremo, no. 173, Dec. 23, 1819, Com'dante G'ral de Armas, no. 135, Feb. 1, 1821, and to Com'te G'l de Armas, no. 282, July 20, 1821, ANC-S, Intendencia, Santiago, vol. 1, 1817–25.

18. Intendencia from Dirc[n]. Supremo, no. 121, Oct. 12, 1820, Intendencia to Dirc[n]. Supremo, Oct. 19, 1820, to Gobernadores of Cunic[o] and Fernando, no. 43, Dec. 1, 1820, ANC-S, Intendencia, Santiago, vol. 1, 1817–25; José María de Guzmán to Dirc[n]. Supremo, Mar. 22, 1819, ANC-S, Ministerio de Guerra, Correspondencia 1818–20, vol. 64; Decree, Ministerio de la Guerra, ANC-S, Oficios, 1817–18, vol. 27, no. 26; Feliú Cruz, *La abolición*, 56–58.

19. Hardy to Croker, Secret, no. 90, Sept. 20, 1820, ADM 1/25.

20. Sales de Bohigas, *Sobre esclavos*, 64.

21. Chile, *Boletín de las leyes i decretos del gobierno 1819–1820* (Santiago: Imprenta Nacional, 1900), 273.

22. Anna, *Fall*, chaps. 1 and 5, and pp. 45–46; Semprún and Bullón de Mendoza, *El ejército realista*, 99–102.

23. Bowles to Croker, no. 118, Oct. 10, 1818, ADM 1/24; "Tasación del valor de tres esclavos que pertenecieron al finado insurgente Mateo García Pumacahua," Cuzco, June 7, 1815, BN-L, D8785; John Fisher, "Royalism, Regionalism, and Rebellion in Colonial Peru, 1808–1815," *Hispanic American Historical Review* 52, no. 2 (1979): 245–52; Lynch, *Spanish American Revolutions*, 165–72.

24. "Autos seguidos por Fabián y Juan Arosamena, esclavos de Doña Severina Alfaro, sobre sevicia y les estienda boleta de venta," 1817, AGN-L, Cabildo, Causas Civiles, leg. 36, cuad. 588; "Tasación del valor de tres esclavos que pertenecieron al finado insurgente Mateo García Pumacahua." See also "Expediente que sigue Don Pedro Reyna con José María y Manuel Reyna sobre su venta," Jan. 11, 1830, AGN-L, Expedientes Judiciales, Causas Civiles, leg. 86, cuad. 4.

25. "Título de Comandante del Escuadrón de Pardos con grado de Teniente Coronel, librado en favor del de igual casta, Don Marín Oviedo," Lima, Jan. 7, 1818, BN-L, D406;

various cases, AGN-L, Real Audiencia, Causas Criminales, 1808–21, legs. 112–42; Anna, *Fall*, 93–99, 156–58; Héctor Centurión Vallejo, *Esclavitud y manumisión de negros en Trujillo* (Trujillo: n.p., 1954), 9–10; Alberto Flores Galindo, "Bandidos de la costa," and Carmen Vivanco Lara, "Bandolerismo colonial peruano, 1760–1810: Caracterización de una respuesta popular y causas económicas," in *Bandoleros, abigeos y montoneros: criminalidad y violencia en el Perú, siglos XVIII–XX*, ed. Carlos Aguirre and Charles Walker (Lima: Instituto de Apoyo Agrario, 1990), 25–68. See also AA-L, Causas de Negros, 1799–14, leg. 35.

26. Quoted in Anna, *Fall*, 151; see also 139.

27. "Expediente que sigue Don Pedro Reyna con José María y Manuel Reyna sobre su venta"; Santiago Tavara, *Abolición de la esclavitud en el Perú* (Lima: José María Monterola, 1855), 29.

28. "Ajustamiento del haber vencido de los oficiales y demas individuos del Cuerpo Pardos en el Callao," Lima, July 30, 1815, BN-L, D279; "Autos criminales seguidos por Pío Molina, cabo retirado de una de las compañías de pardos libres," 1810, AGN-L, Auditoria General de Guerra, Causas Penales, leg. 5, cuad. 98; Robert Proctor, *Narrative of a Journey across the Cordillera of the Andes, and of a Residence in Lima, and other Parts of Peru, in the Years 1823 and 1824* (London: A. Constable and Co. Edinburgh, 1825), 356; Domínguez, *Insurrection*, 262; Semprún and Bullón de Mendoza, *El ejército realista*, 96–97.

29. "Expediente promovido ante el Superior Gobierno por Dña María del Carmen Gomez," 1818, AGN-L, Superior Gobierno, leg. 36, cuad. 1268. See also "Expediente sobre la petición presentada por el soldado Esteban Rozas," Apr. 6, 1818, BN-L, D409.

30. "Autos criminales seguidos de oficio contra los soldados José Dolores, José Sanchez, y Blas García," 1817, AGN-L, Auditoria General de Guerra, Causas Penales, leg. 7, cuad. 156; "Seguidos por don Ramón Ovalle, sobre que se le entregue a su esclavo Rodulfo," 1814, AGN-L, Causas Civiles, leg. 19, cuad. 320; Hünefeldt, *Paying the Price*, 152.

31. Bowles to Croker, Secret, no. 57, Jan. 4, 1818, ADM 1/23; "Autos criminales seguidos de oficio por la Real Justicia contra los soldados cazadores de morenos libres," 1817 AGN-L, Real Audiencia, Causas Criminales, leg. 136, cuad. 1665; Sales de Bohigas, *Sobre esclavos*, 128n79.

32. Bowles to Croker, Most Secret, no. 85, June 10, 1818, ADM 1/23.

33. Argentina, *Documentos*, 7:51–53.

34. Italics in the original. Argentina, *Documentos*, 11:257. San Martín, like other independence figures, frequently made the analogy of colonial rule with slavery. See Peter Blanchard, "The Language of Liberation: Slave Voices in the Wars of Independence," *Hispanic American Historical Review* 82, no. 3 (1993): 511–12.

35. *Gaceta del Gobierno de Lima*, Apr. 7, May 12, 19, 1819; *Gaceta Extraordinaria del Gobierno de Lima*, May 15, 1819; Argentina, *Documentos*, 7:399; Miller, *Memoirs*, 1:219.

36. Miller, *Memoirs*, 1:287–88.

37. Ella Dunbar Temple, ed., *La acción patriótica del pueblo en la emancipación: Guerrillas y montoneras*, in Perú, *Colección documental de la independencia del Perú* (Lima: Comisión Nacional del Sesquicentenario de la Independencia del Perú, 1971), tomo 5, 1:250–51.

38. Félix D'Olhaberriague y Blanco, June 19, 1821, AGI, Lima 1023. See also *Gaceta de Buenos Aires*, Nov. 29, 1820; Cabezudo to Juan de Dios Cabezudo, Dec. 28, 1820, Argentina, *Documentos*, 5:147; Miller, *Memoirs*, 1:280, 305.

39. Letter of Mercadillo, May 15, 1821, ANE-Q, Milicias, caja 7, 1820–23, 12-V-1821.

40. Daniel Florencio O'Leary, *Memorias del General O'Leary* (Caracas: Ministerio de la Defensa, 1980), 5:294; Proctor, *Narrative*, 164; John Fisher, *Bourbon Peru, 1750–1824* (Liverpool: Liverpool University Press, 2003), 133n83.

41. Miller, *Memoirs*, 1:352–53; Dunbar Temple, *La acción patriótica*, 7:371–86.

42. Vivanco Lara, "Bandolerismo"; Flores Galindo, "Bandidos"; Charles Walker, "Montoneros, bandoleros, malhechores: Criminalidad y política en las primeras décadas republicanas," and Carlos Aguirre, "Cimarronaje, bandolerismo y desintegración esclavista: Lima, 1821–1854," in Aguirre and Walker, *Bandoleros*, 25–68, 105–82; Gustavo Vergara Arias, *Montoneras y guerrillas en la etapa de la emancipación del Perú (1820–1825)* (Lima: Imprenta y Litografía "Salesiana," 1973).

43. *Gaceta del Gobierno de Lima*, Aug. 12, 1820.

44. Hardy to Croker, no. 25, Mar. 22, 1821, ADM 1/26, Secret, no. 110, Nov. 30, 1821, ADM 1/27; Lynch, *Spanish American Revolutions*, 178.

45. AGN-L, Protocolos, Vicente García, no. 255, 1820–25, 33.

46. "Virreynato, Alistamiento de negros," Lima, Feb. 18, 1821, BN-L, D5985; *Gaceta de Buenos Aires*, Nov. 29, 1820; Anna, *Fall*, 172; Alejandro Reyes Flores, *Esclavitud en Lima 1800–1840* (Lima: Universidad Nacional Mayor de San Marcos, 1985), 39.

47. Anna, *Fall*, 167–68, chap. 8; Lynch, *Spanish American Revolutions*, 176–80.

48. Quoted in Lynch, *Spanish American Revolutions*, 179.

49. Hardy to Croker, Secret, no. 75, Sept. 14, 1821, ADM 1/26; Anna, *Fall*, 183–84.

50. Peru, *Colección de los bandos publicados por el gobierno de Lima independiente* (Lima: Imprenta de Rio, 1821), located in AGI, Lima 800; Perú, *Colección de leyes, decretos y ordenes desde su independencia en el año de 1821, hasta 31 de diciembre de 1830* (Lima: Imprenta de José Masias, 1831), 1:16, 83.

51. Perú, *Colección*, 1:24, 30; Anna, *Fall*, 197; Tavara, *Abolición*, 7–8.

52. Perú, *Colección*, 1:65.

53. Ibid., 1:74–75.

54. Ibid., 1:80.

55. Ibid., 1:106–7.

56. Torre Tagle's aims were more nationalistic than humanitarian, according to Jean-Pierre Tardieu. See Jean-Pierre Tardieu, *El decreto de Huancayo: Abolición de la esclavitud en el Perú. 3 de diciembre de 1854* (Lima: Fondo Editorial del Congreso del Perú, 2004), 41.

57. Perú, *Colección*, 1:127, 147, 178–80, 184–85, 200; Listas de Revista, Batallón Unión Peruana, 1823, AGN-L, O.L. 71–354; Ministerio de Guerra y Marina to General en Jefe, May 2, 1822, AHM-L, Copiador Comunicaciones del Ministerio de Guerra y Marina, 1821/22, L2; Anna, *Fall*, 202.

58. Monteagudo to Ministerio de Guerra, Apr. 19 and 26, 1822, AHM-L, Manual de Partes, 1821/1822, A1, leg. 25, nos. 111, 115, Freyre to Ministerio de Guerra y Marina, May 7, 1823, leg. 6, no. 14.

59. Ministerio de Guerra y Marina to General de Jefe, Mar. 30 and Apr. 17, 23, and 26, and May 14, 1822, AHM-L, Manual de Partes, 1821/1822, A1; Copiador de Correspondencia del Ministerio de Guerra y Marina, 1821/22, AHM-L, L2; Copiador Correspondencia General con el Intendente del Ejército, 1822/1823, AHM-L, L6; Alvarado to Ministerio de

Guerra y Marina, Apr. 22, 1822, leg. 4, no. 163, Monteagudo to Ministerio de Guerra y Marina, May 13 and 15 and June 14, 1822, leg. 25, nos. 124, 128, and 140, Morales to Ministerio de Guerra y Marina, Sept. 10, 1822, leg. 26, no. 245; Novoa to Ministerio de Guerra y Marina, Sept. 30, 1822, leg. 28, no. 137; Novoa to Guido, Nov. 30, 1822, leg. 28, no. 199; Freyre to Ministerio, June 11, 1823, leg. 6, no. 67, Santa Cruz to Ministerio de Guerra y Marina, Mar. 17 and May 6, 1823, leg. 17, nos. 29 and 92, AHM-L, Ledra D, carpeta 2; "Ocurrencia diaria del Ejército Libertador," 1822, BN-L, D11701; AGN-L, O.L. 38–70, 52–47.

60. Anna, *Fall*, 196, 202; Timothy E. Anna, "Economic Causes of San Martín's Failure in Lima," *Hispanic American Historical Review* 54, no. 4 (1974): 662.

61. AHM-L, Manual de Partes, 1821/1822, A1; AHM-L, Acuerdos del Exmo Sor Marqués de Trujillo, Supremo Delegado del Perú, desde 15 de julio de 1822, B1, Correspondencia General y con los Jefes del Ejército, 1821/22, L2; "Ocurrencia diaria del Ejército Libertador"; Anna, "Economic Causes," 662.

62. Listas de Revista, Batallón Unión Peruana, 1823; "Ocurrencia diaria del Ejército Libertador"; To Mayor de Plaza, Nov. 26, 1822, AHM-L, Acuerdos del Exmo Sor Marqués de Trujillo, Supremo Delegado del Perú, desde 15 de julio de 1822, B1; Min[isterio] de G[uerra] y M[arina] to Genl en Jefe, May 2, 1822, AHM-L, Copiador Correspondencia del Ministerio de Guerra y Marina, 1821/1822, L2; Novoa to Ministerio de Guerra y Marina, Mar. 3, 1822, AHM-L, leg. 27, no. 19; Novoa to Guido, Nov. 27, 1822, AHM-L, leg. 28, no. 196.

63. Ministerio de Guerra y Marina to Diputados del Congreso Constituyente, Sept. 25, 1822, AHM-L, Correspondencia de Ministerio de Guerra y Marina con los Jefes del Ejército Unido, 1822–23, J4.

64. Anna, *Fall*, 196.

65. Ministerio de Guerra to General en Jefe, May 4, 1822, in "Ocurrencia diaria del Ejército Libertador"; Anna, *Fall*, 197.

66. Ricketts to Canning, no. 26, Dec. 27, 1826, FO 61/8; *El Peruano*, May 5, 19, 29, 1855.

67. AGN-L, O.L., 7–3, 20–18, 30–5.

68. Unanue to Ministerio de Guerra y Marina, Mar. 22, 1822, AHM-L, leg. 36, no. 13; AGN-L, Colecciones Santa María, 1823, no. 0585.

69. Anna, *Fall*, 210–11; Lynch, *Spanish American Revolutions*, 186–88.

70. See the case of Pedro García in "Ocurrencia diaria del Ejército Libertador"; Valdivieso to Ministerio de Guerra y Marina, Oct. 2, 1822, AHM-L, leg. 37, no. 46, July 13, 1822, leg. 37, no. 29.

71. AGN-L, Colecciones Santa María, 1822, no. 0522.

72. AHM-L, Acuerdos de la Suprema Junta Gubernativa, 1823, B2.

73. Lynch, *Spanish American Revolutions*, 185, 271.

74. Hardy to Croker, Secret, no. 35, Apr. 21, 1823, ADM 1/28; Prescott to Admiralty, no. 2, Aug. 23, 1822, Sept. 11, 1822, FO 61/1.

75. AGN-BA, Guerra, 21 de enero, 1823, Ejército Libertador del Perú, Campaña de Puertos Intermedios, X–23–2–5; Lynch, *Spanish American Revolutions*, 187–89, 267–68.

76. Perú, *Colección*, 1:322–24, 326–28.

77. AGN-L, O.L. 74–3, 73–41.

78. "Solicitud de Dn. Ibañes Pacheco, español vecino de la Capital," AGN-L, Superior Gobierno, 1823, leg. 38, cuad. 1443.

79. "Expediente sobre el sorteo de esclavos, obrado por la Comisión de Rescates," AGN-L, O.L. 92–9, 92–10, 92–11; Freyre to Ministerio de Hacienda, Apr. 7, 21, and 25, 1823, AGN-L, O.L. 73–10, 73–38, 73–49, 73–52; Escobar to Freyre, May 17, 1823, AGN-L, O.L. 91–38; AHM-L, Manual de Partes, 1823/1824, A3; AHM-L, Acuerdos de la Suprema Junta Gubernativa, 1823, B2; AHM-L, Copiador, Correspondencia con el E. M. J. y Jefes de Cuerpo, 1823, L7; Perú, *Colección*, 1:338.

80. Perú, *Colección*, 1:338, 351.

81. *Gazeta del Gobierno de Lima Independiente*, July 19, 1823; *Gaceta del Gobierno* (Lima), Aug. 9 and Dec. 17, 1823.

82. Vidaurre to Tagle, Aug. 2, 1823, AGN-L, O.L. 83–80.

83. AHM-L, Manual de Partes, 1823/1824, A3.

84. Lecuna and Bierck, *Selected Writings*, 2:374.

85. Ibid., 2:364–66.

86. Prescott to Hardy, May 26, 1823, FO 61/1.

87. Simón B. O'Leary, *Bolívar en el Perú* (Caracas: Archivo General de la Nación, 1971), 30; Lynch, *Spanish American Revolutions*, 268–69.

88. Anna, *Fall*, 216.

89. O'Leary, *Memorias*, 5:29; To Bolívar's secretary, Dec. 23, 1823, AHM-L, Copiador, Correspondencia con el E.M.J. y Jefes de Cuerpo, 1823, L7.

90. Report on . . . Colombia, encl. with Campbell to Planta, no. 1, Nov. 6, 1824, FO 18/3, Watts to Planta, Private, Sept. 13, 1824, FO 18/7; Comandancia General del Istmo to Comandante General of Guayaquil, Nov. 20, 1823, AHM-G, Diversos Funcionarios, 1823, vol. 2, no. 52, fol. 175; Salom to Intendente of Guayaquil, Apr. 19, 1824, AHM-G, Diversos Funcionarios, 1824, vol. 2, no. 61, fol. 161; Helg, *Equality*, 176, 189.

91. Report on . . . Colombia.

92. Parish to Canning, no. 11, Apr. 25, 1824, FO 6/3; Henderson to Canning, no. 5, Apr. 29, 1824, FO 18/4; Martin to Eyre, Feb. 26, 1824, encl. with Croker to Planta July 5, 1824, FO 61/4; Narrative of the proceedings of the Independent Army under General Bolivar, abstracted from the Journal of an English Officer serving under him, FO 61/6; Proctor, *Narrative*, 339–57; Anna, *Fall*, 222–24. See also José Espinar to Sec. de Estado de Marina y Guerra, Feb. 9, 1824, AGN-B, Archivo Restrepo, caja 7, fondo 1, vol. 17, fols. 99–101.

93. Martínez to Ministerio de Estado del Departamento de Guerra y Marina, Mar. 20 and Nov. 5, 1824, and Correa to Ministerio, May 30, 1824, both in AGN-BA, Guerra, Ejército de los Andes, 1823–26, X–4–4–1; "Sublevación del Callao 1824," in Argentina, *Biblioteca de mayo*, tomo 17, part 2, chap. 11; Proctor, *Narrative*, 338.

94. Rowcroft, Private, June 15, 1824, FO 61/2; *El Centinela en Campaña* (Huánuco), July 11, 1824. In February 1825 two of the surviving leaders of the mutiny were arrested as traitors in Peru, expelled from the country, and then rearrested in Chile. Matías Muñoz and Francisco Molina were brought to trial in Buenos Aires in 1826 and in November condemned to be strangled, but the garrote was not in a state of service. See Gutierrez de la

Fuente to Min° de Guerra y Marina, Feb. 5, 16, and 18, 1825, AHM-L, leg. 11, nos. 263, 286, 293; AGN-BA, Guerra, Ejército de los Andes, 1823–26, X–4–4–1.

95. Hamilton to Planta, Private, Apr. 18, 1824, FO 18/3; Lynch, *Spanish American Revolutions*, 271; Nicolás Rebaza, *Anales del departamento de La Libertad en la guerra de la independencia* (Trujillo: Impr. de "El Obrero del Norte," 1898), 235–36; Vergara Arias, *Montoneras*, 145.

96. Lecuna and Bierck, *Selected Writings*, 2:410.

97. "Expediente que sigue Dª Paula Requena contra Dn José Relaize sobre la venta de un criado," Aug. 11, 1828, AGN-L, Expedientes Judiciales, Causas Civiles, leg. 65, cuad. 4.

98. Rowcroft, Private, June 22, 1824, FO 61/2.

99. *Gaceta del Gobierno* (Trujillo), May 1, 1824.

100. Rowcroft to Planta, no. 6, July 22, 1824, FO 61/2.

101. At the end of the last campaign, Spanish-born soldiers comprised 5 percent of both the royalist and patriot armies. See Semprún and Bullón de Mendoza, *El ejército realista*, 292.

102. Quoted in O'Leary, *Bolívar*, 45.

CHAPTER 6: RECRUITMENT AND RESISTANCE

1. Miller, *Memoirs*, 1:271, 272.

2. *Gaceta de Buenos Aires*, July 19, 1810.

3. "Domingo—negro esclavo con causa contra Antonio Apirón, 1818," AGN-BA, Admin., leg. 29, exp. 986, IX–23–8–3, Tribunal de Cuentas, 1813–17, X–41–4–5.

4. The trial court transposed the names of the slave and his owner. See "Expediente formado por Don José Antonio Ovalle Soto sobre la libertad de su esclavo, Francisco," 1814, ANC-S, Capitanía General, Causas Particulares, vol. 109, no. 1940, fol. 398.

5. Hünefeldt, *Paying*, 35.

6. "Lorenzo Villanueva, pardo esclavo de Dⁿ Juan Antonio de Sta. Coloma, solicitando que se le otorgue papel de venta," 1812, AGN-BA, Admin., leg. 29, exp. 997, IX–23–8–3. For the rhetoric of the time, see Blanchard, "The Language," 499–523.

7. AGN-BA, Sol. Mil., 1815, X–8–7–4.

8. Voelz, *Slave and Soldier*, chap. 21.

9. In the Banda Oriental, the wage rate for slaves who served as porters was six pesos per month. See AGN-BA, Banda Oriental, 1811–14, X–42–7–3, Guerra, Ejército Sitiador Banda Oriental, 1812–14, X–7–9–7.

10. The regular rhythm was 75 to 80 steps per minute; a drumroll was 125 to 130. See ANC-S, Fondo Varios, Batallón de Granaderos de Chile, vol. 238B, 4206–15.

11. AGN-BA, Sol. Mil., 1815, X–8–7–6, Sumarios Militares, Letra G, exp. 406, X–29–11–6.

12. Espejo, "El paso," 14043–44, 14113; Miller, *Memoirs*, 1:272; Bernand, "La población," 128.

13. Voelz, *Slave and Soldier*, 413–14.

14. AHPBA-LP, Tribunal de Cuentas, 1813, Civiles y Militares, 14–1–4–1018.

15. AGN-BA, Antanasio Gutierrez, May, 30, 1811, Banda Oriental, Copias de los Documentos Referente al Ejército del Norte, 1811, X–42–7–1.

16. Semprún and Bullón de Mendoza, *El ejército realista*, 89.

17. Holmberg to Supreme Director, Aug. 18, 1814, AGN-BA, Guerra, 1811–16, X–3–2–3.

18. Argentina, *Registro oficial*, 1:393–94.

19. Miller, *Memoirs*, 1:305, 352–53, 2:42–44, 445, 447–48; Rebaza, *Anales*, 8–9; Thibaud, *Repúblicas en armas*, 368. See also "Uniforme que debera usar la oficialidad y tropa del Batallón 'Unión Peruana,'" May 23, 1822, BN-L, D12381.

20. AGN-BA, Salta: Culto, Guerra, Sisa, Correo, Tribunal de Cuentas, Esclavos, Juzgados, 1810–13, Guerra, X–43–8–2; ANC-S, Ejército de Chile, Comisario 1817, vol. 26, Fondo Varios, fol. 41.

21. For an individual to consume eight pounds of meat in a day was highly unlikely. The ration was probably designed to meet the needs of the general's nonmilitary staff, including women, servants, and slaves. Alternatively, he may have distributed or sold the surplus.

22. "Reglamento para la disciplina y subsistencia de las tropas en marcha," Dec. 1819, BN-B, libro 146, no. 200, 112–13; AGN-BA, Banda Oriental, 1811–14, X–42–7–3; ANE-Q, Milicias, 1820–1823, caja 7, Nov. 19, 1822.

23. AGN-B, Archivo Restrepo, caja 6, fondo 1, vol. 10, fols. 302–7.

24. Lynch, *Simón Bolívar*, 108.

25. AGN-BA, Sol. Mil., 1819, X–11–1–7.

26. AGN-BA, Sol. Mil., 1815, X–8–7–5, 1819, X–11–1–7, X–11–3–7; Cutolo, *Nuevo diccionario*, 1:323–24, 7:173–74.

27. Miller, *Memorias*, 2:427; Bernand, "La población," 129.

28. For these and other cases, see AGN-BA, Guerra, Rescate de Esclavos, 1813–17, X–43–6–7, Sol. Civiles y Mil., 1812, X–6–6–13, Gobierno, Sol. Mil., 1817, X–9–7–2, X–9–7–3, X–10–1–1, 1819, X–11–1–6, X–35–8–2, 1820, X–11–9–2, 1822, X–12–10–7; "Expediente promovido por D^n Pedro Giles reclamando un esclabo suyo nombrado Miguel que está sirviendo en la 3ª Compañia del Batallon 2° de Cazadores," 1821, AGN-BA, Admin., leg. 34, exp. 1207, IX–23–9–1; "Dª Luisa Bossorino reclamando al negro José Perez que con el nombre de José Parra ha tomado plaza en un regimiento de linea," 1822, AGN-BA, Admin., leg. 34, exp. 1223, IX–23–9–1.

29. Martínez Montero, "El soldado negro," 274n.

30. "Doña Manuela Tadea Pinazo solicitando la entrega de los esclavos europeos," 1816–17, AGN-BA, Admin., leg. 32, exp. 1123, IX–23–8–6.

31. AGN-BA, Sol. Mil. 1815, X–8–7–5.

32. *Gaceta de Buenos Aires*, Feb. 14, 1821.

33. AGN-BA, Sol. Mil., 1817, X–10–1–1.

34. AGN-B, Archivo Anexo, Solicitudes, tomo 12, 133–44.

35. AGN-L, O.L. 20–24.

36. AGN-L, O.L. 20–24.

37. AGN-BA, Sol. Mil., 1815, X–8–7–6.

38. AGN-BA, Sol. Mil., 1815, X–8–7–4.

39. AGN-C, La Colonia, Gob. y Cap. Gen., tomo 306, 1818, fol. 302; AGN-B, Archivo Anexo, Solicitudes, tomo 12, 117–31; AHM-L, Manual de Partes, 1823, A2; AHM-L, 1823/1824, A3, 1824 y 1825, A4; AHML, Copiador, Correspondencia con el Jral en Jefe del

Ejército, 1821/1822/1823, L4; Hamnett, "Popular Insurrections," 310. See also "Del General Soublette para los señores de la Junta de Manumisión," Caracas, Jan. 15, 1822, AGN-C, Gran Colombia, Int.-Ven., tomo 59, 1822, fol. 10.

40. Valdivieso to Min. de Guerra, Dec. 5, 1822, AHM-L, 1822–23, leg. 38, no. 101; Rafael Jiménez to Min. de Guerra, Dec. 2, 1823, AHM-L, 1822–23, leg. 10, no. 66; J. G. Pérez to Min. de Estado en Departamento de Guerra, Oct. 13, 1823, leg. 15, no. 63; Valdivieso to Ministerio de Guerra y Marina, May 16, 1823, AHM-L, 1822–23, leg. 20, no. 61.

41. AGN-BA, Sol. Mil., 1817, X–9–7–10.

42. AGN-BA, Guerra, Rescate de Esclavos, 1813–17, X–43–6–7, Sol. Civiles y Mil., 1812, X–6–6–12, Sol. Mil., 1818, X–35–7–9, 1822, X–12–10–7.

43. AGN-BA, Guerra, Rescate de Esclavos, 1813–17, X–43–6–7, Sol. Mil., 1815, X–8–7–6, 1816, X–35–7–8, 1817, X–9–7–10, 1818, X–35–7–9, 1822, X–12–10–7; Bernand, "La población," 105, 113–14.

44. "El ciudadano Vicente Rosas, reclamando su esclavo Joaquín Mosquera o su valor," AHG-G, 1821, no. 1427.

45. See Miguel A. Rosal, "Diversos aspectos relacionados con la esclavitud en el Río de la Plata a través del estudio de testamentos de afroporteños, 1750–1810," *Revista de Indias* 56, no. 206 (1996): 227–30.

46. AGN-BA, Guerra, Rescate de Esclavos, 1813–17, X–43–6–7, Sol. Mil., 1815, X–8–7–6, 1822, X–12–10–7.

47. In Buenos Aires, the Battalion of Invalids was used for night patrols and incorporated the aged as well as invalids. One soldier serving in 1816 was Mateo Arroyo, who was seventy-eight years old. See AGN-BA, Sol. Mil., 1816, X–35–7–8.

48. AGN-BA, Gobierno, Sol. Mil., 1817, X–9–7–2.

49. AGN-BA, Sol. Mil., 1819, X–11–1–6.

50. AGN-BA, Sol. Mil., 1817, X–9–7–10.

51. AGN-BA, Sol. Mil., 1815, X–8–7–5.

52. Argentina, *Biblioteca de mayo*, 14:12681–95. See also Thibaud, *Repúblicas en armas*, 356–59.

53. Soler to Head of State, Oct. 24, 1812, AGN-BA, Guerra, 1811–16, X–3–2–3. For the same assessment from a Venezuelan royalist viewpoint, see Morillo to Ramón Correa, Nov. 17, 1819, AGN-B, Archivo Restrepo, caja 9, fondo 1, vol. 21, fols. 265–66.

54. Rowcroft to Canning, Private, Oct. 15, 1824, FO 61/3.

55. Thibaud, *Repúblicas en armas*, 423.

56. Hasbrouck, *Foreign Legionaries*, 97; Masur, *Simon Bolivar*, 240.

57. Argentina, *Documentos*, 6:81.

58. Proctor, *Narrative*, 139.

59. Stoan, *Pablo Morillo*, 185.

60. O'Leary, *Memorias*, 1:123, 201.

61. AGN-B, República, Guerra y Marina, tomo 56, fols. 92–97.

62. Argentina, *Biblioteca de mayo*, 14:13249; Argentina, *Documentos*, 5:349–526; O'Leary, *Memorias*, 1:83.

63. Stoan, *Pablo Morillo*, chap. 6.

64. Letter from L. F. de Icasa, AHBM-G, Copias de Documentos Auténticos, 1820–1909, no. 36, fol. 37. See also Thibaud, *Repúblicas en armas*, 444–45.

65. Anna, *Fall*, 204. See also Anna, "Economic Causes," 657–81.

66. Narrative of the proceedings of the independent army under General Bolivar, abstracted from the journal of an English officer serving under him, FO 61/6; Kelly to Rowcroft, Sept. 5, 1824, FO 61/3.

67. AHPBA-LP, Tribunal de Cuentas, 1819, Civiles y Militares, 14–1–10–1024.

68. Stoan, *Pablo Morillo*, 185.

69. O'Leary, *Memorias*, 5:24.

70. AGN-BA, Ejército de los Andes, 1816, X–4–2–6; "Sobre . . . los presidarios Antonio Pujol, Marcelino Soria, y Miguel Ferrer," AGN-BA, Guerra, 1815, X–10–4–6.

71. AGN-BA, Sol. Civiles y Mil., 1816, X–9–2–4; Pedro Cunill Grau, "El mito del ordenamiento espacial colonial ante las realidades de la geografía de la insurgencia en tiempos de Antonio José de Sucre, Gran Mariscal de Ayacucho," in *Insurgencia y revolución: Antonio José de Sucre y la independencia de los pueblos de América*, ed. José Maria Cadenas (Seville: Universidad Internacional de Andalucía, Colección Encuentros Iberoamericanos, 1996), 40–44; Rebecca Earle, "'A Grave for Europeans'? Disease, Death and the Spanish-American Revolutions," in *The Wars of Independence in Spanish America*, ed. Christon I. Archer (Wilmington, DE: Scholarly Resources Inc., 2000), 283–97; Drusilla Scott, *Mary English: A Friend of Bolívar* (Lewes, U.K.: The Book Guild, 1991), 73.

72. Lecuna and Bierck, *Selected Writings*, 1:231–32.

73. Haigh, *Sketches*, 127, 233–34.

74. ANE-Q, Esclavos, caja 21, 1811–18, exp. 10.

75. AGN-BA, Sol. Mil., 1810–13, X–35–7–6. For cases of wounded soldiers from primarily black units, see AGN, Guerra, Ejército Auxiliar del Perú, 1812, X–3–10–3, Guerra, Sol. Mil., 1812, X–6–5–7, Gobierno, Sol. Mil., 1817, X–9–7–2, Sol. Mil., 1817, X–9–7–3, 1817, X–10–1–1.

76. AGN-BA, Sol. Mil., 1817, X–10–1–1.

77. Pedro de Urquinana, Apr. 15, 1814, AGI, Caracas 437a.

78. Pedro Carrasco to Belgrano, AGN-BA, Guerra, Ejército Auxiliar del Perú, 1812, X–3–10–4.

79. Rowcroft to Canning, Oct. 15, 1824, Private, FO 61/3.

80. Oficio of Morillo to Capt. General, May 31, 1817, AGI, Caracas 386,

81. O'Leary, *Memorias*, 1:200, 126; Thibaud, *Repúblicas en armas*, 359–62. For a description of postwar hospital care that indicated conditions had not improved, at least in Guayaquil, see Valdés to intendant of Department, June 11, 1826, AHM-G, Comandancias, 1826, no. 80, fols. 100–101.

82. For examples of San Martín's efforts in this regard, see AGN-BA, Guerra, Ejército Sitiador Banda Oriental, 1812–14, X–7–9–7; AGN-BA, Tribunal de Presas, Junta Electoral, Provisor, Asesora, Prisioneros, 1819, X–11–5–6; Argentina, *Documentos*, 5:609–44; San Martín to Pezuela, Nov. 9, 1821 [*sic* 1820], AGI, Lima 800.

83. Sucre to Int't of Dept., Mar. 29, 1823, Fundación John Boulton, Caracas, Venezuela, Archivo Sucre, Carpeta C-084; Halperín-Donghi, *Politics*, 200; O'Leary, *Bolívar*, 61, 111, 164.

84. Espejo, "El paso," 14122.

85. Spanish regulations concerning capital punishment, July 28, 1817, AGI, Santa Fe 668.

86. Argentina, *Documentos,* 8:139–40.

87. Soler to Sarratea, Feb. 6, 1813, AGN-BA, Guerra, 1811–16, X–3–2–3.

88. Miller, *Memoirs,* 1:335; Helg, *Liberty,* 153.

89. "Expediente promovido por Doña Juan Inés Pérez, sobre la devolución de 4 esclavos, 1815," AGN-BA, Admin., leg. 28, exp. 970, IX–23–8–2.

90. "Comunicación de Miguel Vásquez para el Gobernador Político," Caracas, Dec. 6, 1821, and "Borrador referente al esclavo Tomás, que reclama el doctor Escalona," Caracas, Dec. 6, 1821, AGN-C, Gran Colombia, Int.-Ven., tomo 50, 1821, fols. 51 and 59.

91. Quoted in Hünefeldt, *Paying,* 87.

92. *Gazeta de Buenos-Ayres,* Aug. 25, 1819; AGN-BA, Policía Ordenes Superiores, Feb. 6, 1820, tomo 1, no. 182, X–32–10–1.

93. "Autos seguidos por Domingo Ordois contra D. José Aniceto de Arróspide sobre su libertad," AGN-L, Cabildo—Causas Civiles, 1813, leg. 26, cuad. 421.

94. AGN-BA, Sol. Mil., 1815, X–8–7–4.

95. AHM-G, Diversos Funcionarios, 1822, no. 48, fol. 61.

96. AGN-BA, Sol. Civiles y Mil., 1812, X–6–6–12.

97. "De Pedro Briceño Méndez para el Comandante General del Departamento de Venezuela. Transcribe oficio del Comandante General de Cundinamarca, Bogotá," Sept. 10, 1822, AGN-C, Gran Colombia, Int.-Ven., tomo 106, 1822, fol. 252; AGN-BA, Guerra, Sol. Civiles y Mil., 1813, X–6–9–1, Sol. Mil., 1820, X–11–9–2.

98. AGN-BA, Sol. Mil, 1817, X–10–1–1. This file contains numerous requests by soldiers asking for release because of various injuries, such as lost limbs and illnesses suffered in campaigns in the Banda Oriental, Upper Peru, Paraguay, and Argentina.

99. AGN-BA, Sol. Mil., 1817, X–10–1–1.

100. For examples from Colombia, see AGN-B, República, Guerra y Marina, tomos 56 and 58, fols. 213, 215, 219, 256, 265, 315, 383.

101. For example, Boves started out supporting the patriots. For some of the Peruvian leaders who changed sides, see Cecilia Méndez, *The Plebeian Republic: The Huanta Rebellion and the Making of the Peruvian State, 1820–1850* (Durham, NC: Duke University Press, 2005), 59.

102. Semprún and Bullón de Mendoza, *El ejército realista,* chap. 8.

103. Andrews, *Afro-Argentines,* 117; Thibaud, *Repúblicas en armas,* 417, 420, 457, 459–65.

104. San Martín to Balcarce, July 6, 1815, AGN-BA, Ejército de los Andes, 1814–15, X–4–2–5; Argentina, *Documentos,* 2:174.

105. Lecuna and Bierck, *Selected Writings,* 1:135, 142.

106. Ibid., 1:217, 2:412.

107. Domínguez, *Insurrection,* 211–13; Woodward, "The Spanish Army," 590–93.

108. Clissold, *Bernardo O'Higgins,* 190.

109. AHM-L, Ministerio de Guerra y Marina to Commander in Chief, Feb. 5, 1822, Copiador de Correspondencía de Ministerio de Guerra y Marina, 1821/1822, L2; AHM-L,

Alvarado to Ministero de Guerra y Marina, Aug. 10, 1822, leg. 7, no. 317, Aug. 19, 1822, leg. 7, no. 327, Carreño to Minister de Guerra y Marina, Aug. 26, 1822, leg. 17, no. 30, Ribadeneira y Tejada to Ministerio de Guerra y Marina, Mar. 14, 1822, leg. 33, no. 8.

110. AGN-BA, Guerra, Rescate de Esclavos, 1813–17, X–43–6–7, Guerra, 1811–16, X–3–2–3; *Gaceta de Buenos Ayres,* Nov. 1, 1820.

111. Honorario to Supreme Director of the State of Chile, Dec. 14, 1818, ANC-S, Ministerio de Guerra, Provincia de Santiago i sus Departamentos, 1817–28, tomo 18.

112. Reyes Flores, *Esclavitud,* 39.

113. AHM-L, Zufiátegui to Ministerio de Guerra y Marina, Apr. 2, 1822, leg. 39, no. 52.

114. AGN-BA, Ejército de los Andes, 1816, X–4–2–6, Guerra, 1815–16, X–39–8–5, 1818, X–10–4–6, Sumarios Militares, Letra G, exp. 436, X–29–11–6; Andrews, *Afro-Argentines,* 117; Frigerio, "Con sangre de negros," 61.

115. Gen. J. Lara to Government, Dec. 9, 1822, AGN-B, Fondo EOR, caja No. 17, Comandancia Militar, carpeta 68, fol. 25.

116. Hardy to Croker, Secret, no. 127, Dec. 12, 1820, ADM 1/26; ANE-Q, Criminales, caja 228, 1821–22, exp. 22; *Gaceta del Gobierno de Lima,* Aug. 31, 1820.

117. AGN-BA, Sol. Mil., 1817, X–10–1–1.

118. AGN-BA, Solicitudes, Protección de Esclavos, 1816, X–22–1–2.

119. AGN-BA, Sol. Mil., 1822, X–12–10–7. See also the case of the Ecuadorian slave Fermín Padilla who despite being permitted by his owner to serve and fight with Sucre at Pichincha, was reclaimed. ANE-Q, Fondo Especial, caja 240, 1822, vol. 5, no. 106.

120. AGN-BA, Sol. Mil., 1817, X–9–7–10.

121. "Manuel Garmendia, moreno esclavo, sobre su libertad," AGN-BA, Admin., leg. 33, exp. 1142, IX–23–8–7.

CHAPTER 7: THE PERSONAL WAR OF SLAVE WOMEN

1. "La morena Juliana García, esclava que fué de Don Pedro García, reclamando su libertad," 1818, AGN-BA, Admin., leg. 33, exp. 1179, IX–23–8–7.

2. Evelyn Cherpak, "The Participation of Women in the Independence Movement in Gran Colombia, 1780–11830," in *Latin American Women: Historical Perspectives,* ed. Asunción Lavrin (Westport, CT: Greenwood Press, 1978), 219–34; Rebecca Earle, "Rape and the Anxious Republic: Revolutionary Colombia, 1810–1830," in *Hidden Histories of Gender and the State in Latin America,* ed. Elizabeth Dore and Maxine Molyneux (Durham, NC: Duke University Press, 2000), 128–29, 132–33; Prieto de Zegarra, *Mujer,* 2:162–64, 169–70, 240, 278; Ermila Troconis de Veracoechea, *Indias, esclavas, mantuanas y primeras damas* (Caracas: Alfadil Ediciones, 1990), 127–52.

3. "[Memoria militar del General Pezuela (1813–1815)]," in *Memorias, diarios y crónicas,* tomo 26, vol. 1 of *Perú, Colección,* 280; Prieto de Zegarra, *Mujer,* 2:162–64, 169–70.

4. Rafael Antonio Díaz Díaz, *Esclavitud, región y ciudad: El sistema esclavista urbano-regional en Santafé de Bogotá, 1700–1750* (Bogotá: Centro Editorial Javeriano, CEJA, 2001), 63–65.

5. Marta B. Goldberg, "Mujer negra rioplatense (1750–1840)," in *La mitad del país: La*

mujer en la sociedad argentina, ed. Lidia Knecher and Marta Panaia (Tucumán: Bibliotecas Universitarias, 1994), 74.

6. For an overview of female slave life in Río de la Plata during the independence period, see Goldberg, "Mujer negra rioplatense," 67–81. For Lima, see Hünefeldt, *Paying*. See also John Miers, *Travels in Chile and La Plata, Including Accounts Respecting the Geography, Geology, Statistics, Government, Finances, Agriculture, Manners, and Customs, and the Mining Operations in Chile; Collected during a Residence of Several Years in These Countries* (New York: AMS Press, [1970]), 1:5, 156; Andrews, *Afro-Argentines*, 95; Frigerio, "Con sangre de negros," 50; Goldberg and Mallo, "La población africana," 36, 37, 46; Halperín-Donghi, *Politics*, 17, 24, 41–43, 49.

7. Andrews, *Afro-Argentines*, 42–44; Goldberg, "Mujer negra," 69–70; Halperín-Donghi, *Politics*, 40; Johnson, "Manumission," 262, 263, 273–75, 277.

8. "Expediente promovido por Juana Mesagas esclava del Teniente Coronel Don Juan Manuel Cabot, sobre el rescate de dos hijos que quel este la compró," 1821, AGN-BA, Admin., leg. 34, exp. 1201, IX–23–9–1.

9. Salazar to Ministerio de Marina, Nov. 19, 1811, AGI, Estado, 79, no. 31; José Artigas, Nov. 3, 1811, AGI, Buenos Aires, 317; AGN-BA, Gobierno, Correspondencia del Gobierno de Buenos Aires con Elío y Vigodet, 1810–814, X–1–5–10; Pereda Valdes, *Negros esclavos*, 120–23.

10. Masur, *Simon Bolívar*, 264.

11. Quoted in Víctor Barrionuevo Imposti, "La mujer en las campañas san martinia-ras," *Todo Es Historia*, supplement no. 29 (1970): 20.

12. Manuela Sáenz, Bolívar's longtime lover, and her accompanying escort of two black females were notorious for dressing in military uniforms in public. See Lynch, *Simón Bolívar*, 180; Pamela S. Murray, "'Loca' or 'Libertadora'? Manuela Sáenz in the Eyes of History and Historians, 1900–c.1990," *Journal of Latin American Studies* 33, no. 2 (2001): 294–96. In Mexico, donning male attire seems to have been a prerequisite for women to engage in military service at different times during its history. See Elizabeth Salas, *Soldaderas in the Mexican Military: Myth and History* (Austin: University of Texas Press, 1990), chaps. 2, 5.

13. Cherpak, "The Participation," 223.

14. Argentina, *Biblioteca de mayo*, 15:13166.

15. "Expediente promovido por Juana de la Patria, emigrada de Potosí, sobre su livertad," 1817, AGN-BA, Admin., 1816–817, leg. 32, exp. 1113, IX–23–8–6.

16. José Artigas, Nov. 3, 1811, AGI, Buenos Aires 317; "Memoria del Sr. General D. Nicolás de Vedia," 107.

17. AGN-BA, Guerra, Sol. Mil., 1812, X–6–5–7.

18. Páez, *Autobiografía*, 1:118, 141. See also Troconis de Veracoechea, *Indias*, 133, 136, 147.

19. See, for example, the request in 1822 of a sergeant and two soldiers that their wives be permitted to embark from Cartagena. AGN-B, Fondo E.O.R., caja 15, carpeta 60, fol. 33.

20. ["Memoria militar"], 248.

21. Museo Mitre, *Documentos del archivo de Belgrano* (Buenos Aires: Imprenta de Coni Hermanos, 1916), 6:607.

22. Halperín-Donghi, *Politics*, 381.

23. AGN-B, Colonia, Miscelánea, tomo 81, 10–12.

24. Bernand, "La población," 139.

25. Argentina, *Biblioteca de mayo*, 15:13508; AGN-BA, Ejército de los Andes, Enero-Junio 1817, X–4–2–8; Dunbar Temple, "La acción patriótica," tomo 5, vol. 1:418–19, 429.

26. AGN-BA, Sol. Mil., 1818, X–35–7–9.

27. Redhead to Bowles, May 16, 1817, enclosure with Bowles to Croker, Secret, no. 37, May 24, 1817, ADM 1/23; Fisher, *Bourbon Peru*, 131n57. See also Earle, "Rape and the Anxious Republic," 134–36.

28. Andrews, *Afro-Latin America*, 31–33; Hünefeldt, *Paying*, 144–66.

29. "Expediente formado por el negro Francisco, esclavo de Dⁿ José Alberto Calsena y Echevarría: reclamando su libertad," 1813, AGN-BA, Admin., leg. 29, exp. 984, IX–23–8–3.

30. "Solicitando carta de libertad," AGN-BA, Admin., leg. 33, exp. 1144, IX–23–8–7, Sol. Mil., 1815, X–8–7–6.

31. "La morena Juliana García, esclava que fué de Don Pedro García, reclamando su libertad," 1818.

32. Martínez Montero, "Fugas y castigos," 248–49.

33. AGN-L, 1823, O.L. 71–265.

34. "Domingo Miguens solicitando la entrega de una hija," 1818, AGN-BA, Admin., 1818–20, leg. 33, exp. 1191, IX–23–8–7.

35. AGN-BA, Sol. Mil., 1818, X–10–9–5.

36. AGN-BA, Sol. Mil., 1815, X–8–7–4.

37. AGN-BA, Sol. Mil., 1818, X–10–9–5.

38. "José Antonio Albán, sobre tasación de su esposa María Antonia, esclava del Coronel Don Agustín Arenas," 1819, AGN-BA, Admin., leg. 33, exp. 1175, IX–23–8–7.

39. AGN-BA, Sol. Mil., 1817, X–10–1–1.

40. AGN-BA, Sol. Mil., 1822, X–12–10–7.

41. The lottery referred to the freeing of a certain number of Lima slaves annually in recognition of their contribution to the defense of Lima against the royalist attack in September 1821. See above page 100. See also Alvarado to Min° de Guerra y Marina, Feb. 11, Feb. 16, and Sept. 13 1822, AHM-L, leg. 2, nos. 67, and 74, and leg. 7, no. 345.

42. Alvarado to Min° de Guerra y Marina, Feb. 16, 1822, AHM-L, leg. 2, no. 74; AGN-L, O.L. 71–264.

43. In cases where money was assigned to a wife, the soldier may have been recognizing his obligation as a husband. For a brief discussion of a husband's spousal obligations, see Sonya Lipsett-Rivera, "Marriage and Family Relations in Mexico during the Transition from Colony to Nation," in *State and Society in Spanish America during the Age of Revolution*, ed. Victor M. Uribe-Uran (Wilmington, DE: Scholarly Resources, 2001), 125–28.

44. AGN-BA, Sol. Mil., 1815, X–8–7–6, 1819, X–11–3–7; Cutolo, *Nuevo diccionario*, 7:173–74.

45. AGN-BA, Sol. Mil., 1815, X–8–7–6.

46. AGN-BA, Sol. Mil., 1815, X–8–7–5, 1819, X–11–1–7. Venezuelan soldiers were also assigning money to their wives. See Troconis de Veracoechea, *Indias*, 146–47.

47. AGN-BA, Sol. Mil., 1814–1815, X–35–7–7.

48. AGN-BA, Sol. Mil., 1824, X–13–4–8.

49. AGN-BA, Sol. Civiles y Mil., 1816, X–9–2–4, Sol. Mil., 1819, X–11–1–6, X–11–1–7.

50. AGN BA, Sol. Civiles y Mil., 1816, X–9–2–4.

51. AGN-BA, Sol. Mil., 1817, X–13–1–4.

52. AGN-BA, Sol. Mil., 1817, X–10–1–1.

53. AGN-BA, Sol. Mil., 1818, X–35–7–9.

54. AGN-BA, Sol. Mil., 1815, X–8–7–6, 1816, X–35–7–8, 1817, X–9–7–10, 1819, X–11–1–6, Sol. Civiles y Mil., 1816, X–9–2–4, Gobierno, Sol. Mil., 1827, X–9–7–2; AHPBA-LP, Tribunal de Cuentas, Civiles y Militares, 1817 and 1818, 14–1–8–1022.

55. AGN-BA, Sol. Mil., 1810–1813, X–35–7–6.

56. "Expediente promovido ante el Superior Gobierno por Dña María del Carmen Gomez," AGN-L, Superior Gobierno, 1818, leg. 36, cuad. 1268.

57. AGN-BA, Sol. Mil., 1816, X–35–7–8, 1818, X–10–9–5. In Venezuela the same concern is evident. In one case, the mother of a soldier who had served the republican forces for eleven years asked for his license permitting his release. See "Representación que hace María del Carmen Colmenares ante el General en Jefe del Ejército," Maracay, July 7, 1823, AGN-C, Gran Colombia, Int.-Ven., tomo 145, 1823, fol. 184.

58. AGN-L, Colecciones Santa María, 1823, O585; AA-L, Causas de Negros, 1825, leg. 306, exps. 30–32.

59. "Los que sigue María Anselma Vellodas con su ama, Dᵃ Mariana Melendez, sobre su libertad y la de dos hijos suyos," Dec. 7, 1822, AGN-L, Expedientes Judiciales, Causas Civiles, leg. 14, cuad. 3; "Autos que sigue Clara LaValle con Doña Mercedes Palacios," Sept. 20, 1823, AGN-L, Expedientes Judiciales, Causas Civiles, leg. 17, cuad. 7.

60. These averages are based on figures found in the following notarial records: AGN-BA, Protocolos, Escribanos, Juan José de Rocha, registro 2, 1810; Juan Cortes, registro 7, 1813; I. A. Agrelo, 1813–14; José Manuel Godoy, 1819–21.

61. "Don Francisco de Paula Ramiro, sobre que Doña María Petrona Montero lleva la esclaba llamada Juana, que le vendió," AGN-BA, Admin., 1808, leg. 22, exp. 713, IX–23–7–3; "Expediente promovido por el Señor Regidor Protector de esclavos en representación de la criada nombrada Juana . . . ," AGN-BA, Admin., 1816–17, leg. 30, exp. 1030, IX–23–8–4; "El Coronel Don Cornelio Zelaya, con su esclava Marta, sobre la libertad de esta," AGN-BA, Admin., 1816–17, leg. 32, exp. 1097; "Doña Manuela Nuñez que ha comprada a Don Angel Sanches una negra llamada Inés," AGN-BA, Admin., 1816–17, leg. 32, exp. 1128, IX–23–8–6.

62. AGN-BA, Protocolos, Escribanos, Juan José de Rocha, registro 2, 1810; Justo José Nuñez, 1810–12, 1813–15; I. A. Agrelo, 1813–14; Juan Cortes, registro 7, 1813; José Manuel Godoy, 1819–21; Narciso Yranzuaga, 1820; Manuel de Llames, 1825.

63. "El que fue Alcalde de 1a nominación, el Señor Francisco Bernal, quien entregó este cuaderno para que lo archive," AHG-G, 1823, no. 1546.

64. Josefa Ramírez to the intendent, Caracas, July 22, 1823, AGN-C, Gran Colombia, Int.-Ven., tomo 146, 1823, fol. 296; "Representación que hace Antonio Delgado ante el Intendente Departamental," Valencia, Aug. 7, 1823, AGN-C, Gran Colombia, Int.-Ven., tomo 148, 1823, fol. 154.

65. Camilla Townsend, "'Half My Body Free, the Other Half Enslaved': The Politics of the Slaves of Guayas at the End of the Colonial Era," *Colonial Latin American Review* 7, no. 1 (1998): 105–28. A modified version of this article is Camilla Townsend, "Angela Batallas: A Fight for Freedom in Guayaquil," in *The Human Tradition in Colonial Latin America*, ed. Kenneth J. Andrien (Wilmington, DE: Scholarly Resources, 2002), 293–307. The original document is "Angela Batallas contra su amo Ildefonso Coronel, sobre su libertad," 1823, AHG-G, no. 698.

66. "Asuntos promovidos por María del Carmen Sarria, negra esclava de Don Francisco Aviles," Oct. 20, 1823, AGN-L, Expedientes Judiciales, Causas Civiles, 1823, cuad. 14, leg. 17.

67. "Lucas Rivadavia, esclavo de Don Bernardino Rivadavia . . . sirva en el Cuerpo de Libertos," 1813–14, AGN-BA, Admin., leg. 30, exp. 1025, IX–23–8–4. For another example of a mother interceding on behalf of her son, who had been sold to the state for military service, see the case of Feliciana Herrera, a free *parda* from Buenos Aires, in AGN-BA, Sol. Mil., 1820, X–11–9–2.

CHAPTER 8: THE SURVIVAL OF SLAVERY

1. Feliú Cruz, *La abolición*, 59, 66–68, 73, 98, 102–4, chap. 7.

2. Enclosure with Canning to Rowcroft, no. 2, Dec. 15, 1823, FO 61/1.

3. Lynch, *Simón Bolívar*, 151–53, 203; Salcedo-Bastardo, *Bolívar*, 105, 109.

4. Crl. Francisco de Buenza to José Prieto, Feb. 11, 1828, AHM-L, leg. 5-B-1, no. 181.

5. Aguirre, *Breve historia*, 245–53.

6. ANE-Q, Esclavos, caja 23, 1825–30, exps. 3 and 6.

7. "Pablo Delgado para el Vicepresidente," Ocumare de la Costa, Jan. 27, 1822, AGN-C, Gran Colombia, Int.-Ven., tomo 63, 1822, fol. 184.

8. AGN-L, O.L., 7–3, 20–18, 30–5.

9. Ricketts to Canning, no. 26, Dec. 27, 1826, FO 61/8. See also *El Comercio* (Lima), Apr. 27, 1841.

10. "Representación del Administrador de la Obra Pía de Chuao, Bartolomé Manrique al intendente," Caracas, Mar. 8, 1822, AGN-C, Gran Colombia, Int.-Ven., tomo 4, 1822, fol. 190.

11. "Oficio de Juan Félix Ovalles, Comisario de Nirgua, al Jefe de Estado Mayor del Ejército," Canoabo, June 24, 1822, AGN-C, Gran Colombia, Guerra y Marina, tomo 21, 1822, fol. 204; "Oficio del Comandante Político y Militar del Cantón de Nirgua, al Comandante General de la Línea contra Puerto Cabello," Nirgua, June 17, 1822, AGN-C, Gran Colombia, Guerra y Marina, tomo 22, 1822, fol. 288; "Comunicación de Juan Antonio de Acha para el Intendente del Departamento," Choroní, May 6, 1822, AGN-C, Gran Colombia, Intendencia de Venezuela, tomo 83, 1822, fol. 329; "Oficio del Juez Político de Ocumare al Intendente," Sabana de Ocumare, June 1, 1823, AGN-C, Gran Colombia, Intendencia de Venezuela, tomo 10, 1823, fol. 35; "J. Escalona para el Intendente Departamental," Caracas, Aug. 1, 1823, AGN-C, Gran Colombia, Intendencia de Venezuela, tomo 148, 1823, fol. 31.

12. Lecuna and Bierck, *Selected Writings*, 2:512. See also O'Leary, *Bolívar*, 332–33.

13. AHM-G, Diversos Ministerios, 1822, no. 46, fol. 112; ANE-Q, Milicias, caja 7, 1820–23, Nov. 4, 1823; Russell Lohse, "Reconciling Freedom with the Rights of Property: Slave Emancipation in Colombia, 1821–1852, with Special Reference to La Plata," *Journal of Negro History* 86, no. 3 (2001): 205; Rout, *African Experience*, 226.

14. Andrews, *Afro-Argentines*, 34; Peter Blanchard, *Slavery and Abolition in Early Republican Peru* (Wilmington, DE: Scholarly Resources, Inc., 1992), 12.

15. For the case of the Colombian Caribbean, see Helg, *Liberty*, 180–84, 188, 235.

16. "Expediente sobre los autos seguidos por la esclava Isabel Verano, para cambiar de amo," Huaura, Oct. 17, 1825, BN-L, D12586. See also AGN-L, Expedientes Judiciales, Causas Civiles, 1826, leg. 33, cuads. 1, 2, 3, and 11; ANE-Q, Esclavos, caja 22, 1818–24, exp.17.

17. Perú, *Colección*, 1:106–7, 322–24, 326, 351, 2:96, 159–60, 167–69, 182; *El Imparcial del Ecuador* (Quito), Dec. 17, 1827; Blanchard, *Slavery and Abolition*, chap. 3; Colmenares, "Popayán," 163–64; Camilo Destruge, "La esclavitud en el Ecuador," *Boletín de la Biblioteca Municipal de Guayaquil*, no. 28 (1912): 52–53; Lynch, *Argentine Dictator*, 122.

18. Quoted in Lynch, *Spanish American Revolutions*, 225. See also Peter Blanchard, "Pan Americanism and Slavery in the Era of Latin American Independence," in *Beyond the Ideal: Pan Americanism in Inter-American Affairs*, ed. David Sheinin (Westport, CT: Praeger, 2000), 12.

19. Aline Helg makes this point for Colombia, but it applies more broadly. See Helg, *Liberty*, 168.

20. Aline Helg, "Simón Bolívar and the Spectre of *Pardocracia:* José Padilla in Post-Independence Cartagena," *Journal of Latin American Studies* 35, no. 3 (2003): 450–53, 455; Helg, *Liberty and Equality*, 196–11; Lasso, "Haiti as an Image," 184–86.

21. Reid Andrews has written that fewer than 150 returned. Francisco Morrone gives a figure of 159. Andrews, *Afro-Argentines*, 117, 118; Morrone, "La participación," 356.

22. AGN-BA, Guerra, Ejército de los Andes, 1823–826, X–4–4–1.

23. Miller, *Memoirs*, 2:427; Helg, *Liberty*, 175; Izard, *El miedo*, 158–63; Lynch, *Spanish American Revolutions*, 222–24.

24. Espejo, "El paso de los Andes," 14105; AGN-BA, Sol. Mil., 1817, X–10–1–1; AGN-BA, Gobierno, Sol. Mil., 1817, X–9–7–2; Klachko, "Le processus," 143.

25. For the cases of two Venezuelan slaves who expressed a desire to return to their owners, see "El Coronel Juan Padrón, a nombre de la Señora Teresa Gutierrez de Malo, reclama un esclavo," AGN-C, República, Secretaría del Interior y Justicia, tomo 4, 1830, fol. 246; and "Sobre el reclamo que hace Pedro Elisaldy de dos esclavos de su propiedad," AGN-C, República, Secretaría del Interior y Justicia, tomo 18, 1831, fol. 411.

26. See, for example, "Peticiones presentadas por varios negros para que se les expida licencia para que pueden contraer matrimonio," Lima, Nov. 4, 1828, BN-L, D10859, which contains several Peruvian cases of soldiers marrying slaves, including one of a black soldier from Buenos Aires who was marrying a fourteen-year-old. In another instance, a former Peruvian slave named Manuel Inosencio Aparicio, who had been drafted into the patriot army shortly after it entered Lima and subsequently served in the militia, moved to Chile after the war and in 1835, after fourteen years of separation, wrote to the archbish-

opric of Lima inquiring about the wife he had left behind, whom he believed had died, as he was "resolved" to remarry. Unfortunately for his plans, his wife was found to be still alive. See AA-L, Causas de Negros, leg. 36, exp.51, 1835.

27. Colonel Francis Hall, "Treatise on Colombia," enclosure with Sutherland to Canning, no. 1, Mar. 11, 1824, FO 18/8. The decline in Colombia was also significant. See Helg, *Liberty*, 167–68.

28. Enclosure with Hullett to Canning, July 31, 1824, FO 6/6.

29. Rowcroft, Private, Oct. 11, 1824, FO 61/3.

30. Legaciones y Oficios al Intendente, 1823, AHM-G, no. 55, fol. 60.

31. "De José Joaquín y Juan Hernández sin destinatario," Caracas, Dec. 19, 1822, AGN-C, Gran Colombia, Int.-Ven., tomo 123, 1822, fol. 246; Perú, *Colección*, 1:30.

32. "Sobre que se declare la libertad que reclama Timoteo a su ama," AGN-L, Corte Superior de Justicia, Causas Civiles, 1825, leg. 29, cuad. 17.

33. Andrews, *Afro-Argentines*, 51–52; Klachko, "Le processus," 126.

34. Andrews, *Afro-Argentines*, 53; Goldberg, "Mujer negra," 75; Goldberg, "La población negra," 84–86; Goldberg and Mallo, "La población africana," 18; Masini, *La esclavitud*, 51; Williams, "Observations," 420.

35. AGN-B, Notaria, Eugenio de Elorga, 1824, tomo 244, 1825, tomo 245, 1826, tomo 246, 1827, tomo 247, and 1828, tomo 250.

36. In Uruguay, the proportion of slaves rose between 1810 and 1832 as a result of Brazilian domination and illegal imports. See Williams, "Observations," 414. For details of the ineffectiveness of the manumission juntas in Ecuador and Colombia, see AHM-G, Diversos Funcionarios, 1824, vol. 1, no. 61, fol. 113, and vol. 3, no. 62, fol. 104; Helg, *Liberty*, 169–72; Lohse, "Reconciling Freedom," 206–7. In Venezuela, only sixty-nine slaves were freed by 1829, and an average of twenty-five were freed annually in the years afterwards. See Izard, *El miedo*, 63–64; John V. Lombardi, "Manumission, *Manumisos*, and *Aprendizaje* in Republican Venezuela," *Hispanic American Historical Review* 49, no. 4 (1969): 666.

37. "El Señor Procurador General en defensa de José Hurtado y otros contra el ciudadano Francisco Granja sobre libertad de sus protegidos," AHG-G, 1823, no. 784.

38. ANE-Q, Criminales, caja 230, 1823–24, exp. 18.

39. For the lack of unity between *pardos* and blacks in Colombia, see Helg, *Liberty*, 184.

40. Bowles to Croker, Secret, no. 113, Oct. 3, 1818, ADM 1/23; Bowles to Croker, Secret, no. 165 Feb. 27, 1819, ADM 1/24.

41. Rebaza, *Anales*, 235–36.

42. Campbell to Canning, no. 102, Oct. 7, 1826, FO 18/28.

43. Lecuna and Bierck, *Selected Writings*, 2:613.

44. Lecuna and Bierck, *Selected Writings*, 2:480, 495; Jorge Basadre, *Historia de la república del Perú, 1822–1933*, 6th ed. (Lima: Editorial Universitaria, 1969–1970), 1:200–201.

45. J. J. Santana to Secretary of War, Sept. 26, 1823, AGN-B, Archivo Restrepo, caja 7, fondo 1, vol. 7, fols. 126–27.

46. Lecuna and Bierck, *Selected Writings*, 2:526, 530, 535, 537, 547, 550; AGN-B, Fondo E. O. R., caja 15, carpeta 60, fols. 140, 142; Campbell to Canning, no. 137, Dec. 21, 1826, FO 18/28.

47. Watts to Canning, no. 8, Jan. 24, 1826, FO 18/31.

48. Ricketts to Planta, Jan. 30, Ricketts to Canning, Secret, Feb. 6, no. 8, Mar. 31, 1827, FO 61/11; Basadre, *Historia*, 1:193–94.

49. Salom to Heres, Jan. 27, 1825, Jan. 30, 1825, Feb. 1, 1825, and May 8, 1825, AHM-L, Ministerio de Guerra y Marina, leg. 24, nos. 8, 14, 21, and 171; Figueredo to Ministerio de Departamento de Guerra, Jan. 2 and June 21, 1825, AHM-L, leg. 9, nos. 38 and 85; Figueredo to Ministerio de Guerra y Marina, May 21, June 11, and June 18, 1825, AHM-L, leg. 9, nos. 74, 80, and 83.

50. Salom to Ministerio de Guerra, June 1, 1825, AHM-L, leg. 25, no. 212; Salazar to Ministerio de Guerra y Marina, May 4, May 6, and May 17, 1825, AHM-L, leg. 25, nos. 48, 654, and 673.

51. "D. Mariano Reyna sobre la devolución de un esclavo suyo que está sirviendo a la Patria, y en la actualidad en el Resguardo Militar del Callao," AGN-L, P.L. 6–189, 1826; Figueredo to Ministerio de Guerra y Marina, Jan. 14, 1826, AHM-L, leg. 7, no. 6.

52. Figueredo to Ministerio de Guerra y Marina, Mar. 29, 1826, AHM-L, leg. 9, no. 228; Salazar to Ministerio de Guerra, June 12, 1826, AHM-L, leg. 25, no. 10.

53. "Expediente promovido por D. Vicente del Castillo, solicitando le se devuelto un esclavo negro de su propiedad llamado Manuel del Castillo, enrolado en la artilleria," AGN-L, O.L. 145–561, 1826.

54. Larenas to Figueredo, July 8, 1826, AHM-L, leg. 15, no. 59; Salazar to Ministerio de Guerra, July 22, 1826, AHM-L, leg. 25, no. 67.

55. *Gaceta del Gobierno Estraordinaria*, Jan. 23, 1826, enclosed with Ricketts to Canning, no. 1, Jan. 23, 1826, FO 61/7; Tavara, *Abolición*, 12.

56. See, for example, José María Pérez to the intendente, Caracas, Aug. 27, 1823, AGN-C, Gran Colombia, Int.-Ven., tomo 149, 1823, fol. 224.

57. "Borrador: Se ordena excluir del servicio a un esclavo de la propiedad del señor Pedro Manuel Oropeza," Dec. 4, 1821, AGN-C, Gran Colombia, Int.-Ven., tomo 49, 1821, fol. 389; "Comunicación a F. Avendeño para el Gobernador Político de Caracas," La Guaira, Dec. 5, 1821, AGN-C, Gran Colombia, Int.-Ven., tomo 50, 1821, fol. 9; "Comunicación de C. Soublette para el Gobernador Político de esta Provincia," Caracas, Dec. 12, 1821, AGN-C, Gran Colombia, Int.-Ven., tomo 50, 1821, fol. 310.

58. "Expediente obrado a instancia del C. Tomás Pérez reclamando la entrega de un esclavo nombrado Felipe perteneciente a su suegro Antonio Montes de Oca que se ha alistado en el Batallón de Arisuategui, o que se admita su valor en pago de lo que deba satisfacer en la administración de secuestro," AANH-C, Civiles-Esclavos, 1825, caja 19, exp. 3.

59. "Representación de la Señora Rosalia de la Madriz al Intendente," Caracas, May 7, 1822, AGN-C, Gran Colombia, Int.-Ven., tomo 4, 1822, fol. 339; "Solicitud de José Bernardo Arévalo," Ocumare, May 7, 1822, AGN-C, Gran Colombia, Int.-Ven., tomo 83, 1822, fol. 346; "Representación que hace María Teresa Velez Cossio ante el Intendente Departamental," Caracas, July 18, 1822, AGN-C, Gran Colombia, Int.-Ven., tomo 148, 1823, fol. 139; "De C. Soublette para el Tesorero de los fondos de Manumisión," Caracas, June 7, 1823, AGN-C, Gran Colombia, Int.-Ven., tomo 142, 1823, fol. 229; "La Señora Rosa Ramona Pérez cobrando trescientos pesos contra los fondos centrales de manumisión por

valor de su esclavo José Cirilo que tomó service en los ejércitos de la República," AGN-C, República, Secretaria del Interior y Justicia, tomo 1, 1830, fol. 169; "La Señora Manuela Suárez de Urbina reclamando el valor de un esclavo de su propiedad que tomó servicio en los ejércitos de la República," AGN-C, República, Secretaria del Interior y Justicia, tomo 23, 1831, fol. 142. See also "El Sindico Procurador municipal de este canton demandando al Sõr Domíngo Vargas la libertad de Andrés Vargas, su siervo, por haber servido en los ejércitos de la República," AANH-C, Civiles-Esclavos, 1828-IRV, exp. 3; "El Sõr Candelario Espinosa cobrando al Estado el valor de su esclavo, Silvestre, que tomó las armas en defensa de la República," AANH-C, 1829-ACEF, exp. 3.

60. See, for example, documents concerning the slave José Agustín, who enlisted in the Batallón Granaderos de la Guardia, Mar. 7, 1837, AGN-C, Gran Colombia, Int.-Ven., tomo 9, 1823, fols. 76–84; "El Señor Ramón Fuenmayor sobre que se le abone el resto del valor de su esclavo José Antonio Sambrano que fué declarado libre por la Dirección de Manumisión en 1830," AGN-C, República, Secretaria del Interior y Justicia, tomo 21, 1831, fol. 123.

61. "El Señor Procurador Municipal en defensa de Alexandro Campusano, esclavo, sobre se le declare exento del servicio de esclavitud," AHG-G, 1826, no. 5996. For other cases, see "El Señor Procurador Municipal, por Manuel José Martínez, sobre su libertad en consideración a los servicios hechos de soldado," AHG-G, 1826, no. 6242; "El Señor Procurador Municipal en defense de Diego Penedo, sobre se le declare libre," AHG-G, 1826, no. 6196; ANE-Q, Fondo Especial, caja 244, 1823, vol. 2, no. 170; Manuel Valdés to Intendant of Departamento, Guayaquil, Feb 24, 1826, AHM-G, Comandancias Militares, 1826, no. 80, fol. 30.

62. ANE-Q, Esclavos, caja 22, 1818–24, exp. 19.

63. "El Señor Procurador Municipal en defensa de Teodoro Samora, sobre su libertad en virtud de haber servido a la Patria," AHG-G, 1826, no. 6238.

64. "El Señor Procurador Municipal en defensa de Antonio Quiñones sobre se le declare libre en atención a los servicios hechos a la República," AHG-G, 1826, no. 6207. See also "El Señor Procurador Municipal en defensa de Toribio Lazo con la Sra Rosa Lazo sobre la libertad de esta esclavo por haber servido a la Patria," AHG-G, 1826, no. 8317.

65. "El Señor Procurador Municipal, por el esclavo Jacinto Santos, sobre se le declare libre por servicio hecho de soldado en la República," AHG-G, 1826, no. 6007. The same argument, that freedom should not be granted for brief service, was being made in Venezuela. See "José de Jesús Malpica, esclavo de los herederos de Melchor Canivel, sobre su libertad," AANH-C, Civiles-Esclavos, 1827-CMPR, exp. 2.

66. ANE-Q, Esclavos, caja 22, 1818–24, exp. 21; Francisco Gerónimo Cicero, slave of Hacienda Saldaña, BN-B, tomo 329, no. 961, 103–6.

67. AGN-BA, Sol. Mil., 1824, X–13–4–8.

68. Ibid.

69. "Expediente sobre la petición presentada por Angela Zagal, para que se deja sin efecto la solicitud presentada por un esclavo de su propiedad y se le ponga bajo su dominio," Lima, May 28, 1828, BN-L, D10936.

70. Perú, *Colección*, 3:249. For further claims, see Fuente to Ministerio de Guerra y Marina, Mar. 5, 1828, AHM-L, leg. 9, no. 77; Gamarra to Ministerio de Estado en el Depar-

tamento de Guerra y Marina, Aug. 26, 1828, AHM-L, leg. 11, no. 49; Morales to Ministerio de Guerra y Marina, Feb. 28, 1828, AHM-L, leg. 22, no. 180; "Expediente seguido por Don Isidro Pisarro sobre el reojo de su esclavo Nicolas Torralva," AGN-L, Expedientes Judiciales, Causas Civiles, 1826, leg. 34, cuad. 7.

71. Dunbar Temple, *La acción patriótica*, 6:420–46.

72. "Expediente seguido por José Ambrosio Surarregui reclamando su libertad por haver servido a las tropas de la República," AANH-C, Civiles-Esclavos, 1829-LRST, exp. 6.

73. "Documentos sobre servicio de dos esclavos, José Estebán y Jacobo, en la Batallón de Granaderos," Caracas, Aug. 18, 1823–Oct. 10, 1840, AGN-C, Gran Colombia, Int.-Ven., tomo 9, 1823.

74. AGN-C, Revolución y Gran Colombia, Ilustres Próceres, Toribio Gascue, letra G, tomo 33, fol. 315.

75. *La Miscelánea* (Lima), June 26, 1830.

76. For a brief overview of some of the postwar hostilities, see Lynch, *Spanish American Revolutions*, 67–71, 103–5, 353–56.

77. Hardy to Croker, Secret, no. 69, July 11, 1820, ADM 1/25; Masini, *La esclavitud*, 34–35.

78. Ponsonby to Canning, no. 38, Dec. 30, 1826, FO 6/13. Among the veterans was Lorenzo Barcala, who subsequently served in both the Argentine civil wars and the war against Brazil. See Cutolo, *Nuevo diccionario*, 1:323–24. See also Andrews, *Afro-Argentines*, 117.

79. General José María Plaza, Piura, to Ministerio de Guerra y Marina, Mar. 21, 1828, AHM-L, Ministerio de Guerra y Marina, leg. 28, no. 462; "El Señor José Santa-Coloma reclama la entrega de su esclavo Pedro Franco, y acredita su buena conducta," AHG-G, 1830, no. 501; "La Señora Juana Avellán sobre el pago del valor de su esclavo José María Indaburu, que se tomó para el servicio militar," AHG-G, 1829, no. 7583.

BIBLIOGRAPHY

ARCHIVAL SOURCES

Argentina:

Archivo General de la Nación, Buenos Aires, especially Administrativos, Ejército de los
  Andes, Gobierno, Guerra, Hacienda, Protocolos, Rescate de Esclavos, Solicitudes Mili-
  tares, and Tribunal de Cuentas
Archivo Histórico de la Provincia de Buenos Aires, La Plata, especially Tribunal de Cuentas

Chile:

Archivo Nacional de Chile, Santiago, especially Causas Particulares, Ejército de Chile,
  Fondo Varios, Intendencia, and Ministerio de Guerra

Colombia:

Archivo General de la Nación, Bogotá, especially Archivo Anexo, Archivo Restrepo, Esclavos, Fondo E. O. R., Guerra y Marina, Negros y Esclavos, Notaria, and Solicitudes
Biblioteca Nacional, Bogotá

Ecuador:

Archivo Histórico Municipal "Camilo Destruge," Guayaquil, especially Comandancias, Di-
  versos Funcionarios, Diversos Ministerios, Legaciones y Oficios al Intendente, and
  Listas de Revistas y Estados
Archivo Histórico de Guayas, Guayaquil
Archivo Nacional del Ecuador, Quito, especially Criminales, Esclavos, Fondo Especial, and
  Milicias

England:

Public Record Office, London, Admiralty, file 1 and Foreign Office, files 6, 18, and 61

Peru:

Archivo Arzobispal, Lima, especially Causas de Negros

Archivo General de la Nación, Lima, especially Causas Civiles, Causas Criminales, Colecciones Santa María, Ejército, Protocolos, Real Hacienda, and Superior Gobierno

Archivo Histórico Militar, Lima, especially Acuerdo de la Suprema Junta Gobernativa, Correspondencia, and Manual de Partes

Biblioteca Nacional, Lima

Spain:

Archivo General de Indias, Seville, especially Buenos Aires, Caracas, Estado, Lima, and Santa Fe

Uruguay:

Casa de Lavalleja, Montevideo, especially Colección de Manuscritos Pablo Blanco Acevedo

Venezuela:

Archivo de la Academia Nacional de la Historia, Caracas, Civiles-Esclavos

Archivo Arzobispal, Caracas, especially Judiciales

Archivo General de la Nación, Caracas, especially Archivo de Aragua, Gobernación y Capitanía General, Ilustres Próceres, Intendencia de Venezuela, and Secretaria del Interior y Justicia

Fundación Bolton, Caracas, Archivo Sucre

PRIMARY SOURCES

Aguirre, José María. "Compendio de las campañas del Ejército de los Andes." In Argentina, Comisión Nacional del Centenario, *Documentos del archivo de San Martín*, vol. 10, 213–28. Buenos Aires: Imprenta de Coni Hermanos, 1910–11.

"Antecedentes y organización del Ejército de los Andes." In Argentina, Senado de la Nación, *Biblioteca de mayo*, vol. 17, part 1.

Argentina. *Registro oficial de la república Argentina que comprende los documentos expedidos desde 1810 hasta 1872*. 2 vols. Buenos Aires: "La República," 1879.

———. Comisión Nacional del Centenario. *Documentos del archivo de San Martín*. 12 vols. Buenos Aires: Imprenta de Coni Hermanos, 1910–11.

———. Senado de la Nación. *Biblioteca de mayo: Colección de obras y documentos para la historia Argentina*. 17 vols. Buenos Aires: Imprenta del Congreso de la Nación, 1960–63.

Cartas Santander-Bolívar. 6 vols. Bogotá: Biblioteca de la Presidencia de la República, 1988–90.

Chile. *Boletín de las leyes i decretos del gobierno 1819–1820*. Santiago: Imprenta Nacional, 1900.

Cochrane, Charles Stuart. *Journal of a Residence and Travels in Colombia, during the Years 1823 and 1824*. 2 vols. London: Henry Colburn, 1825.

Dunbar Temple, Ella, ed. *La acción patriótica del pueblo en la emancipación: Guerrillas y montoneras*. Tomo 5, vols. 1–6, of Perú, *Colección documental de la independencia del Perú*.

Haigh, Samuel. *Sketches of Buenos Ayres, Chile, and Peru.* London: Effingham Wilson, 1831.

Lecuna, Vicente, comp., and Harold A. Bierck Jr., ed. *Selected Writings of Bolívar.* Translated by Lewis Bertrand. 2 vols. New York: The Colonial Press Inc., 1951.

"Memoria del Sr. General D. Nicolás de Vedia." *Boletín Histórico, Estado Mayor General del Ejército* 96–97 (1963): 101–11.

"[Memoria militar del General Pezuela (1813–1815)]." In *Memorias, diarios y crónicas*, 241–345. Edited by Félix Denegri Luna. Tomo 26, vol. 1 of *Perú, Colección documental de la independencia del Perú.*

"Memorias de Dámaso de Uriburu." In Argentina, Senado de la Nación, *Biblioteca de mayo*, vol. 1.

Miers, John. *Travels in Chile and La Plata, Including Accounts Respecting the Geography, Geology, Statistics, Government, Finances, Agriculture, Manners, and Customs, and the Mining Operations in Chile; Collected during a Residence of Several Years in these Countries.* 2 vols. 1826; New York: AMS Press, [1970].

Miller, John. *Memoirs of General Miller, in the Service of the Republic of Peru.* 2nd ed. 2 vols. London: Longman, Rees, Orme, Brown, and Green, 1829.

Museo Mitre. *Documentos del archivo de Belgrano.* 7 vols. Buenos Aires: Imprenta de Coni Hermanos, 1913–17.

O'Leary, Daniel Florencio. *Memorias del General O'Leary.* 34 vols. Caracas: Ministerio de la Defensa, 1980.

O'Leary, Simón B. *Bolívar en el Perú.* Caracas: Archivo General de la Nación, 1971.

Páez, José Antonio. *Autobiografía del General José Antonio Páez.* 2 vols. Caracas: Petróleos de Venezuela, 1990.

Perú. *Colección de leyes, decretos y ordenes desde su independencia en el año de 1821, hasta 31 de diciembre de 1830.* 7 vols. Lima: Imprenta de José Masias, 1831.

———. *Colección de los bandos publicados por el gobierno de Lima independiente.* Lima: Imprenta de Río, 1821.

———. *Colección documental de la independencia del Perú.* 30 vols. Lima: Comisión Nacional del Sesquicentenario de la Independencia del Perú, 1971.

Proctor, Robert. *Narrative of a Journey across the Cordillera of the Andes, and of a Residence in Lima, and Other Parts of Peru, in the Years 1823 and 1824.* London: A. Constable and Co. Edinburgh, 1825.

"República Oriental del Uruguay, Estado Mayor General del Ejército, Sección 'Historia y Archivo.'" *Boletín Histórico del Estado Mayor General del Ejército* (Montevideo) 100–103 (1964): 63.

Newspapers

Boletín de Cartagena, 1815.

Correo del Orinoco, Angostura, Venezuela, 1818, 1820, 1821.

El Centinela en Campaña, Huánuco, Peru, 1824.

El Comercio, Lima, 1841.

Gaceta de Buenos Aires, 1810, 1811, 1820, 1821.

Gaceta del Gobierno, Trujillo, Peru, 1824.

Gaceta del Gobierno de Lima, 1819, 1820, 1823, 1825.
Gaceta Extraordinaria de Buenos Aires, 1812.
Gaceta Extraordinaria del Gobierno de Lima, 1819.
Gaceta Ministerial del Gobierno de Buenos Ayres, 1813.
Gazeta de Buenos-Ayres, 1819.
Gazeta del Gobierno de Lima Independiente, 1823.
Gazeta del Gobierno Estraordinaria, Lima, 1826.
El Imparcial del Ecuador, Quito, 1827.
La Miscelánea, Lima, 1830.
El Peruano, Lima, 1826, 1855.
Suplemento a la Gaceta de Buenos Aires, 1812.
Suplemento a la Gaceta Ministerial, Buenos Aires, 1812.

SECONDARY SOURCES

Aguirre, Carlos. *Agentes de su propia libertad: Los esclavos de Lima y la desintegración de la esclavitud 1821–1854.* Lima: Pontificia Universidad Católica del Perú, Fonda Editorial, 1993.

———. *Breve historia del esclavitud en el Perú: Una herida que no deja de sangrar.* Lima: Fondo Editorial del Congreso del Perú, 2005.

———. "Cimarronaje, bandolerismo y desintegración esclavista: Lima, 1821–1854." In Aguirre and Walker, *Bandoleros, abigeos y montoneros,* 137–82.

Aguirre, Carlos, and Charles Walter, eds. *Bandoleros, abigeos y montoneros: Criminalidad y violencia en el Perú, siglos XVIII–XX.* Lima: Instituto de Apoyo Agrario, 1990.

Anderson, Benedict. *Imagined Communities: Reflections on the Origin and Spread of Nationalism.* 2nd ed. London: Verso, 1991.

Andrews, George Reid. *The Afro-Argentines of Buenos Aires, 1800–1900.* Madison: University of Wisconsin Press, 1980.

———. *Afro–Latin America, 1800–2000.* New York: Oxford University Press, 2004.

Anna, Timothy E. "Economic Causes of San Martín's Failure in Lima." *Hispanic American Historical Review* 54, no. 4 (1974): 657–81.

———. *The Fall of the Royal Government in Peru.* Lincoln: University of Nebraska Press, 1979.

———. "Spain and the Breakdown of the Imperial Ethos: The Problem of Equality." *Hispanic American Historical Review* 62, no. 2 (1982): 254–72.

Archer, Christon I. *The Army in Bourbon Mexico, 1760–1810.* Albuquerque: University of New Mexico Press, 1977.

Barrionuevo Imposti, Víctor. *Los esclavos de San Luis en el Ejército de los Andes y otros documentos sanmartinianos.* Villa Dolores, Argentina: Tallares Gráficos "Democracia," 1947.

———. "La mujer en las campañas san martiniaras." *Todo Es Historia,* supplement no. 29 (1970): 1–31.

Basadre, Jorge. *Historia de la república del Perú, 1822–1933.* 6th ed. 16 vols. Lima: Editorial Universitaria, 1969–70.

Bernand, Carmen. "La población negra de Buenos Aires (1777–1862)." In Mónica Quijada, Carmen Bernand, and Arnd Schneider, *Homogeneidad y nación con un estudio de caso: Argentina, siglos XIX y XX*, 93–140. Madrid: Consejo Superior de Investigaciones Científicas, 2000.

Beverina, Juan. *El virreinato de las provincias del Río de la Plata, su organización militar: Contribución a la "historia del ejército argentino."* 2nd ed. Buenos Aires: Circulo Militar, 1992.

Bierck, Harold A., Jr. "The Struggle for Abolition in Gran Colombia." *Hispanic American Historical Review* 33, no. 3 (1953): 365–86.

Blackburn, Robin. *The Overthrow of Colonial Slavery, 1776–1848*. London: Verso, 1988.

Blanchard, Peter. "The Language of Liberation: Slave Voices in the Wars of Independence." *Hispanic American Historical Review* 82, no. 3 (1993): 499–523.

———. "Pan Americanism and Slavery in the Era of Latin American Independence." In *Beyond the Ideal: Pan Americanism in Inter-American Affairs*, edited by David Sheinin, 9–18. Westport, CT: Praeger, 2000.

———. *Slavery and Abolition in Early Republican Peru*. Wilmington, DE: Scholarly Resources, Inc., 1992.

Bowser, Frederick P. *The African Slave in Colonial Peru, 1524–1650*. Stanford: Stanford University Press, 1974.

Brito Figueroa, Federico. *La estructura económica de Venezuela colonial*. Caracas: Instituto de Investigaciones, Facultad de Economía, Universidad Central de Venezuela, 1963.

Brown, Christopher Leslie, and Philip D. Morgan, eds. *Arming Slaves from Classical Times to the Modern Age*. New Haven: Yale University Press, 2006.

Brown, Matthew. *Adventuring through Spanish Colonies: Simón Bolívar, Foreign Mercenaries and the Birth of New Nations*. Liverpool: Liverpool University Press, 2006.

Bryant, Sherwin K. "Enslaved Rebels, Fugitives, and Litigants: The Resistance Continuum in Colonial Quito." *Colonial Latin American Review* 13, no. 1 (2004): 7–46.

Bushnell, David. *Simón Bolívar: Liberation and Disappointment*. New York: Pearson Longman, 2004.

Campbell, Leon G. "The Army of Peru and the Túpac Amaru Revolt, 1780–1783." *Hispanic American Historical Review* 56, no. 1 (1979): 31–57.

———. *The Military and Society in Colonial Peru, 1750–1810*. Philadelphia: American Philosophical Society, 1978.

Carvalho Neto, Paulo de, ed. *El negro uruguayo (hasta la abolición)*. Quito: Editorial Universitaria, 1965.

Castellano Sáenz Cavia, Rafael M. "La abolición de la esclavitud en las Provincias Unidas del Río de la Plata (1810–1860)." *Revista de Historia del Derecho* (Buenos Aires) 9 (1981): 55–157.

Centurión Vallejo, Héctor. *Esclavitud y manumisión de negros en Trujillo*. Trujillo: n.p., 1954.

Chaves, María Eugenia. *María Chiquinquirá Díaz, una esclava del siglo XVIII: Acerca de las identidades de amo y esclavo en el puerto colonial de Guayaquil*. Guayaquil: Archivo Histórico del Guayas, 1998.

Cherpak, Evelyn. "The Participation of Women in the Independence Movement in Gran

Colombia, 1780–1830." In *Latin American Women: Historical Perspectives*, edited by
Asunción Lavrin, 219–34. Westport, CT: Greenwood Press, 1978.

Childs, Matt D. "'A Black French General Arrived to Conquer the Island': Images of the
Haitian Revolution in Cuba's 1812 Aponte Rebellion." In *The Impact of the Haitian Revolution in the Atlantic World*, edited by David Geggus, 135–56.

———. *The 1812 Aponte Rebellion in Cuba and the Struggle against Atlantic Slavery*. Chapel
Hill: University of North Carolina Press, 2006.

Clissold, Stephen. *Bernardo O'Higgins and the Independence of Chile*. London: Rupert Hart-
Davis, 1968.

Collier, Simon, and William F. Sater. *A History of Chile, 1808–1994*. Cambridge: Cambridge
University Press, 1996.

Colmenares, Germán. "Popayán: Continuidad y descontinuidad regionales en la época de
la independencia." In *América Latina en la época de Simón Bolívar: La formación de las
economías nacionales y los intereses económicas europeos 1800–1850*, edited by Reinhard
Liehr, 157–81. Berlin: Colloquium Verlar, 1989.

Crespi, Liliana M. "Negros apresados en operaciones de corso durante la guerra con el
Brasil (1825–1828)." *Temas de África y Asia* 2 (1993): 109–24.

Cronología militar argentina 1806–1980. Buenos Aires: Editorial CLIO S.A., 1983.

Cunill Grau, Pedro. "El mito del ordenamiento espacial colonial ante las realidades de la
geografía de la insurgencia en tiempos de Antonio José de Sucre, Gran Mariscal de
Ayacucho." In *Insurgencia y revolución: Antonio José de Sucre y la independencia de los pueblos de América*, edited by José María Cadenas, 13–54. Seville: Universidad Internacional de Andalucía, Colección Encuentros Iberoamericanos, 1996.

Curtin, Philip D. *The Atlantic Slave Trade: A Census*. Madison: University of Wisconsin
Press, 1969.

Cushner, Nicholas P. *Lords of the Land: Sugar, Wine, and Jesuit Estates of Coastal Peru, 1600–
1767*. Albany: State University of New York Press, 1980.

Cutolo, Vicente Osvaldo. *Nuevo diccionario biográfico argentino (1750–1930)*. 7 vols. Buenos
Aires: Editorial ELCHE, 1985.

Dávila, Vicente. *Diccionario biográfico de ilustres próceres de la independencia suramericana*. 2
vols. Caracas: Imprenta Bolívar, 1924–26.

Destruge, Camilo. "La esclavitud en el Ecuador." *Boletín de la Biblioteca Municipal de
Guayaquil* 27 (1912): 33–44, 28 (1912): 49–62, and 29 (1912): 65–74.

Díaz Díaz, Rafael Antonio. *Esclavitud, región y ciudad: El sistema esclavista urbano-regional en
Santafé de Bogotá, 1700–1750*. Bogotá: Centro Editorial Javeriano, CEJA, 2001.

Domínguez, Jorge I. *Insurrection or Loyalty: The Breakdown of the Spanish American Empire*.
Cambridge, MA: Harvard University Press, 1980.

Earle, Rebecca A. "'A Grave for Europeans'? Disease, Death and the Spanish-American
Revolutions." In *The Wars of Independence in Spanish America*, edited by Christon I.
Archer, 283–97. Wilmington, DE: Scholarly Resources, Inc., 2000.

———. "Popular Participation in the Wars of Independence in New Granada." In *Independence and Revolution in Spanish America*, edited by Anthony McFarlane and Eduardo
Posada-Carbó, 87–101. London: Institute of Latin American Studies, 1999.

————. "Rape and the Anxious Republic: Revolutionary Colombia, 1810–1830." In *Hidden Histories of Gender and the State in Latin America*, edited by Elizabeth Dore and Maxine Molyneux, 127–46. Durham, NC: Duke University Press, 2000.

————. *Spain and the Independence of Colombia 1810–1825*. Exeter: University of Exeter Press, 2000.

Espejo, Gerónimo. *'El paso de los Andes': Crónica histórica de las operaciones del Ejército de los Andes para la restauración de Chile in 1817*. Buenos Aires: Imprenta y Librería de Mayo, 1882. Reprinted in Argentina, Senado de la Nación, *Biblioteca de mayo*, vol. 16, part 1.

Feliú Cruz, Guillermo. *La abolición de la esclavitud en Chile: Estudio histórico y social*. 2nd ed. Santiago: Editorial Universitaria, 1973.

Fisher, John. *Bourbon Peru, 1750–1824*. Liverpool: Liverpool University Press, 2003.

————. *Government and Society in Colonial Peru: The Intendant System, 1784–1814*. London: Athlone Press, 1970.

————. "Royalism, Regionalism, and Rebellion in Colonial Peru, 1808–1815." *Hispanic American Historical Review* 52, no. 2 (1979): 232–57.

Flores Galindo S., Alberto. *Aristocracia y plebe: Lima, 1760–1830 (estructura de clases y sociedad colonial)*. Lima: Mosca Azul Editores, 1984.

————. "Bandidos de la costa." In Aguirre and Walker, *Bandoleros, abigeos y montoneros*, 57–68 .

Frigerio, José Oscar. "Con sangre de negros se edificó nuestra independencia." *Todo Es Historia* 250 (1988): 48–69.

Gallo, Klaus. *Great Britain and Argentina: From Invasion to Recognition, 1806–26*. Basingstoke, U.K.: Palgrave, 2001.

Geggus, David Patrick, ed. *The Impact of the Haitian Revolution in the Atlantic World*. Columbia: University of South Carolina Press, 2001.

————. "Slave Resistance in the Spanish Caribbean in the Mid-1790s." In *A Turbulent Time: The French Revolution and the Greater Caribbean*, edited by David Barry Gaspar and David Patrick Geggus, 1–50. Bloomington: Indiana University Press, 1997.

Genovese, Eugene D. *From Rebellion to Revolution: Afro-American Slave Revolts in the Making of the Modern World*. Baton Rouge: Louisiana State University Press, 1979.

Goldberg, Marta B. "Mujer negra rioplatense (1750–1840)." In *La mitad del país: La mujer en la sociedad argentina*, edited by Lidia Knecher and Marta Panaia, 67–81. Tucumán: Bibliotecas Universitarias, 1994.

Goldberg, Marta B., and Silvia C. Mallo. "La población africana en Buenos Aires y su campaña: Formas de vida y de subsistencia (1750–1850)." *Temas de África y Asia* 2 (1993): 15–69.

González, Juan Vicente. *José Félix Ribas: Biografía*. Buenos Aires: Ministerio de Educación Nacional de Venezuela, 1946.

Graham, Richard. *Independence in Latin America*. 2nd ed. New York: McGraw-Hill, 1994.

Gutiérrez Azopardo, Ildefonso. *Historia del negro en Colombia ¿Sumisión o rebeldía?* 4th ed. Bogotá: Editorial Nueva América, 1994.

Halperín-Donghi, Tulio. *Politics, Economics and Society in Argentina in the Revolutionary Period*. Translated by Richard Southern. Cambridge: Cambridge University Press, 1975.

Hamnett, Brian R. "Popular Insurrection and Royalist Reaction: Colombian Regions, 1810–1823." In *Reform and Insurrection in Bourbon New Granada and Peru*, edited by John R. Fisher, Allan J. Kuethe, and Anthony McFarlane, 292–326. Baton Rouge: Louisiana State University Press, 1990.

———. "Process and Pattern: A Re-examination of the Ibero-American Independence Movements, 1808–1826." *Journal of Latin American Studies* 29, no. 2 (1997): 279–328.

Hasbrouck, Alfred. *Foreign Legionaries in the Liberation of Spanish South America*. New York: Columbia University Press, 1928.

Helg, Aline. *Liberty and Equality in Caribbean Colombia 1770–1835*. Chapel Hill: University of North Carolina Press, 2004.

———. "The Limits of Equality: Free People of Colour and Slaves during the First Independence of Cartagena, Colombia, 1810–15." *Slavery and Abolition* 20, no. 2 (1999): 1–30.

———. "Simón Bolívar and the Spectre of *Pardocracia*: José Padilla in Post-independence Cartagena." *Journal of Latin American Studies* 35, no. 3 (2003): 447–71.

Hünefeldt, Christine. *Paying the Price of Freedom: Family and Labor among Lima's Slaves, 1800–1854*. Berkeley: University of California Press, 1994.

Izard, Miguel. *El miedo a la revolución: La lucha por la libertad en Venezuela (1777–1830)*. Madrid: Editorial Tecnos, 1979.

James, C. L. R. *The Black Jacobins: Toussaint L'Ouverture and the San Domingo Revolution*. 2nd ed. New York: Vintage Books, 1963.

Johnson, Lyman L. "Manumission in Colonial Buenos Aires, 1776–1810." *Hispanic American Historical Review* 59, no. 2 (1979): 258–79.

Jurado Noboa, Fernando. "Algunas reflexiones sobre la tenencia de los esclavos en la colonia: 1536–1826." *Boletín del Archivo Nacional* (Quito) 22 (1992): 93–101.

———. *Esclavitud en la costa pacífica: Iscuandé, Tumaco, Barbacoas y Esmeraldas, siglos XVI al XIX*. Quito: Ediciones Abya-Yala, 1990.

King, James F. "The Colored Castes and American Representation in the Cortes of Cádiz." *Hispanic American Historical Review* 33, no. 1 (1953): 33–64.

Klachko, Maïté. "Le processus de destruction du système esclavagiste á Buenos Aires 1810–1860." Master's thesis, Université de Paris X Nanterre, 1997.

Klein, Herbert S. "The Colored Militia of Cuba: 1568–1868." *Caribbean Studies* 6, no. 2 (1966): 17–27.

Kuethe, Allan J. *Cuba, 1753–1815: Crown, Military, and Society*. Knoxville: University of Tennessee Press, 1986.

———. *Military Reform and Society in New Granada, 1773–1808*. Gainesville: University Presses of Florida, 1978.

Landers, Jane. "Africans in the Spanish Colonies." *Historical Archaeology* 31, no. 1 (1997): 84–103.

———. *Black Society in Spanish Florida*. Urbana: University of Illinois Press, 1999.

———. "Transforming Bondsmen into Vassals: Arming the Slaves in Colonial Spanish America." In *Arming Slaves: From Classical Times to the Modern Age*, edited by Christopher Leslie Brown and Philip D. Morgan, 120–45. New Haven: Yale University Press, 2006.

Langley, Lester D. *The Americas in the Age of Revolution, 1750–1850.* New Haven: Yale University Press, 1996.

Lasso, Marixa. "Haiti as an Image of Popular Republicanism in Caribbean Colombia: Cartagena Province (1811–1828)." In Geggus, *The Impact of the Haitian Revolution in the Atlantic World,* 176–90.

Lipsett-Rivera, Sonya. "Marriage and Family Relations in Mexico during the Transition from Colony to Nation." In *State and Society in Spanish America during the Age of Revolution,* edited by Victor M. Uribe-Uran, 121–48. Wilmington, DE: Scholarly Resources, 2001.

Lohse, Russell. "Reconciling Freedom with the Rights of Property: Slave Emancipation in Colombia, 1821–1852, with Special Reference to La Plata." *Journal of Negro History* 86, no. 3 (2001): 203–27.

Lombardi, John V. *The Decline and Abolition of Negro Slavery in Venezuela, 1820–1854.* Westport, CT: Greenwood, 1971.

———. "Los esclavos en la legislación republicana de Venezuela." *Boletín Histórico, Federación John Boulton* 13 (Jan. 1962): 43–66.

———. "Los esclavos negros en las guerras venezolanas de la independencia." *Cultura Universitaria* 93 (Oct.–Dec. 1966): 153–68.

———. "Manumission, *Manumisos,* and *Aprendizaje* in Republican Venezuela." *Hispanic American Historical Review* 49, no. 4 (1969): 656–78.

López Domínguez, Luís Horacio, comp. *De Boyacá a Cúcuta: Memoria administrativa 1819–1821.* Bogotá: Biblioteca de la Presidencia de la República, 1990.

Lucena Salmoral, Manuel. *Sangre sobre piel negra: La esclavitud quiteña en el contexto del reformismo borbónico.* Quito: Ediciones Abya-Yala, 1994.

Lynch, John. *Argentine Dictator: Juan Manuel de Rosas, 1829–1852.* Oxford: Clarendon Press, 1981.

———. *Simón Bolívar: A Life.* New Haven: Yale University Press, 2006.

———. *The Spanish American Revolutions 1808–1826.* 2nd ed. New York: W. W. Norton, 1986.

Magallanes, Manuel Vicente. *Historia política de Venezuela.* 7th ed. Caracas: Universidad Central de Venezuela Ediciones de la Biblioteca, 1990.

Martínez Carreras, José U. "España y la abolición de la esclavitud durante el siglo XIX." In *Estudios sobre la abolición de la esclavitud,* edited by Francisco de Solano, 167–79. Madrid: Consejo Superior de Investigaciones Científicas, 1986.

Martínez Montero, Homero. "Fugas y castigos." In Carvalho Neto, *El negro uruguayo,* 218–21.

———. "El soldado negro." In Carvalho Neto, *El negro uruguayo,* 271–82.

Masini, José Luis. *La esclavitud negra en Mendoza: Época independiente.* Mendoza: Talleres Gráficos d'Accurzio, 1962.

Masur, Gerhard. *Simon Bolivar.* Rev. ed. Albuquerque: University of New Mexico Press, 1969.

Mazzeo, Cristina Ana. *El comercio libre en el Perú: Las estrategias de un comerciante criollo, José Antonio de Lavalle y Cortés, 1777–1815.* Lima: Pontificia Universidad Católica del Perú, 1994.

McAlister, Lyle N. *The "Fuero Militar" in New Spain, 1764–1800*. Gainesville: University of Florida Press, 1957.

McKinley, Michael. *Pre-Revolutionary Caracas: Politics, Economy, and Society 1777–1811.* Cambridge: Cambridge University Press, 1985.

Meisel, Seth. "War, Economy, and Society in Post-Independence Córdoba, Argentina." Ph.D. diss., Stanford University, 1998.

Méndez, Cecilia. *The Plebeian Republic: The Huanta Rebellion and the Making of the Peruvian State, 1820–1850*. Durham, NC: Duke University Press, 2005.

Mitre, Bartolomé. *Historia de San Martín y de la emancipación sudamericana*. 3 vols. Buenos Aires: Editorial Universitaria de Buenos Aires, 1968.

Montiel, Hernan Segundo. "Historia parabólica: Los negros en la independencia." *El Nacional* (Caracas), Jan. 15, 1993, 4.

Morrone, Francisco. "La participación del negro en el ejército." In *El negro en la Argentina: Presencia y negación,* edited by Dina V. Picotti, 353–64. Buenos Aires: Editores de América Latina, 2001.

Múnera, Alfonso. *El fracaso de la nación: Región, clase y raza en el Caribe colombiano (1717–1821)*. Bogotá: El Áncora Editores, 1998.

Murray, Pamela S. "'Loca' or 'Libertadora'? Manuela Sáenz in the Eyes of History and Historians, 1900–c.1990." *Journal of Latin American Studies* 33, no. 2 (2001): 291–310.

O'Leary, Daniel Florencio. *Bolívar and the War of Independence*. Translated and edited by Robert F. McNerney Jr. Austin: University of Texas Press, 1970.

O'Phelan Godoy, Scarlett. *Rebellions and Revolts in Eighteenth Century Peru and Upper Peru.* Cologne: Böhlau, 1985.

Palmer, Colin A. *Slaves of the White God: Blacks in Mexico, 1570–1650*. Cambridge, MA: Harvard University Press, 1976.

Parry, J. H. *The Spanish Seaborne Empire*. London: Hutchinson, 1977.

Pereda Valdés, Ildefonso. *El negro en el Uruguay: Pasado y presente*. Montevideo: n.p., 1965.

———. *Negros esclavos y negro libres: Esquema de una sociedad esclavista y aporte del negro en nuestra formación nacional*. Montevideo: Imprenta "Gaceta Comercial," 1941.

Pérez Tenreiro, Tomás. *José Tomás Boves: Primera lanza del rey*. Caracas: La Oficina Técnica del Ministerio de la Defensa, 1969.

Phelan, John Leddy. *The People and the King: The Comunero Revolution in Colombia, 1781*. Madison: University of Wisconsin Press, 1978.

Prieto de Zegarra, Judith. *Mujer, poder, y desarollo en el Perú*. 2 vols. Lima: Editorial DORHCA, 1980.

Rama, Carlos M. "The Passing of the Afro-Uruguayans from Caste Society into Class Society." In *Race and Class in Latin America,* edited by Magnus Mörner, 28–50. New York: Columbia University Press, 1970.

Ramos Guédez, José Marcial. "La insurección de los esclavos negros de Coro en 1795: Algunas ideas en torno a posibles influencias de la revolución francesa." *Revista Universitaria de Ciencias del Hombre . . . Universidad José María Vargas* 2, no. 2 (1989): 103–16.

———. "Simón Bolívar y la abolición de la esclavitud en Venezuela." *Ultimas Noticias, Suplemento Cultural* (Caracas), July 31, 1994, 6–7.

Ramos Pérez, Demetrio. *España en la independencia de América*. Madrid: MAPFRE, 1996.

Rebaza, Nicolás. *Anales del departamento de La Libertad en la guerra de la independencia*. Trujillo: Impr. de "El Obrero del Norte," 1898.

Restall, Matthew. "Black Conquistadors: Armed Africans in Early Spanish America." *The Americas* 57, no. 2 (2000): 167–205.

Reyes Flores, Alejandro. *Esclavitud en Lima 1800–1840*. Lima: Universidad Nacional Mayor de San Marcos, 1985.

Ricoy, Irene S. "San Martín y la formación de batallones de negros en el Ejército de los Andes." *Boletín Informativo, Dirección de Estudios Históricos, Comando General del Ejército* (Buenos Aires) 7–8 (1973): 115–29.

Rodríguez O., Jaime E. *The Independence of Spanish America*. Cambridge: Cambridge University Press, 1998.

Rosal, Miguel A. "Diversos aspectos relacionados con la esclavitud en el Río de la Plata a través del estudio de testamentos de afroporteños, 1750–1810." *Revista de Indias* 56, no. 206 (1996): 219–35.

Rout, Leslie B., Jr. *The African Experience in Spanish America: 1502 to the Present Day*. Cambridge: Cambridge University Press, 1976.

Salas, Elizabeth. *Soldaderas in the Mexican Military: Myth and History*. Austin: University of Texas Press, 1990.

Salcedo-Bastardo, J. L. *Bolívar: A Continent and its Destiny*. Edited and translated by Annella McDermott. Atlantic Highlands, NJ: Humanities Press International, 1977.

Sales de Bohigas, Núria. *Sobre esclavos, reclutas y mercaderes de quintos*. Barcelona: Editorial Ariel, 1974.

Sater, William F. "The Black Experience in Chile." In *Slavery and Race Relations in Latin America*, edited by Robert Brent Toplin, 13–50. Westport, CT: Greenwood Press, 1974.

Scott, Drusilla. *Mary English: A Friend of Bolívar*. Lewes, U.K.: The Book Guild Ltd., 1991.

Semprún, José, and Alfonso Bullón de Mendoza. *El ejército realista en la independencia americana*. Madrid: Editorial MAPFRE, 1992.

Sharp, William Frederick. *Slavery on the Spanish Frontier: The Colombian Chocó, 1680–1810*. Norman: University of Oklahoma Press, 1976.

Slatta, Richard W. *Gauchos and the Vanishing Frontier*. Lincoln: University of Nebraska Press, 1992.

Stoan, Stephen K. *Pablo Morillo and Venezuela, 1815–1820*. Columbus: Ohio State University Press, 1974.

Tardieu, Jean-Pierre. *El decreto de Huancayo: Abolición de la esclavitud en el Perú. 3 de diciembre de 1854*. Lima: Fondo Editorial del Congreso del Perú, 2004.

Tavara, Santiago. *Abolición de la esclavitud en el Perú*. Lima: José María Monterola, 1855.

Thibaud, Clément. *Repúblicas en armas: Los ejércitos bolivarianos en la guerra de independencia en Colombia y Venezuela*. Bogotá: Planeta, 2003.

Thornton, John. *Africa and Africans in the Making of the Atlantic World, 1400–1800*. 2nd ed. Cambridge: Cambridge University Press, 1998.

———. "African Soldiers in the Haitian Revolution." *Journal of Caribbean History* 25, nos. 1 and 2 (1991): 58–80.

Townsend, Camilla. "Angela Batallas: A Fight for Freedom in Guayaquil." In *The Human Tradition in Colonial Latin America*, edited by Kenneth J. Andrien, 293–307. Wilmington, DE: Scholarly Resources, Inc., 2002.

———. "'Half My Body Free, the Other Half Enslaved': The Politics of the Slaves of Guayas at the End of the Colonial Era." *Colonial Latin American Review* 7, no. 1 (1998): 105–28.

Troconis de Veracoechea, Ermila. *Indias, esclavas, mantuanas y primeras damas*. Caracas: Alfadil Ediciones, 1990.

Valencia Villa, Carlos Eduardo. *Alma en boca y huesos en costal: Una aproximación a los contrastes socio-económicos de la esclavitud. Santafé, Mariquita y Mompox 1610–1660*. Bogotá: Instituto Colombiano de Antropología e Historia, 2003.

Vergara Arias, Gustavo. *Montoneras y guerrillas en la etapa de la emancipación del Perú (1820–1825)*. Lima: Imprenta y Litografía "Salesiana," 1973.

Vinson, Ben, III. *Bearing Arms for His Majesty: The Free-Colored Militia in Colonial Mexico*. Stanford: Stanford University Press, 2001.

Vivanco Lara, Carmen. "Bandolerismo colonial peruano, 1760–1810: Caracterización de una respuesta popular y causas económicas." In Aguirre and Walker, *Bandoleros, abigeos y montoneros*, 25–56.

Voelz, Peter M. *Slave and Soldier: The Military Impact of Blacks in the Colonial Americas*. New York: Garland, 1993.

Walker, Charles. "Montoneros, bandoleros, malhechores: Criminalidad y política en las primeras décadas republicanas." In Aguirre and Walker, *Bandoleros, abigeos y montoneros*, 105–36.

Williams, John Hoyt. "Observations on Blacks and Bondage in Uruguay, 1800–1836." *The Americas* 43, no. 4 (1987): 411–27.

Woodward, Margaret L. "The Spanish Army and the Loss of America, 1810–1824." *Hispanic American Historical Review* 48, no. 4 (1968): 586–607.

Wright, Winthrop R. *Café con Leche: Race, Class, and National Image in Venezuela*. Austin: University of Texas Press, 1990.

INDEX

Pezuela, Joaquín de la, 142, 146
Piar, Manuel, 33, 68, 72–73, 166, 200n35
Piñero, Ramón, 29, 31
Pío, Hilario, 97
Pisco, 96, 97, 98
Popayán, 20, 24, 32, 74, 176
Potosí, 145, 151
priests, 26, 27, 40, 49, 51, 124, 135, 151
prisoners of war, 132–33
promotion, 45, 119–20
Puerto Cabello, 83, 163
Pueyrredón, Juan Martín de, 61
Pumacahua, Mateo, 92, 93
Punta Gorda, Company of Pardos of, 57, 58, 118

Quiñones, José Antonio, 176
Quito: reinforcements from, 77; rising, 18–19,
    93; royalists in, 24, 96; slaves in, 7, 8, 68, 84

Ramires, José Gerónimo, 32
Ramírez, María Josefa, 157–58
rape, 29, 147–8
rations, 118–19, 130, 211n21
recruiting laws: in Argentina, 46–50, 59–60,
    134; in Chile, 89, 91; in New Granada, 74; in
    Peru, 98, 100–101, 105; in Venezuela, 26,
    66–67, 71, 80
reenslavement of slave soldiers, 110–11, 133, 162,
    172–79
rescate: in Buenos Aires, 47–48, 53–56, 62; in
    Lima, 101–2, 104, 105
Río de la Plata: British invasion of, 14–15;
    runaways in, 120; slave numbers, 8; troops
    in, 102, 106, 108–10, 118; viceroyalty of, 2,
    37–63
Río de la Plata Regiment, 108–10, 118, 123, 137,
    150–52, 158
Rivadavia, Lucas, 159
Rivadavia, María Dolores, 159
Rodalleja, Mariano Antonio, 32, 131
Rodil, José Ramón, 97, 109–10, 138
Romero, José, 89
Rondeau, José, 40, 41, 45, 58, 124, 125, 148
Rosas, Pedro, 93–94, 155
runaways: in Argentina, 52, 54–55, 58, 120–21,
    123–26, 139; in Banda Oriental, 11, 41–44,
    120–21, 140, 144, 148, 150; before the wars,

14; in Chile, 88, 91; in New Granada, 10, 69;
    in Peru, 93–97, 99, 101, 138; in Venezuela, 11,
    23, 25, 32–33, 134

Salazar, Antonio, 96–97
Salazar, José María, 41–42
Sales de Bohigas, Núria, 2, 3, 92
Salta, 40, 58, 145, 147
San Juan, 55, 59, 62
San Luis, 59, 61, 62
San Martín, José de: and Bólivar, 85, 104;
    in Chile, 3, 89–92, 128, 170; in Cuyo, 38,
    59–63, 120, 133, 136, 138; legislation of,
    99–101, 104, 168; in Peru, 86, 94–104, 129,
    150, 152; relationship with troops, 90, 108,
    128; reorganizing army, 58; and slave women,
    147, 150, 152
Sánchez, Manuel, 131, 156
Santander, Francisco de Paula, 73–77, 81, 82,
    146
Santander Battalion, 83, 125
Santiago, 3, 87, 88, 92, 115, 117
Santos, Ignacio de los, 151
Santos, Jacinto, 176
Sarmiento, Ramón, 69
Sarria, María del Carmen, 158
Sauco, José Apolinario, 44
Sayán, 96, 111, 134
Seventh Regiment (Argentina), 62, 95, 108
Seventh Regiment (Buenos Aires), 55, 58, 119,
    153
Silva, Francisco, 139
Silveira, Antonio José, 51, 52
Sinen, Antonio, 135
Sipe-Sipe, the battle of, 58, 91, 124, 126, 129, 133,
    141, 148
slave soldiers: attributes of, 4; claiming freedom,
    31–32, 41, 91, 135, 139–40, 168, 173, 175–78;
    complimented, 58–59, 70, 90; freeing rela-
    tives, 150–53; from jails, 50, 52, 68, 79, 89,
    91; as non-combatants, 25, 32, 34, 56, 69,
    116–17, 131; promotions of, 62, 119–20; re-
    claimed by owners, 33, 122–24, 133, 172–78;
    support for freedom of, 121–22
slave unrest: in New Granada, 10, 11, 24; in Peru,
    10–11, 92–93, 98–99; postwar, 162–64; in
    Venezuela, 10–11, 23, 26–27, 29, 66, 68